# TWAIN'S
# HEROES

✦❧❦❧✦

# TWAIN'S
# WORLDS

# Andrew Jay Hoffman

# TWAIN'S HEROES

# TWAIN'S WORLDS

Mark Twain's
*Adventures of
Huckleberry Finn,
A Connecticut Yankee in
King Arthur's Court,*
and
*Pudd'nhead Wilson*

University of Pennsylvania Press
Philadelphia

Library of Congress Cataloging-in-Publication Data

Hoffman, Andrew Jay.
Twain's heroes, Twain's worlds : Mark Twain's Adventures of
Huckleberry Finn, A Connecticut Yankee in King Arthur's court, and
Pudd'nhead Wilson / Andrew Jay Hoffman.
p.      cm.
Bibliography: p.
Includes index.
ISBN 0-8122-8139-X
1. Twain, Mark, 1835–1910—Characters—Heroes.   2. Twain, Mark,
1835–1910. Adventures of Huckleberry Finn.   3. Twain, Mark,
1835–1910. Connecticut Yankee in King Arthur's court.   4. Twain,
Mark, 1835–1910. Pudd'nhead Wilson.   5. Heroes in literature.
I. Title.
PS1342.H47H64    1988
813'.4—dc19                                              88-21031
                                                           CIP

# Contents

# Prologue

In one sense, I began this project more than ten years ago, when I was an undergraduate at University of Pennsylvania. I got what I thought of as My Big Break. Running Press, a small Philadelphia publisher, wanted to issue a representative collection of Mark Twain. The task ended up primarily in my inexperienced hands. Months of work became *The Unabridged Mark Twain*, a 1200-page paperback introduced by Kurt Vonnegut. Though a bargain of a book, the volume is not a reliable text. I must take blame for all its shortcomings, from the exclusion of *Pudd'nhead Wilson* to the embarrassingly frequent typographical errors. Mark Twain deserves better than the shabby treatment I gave him. Perhaps this study is my way of paying off my ten-year-old debt for the great pleasure and insight Twain has given me.

Repayment of the debt has taken so long for two reasons. First, I needed to accumulate enough intellectual capital. Recently, the Graduate School of Brown University has given me the time to develop my early critical prejudices into well-grounded beliefs and then to work those beliefs into this book. But this manuscript would never have materialized without the second delay in repayment, a sort of mirroring in miniature of Mark Twain's experience. After graduating from the University of Pennsylvania, I went West, and in San Francisco broke into professional writing. I wrote and edited for publications up and down the West Coast, like Twain earning my livelihood with my pen. Later, I returned East and began working with magazine- and book-publishers of national stature. In time, though, Mark Twain's ghost rose like a band a collection lawyers before me, and I knew I must leave off mimicking Twain and repay the old debt.

In Mark Twain's three most important novels—*Adventures of Huckleberry Finn*(1884), *A Connecticut Yankee in King Arthur's Court* (1889), and *Pudd'nhead Wilson* (1894)—we can see an outline of historical movement. The heroes of these novels do not change very much within the confines of their own works, but as a group the nature of their heroism develops from work to work. We see through their struggles how Twain grappled with the problems heroes present. Mark Twain attempted, through these works, to find a kind of heroism which could at very least survive the world as he saw it. To give his heroes even a chance, he empowered them supernaturally. He idealized them, made more of them than simply realistic characters.

Huck Finn, Hank Morgan, and David Wilson are all symbolic heroes. They are not only flesh, blood, and human crises, but also human emblems—emblems, this book will try to show, of historical dimension. Working in the tradition of Southwestern humorists, Twain mixed the tall-tale heroics of oral storytellers with a nineteenth-century drive toward realism in narrative. The historically verifiable worlds of Twain's fiction strain the seams of their realism by containing their heroes, who originate in a different kind of literature. These characters strike a balance between their traditional heroism and the circumstances they find themselves in by becoming symbols of hope for release from the real worlds those circumstances depict.

I do not mean to say in this argument that Huck, Hank, and Pudd'nhead are simple allegorical figures. As we first encounter them they are very much characters in realistic fictions. But their power as characters outstrips the power each could possibly have as a representation of a single human being. They are heroes—not literary ones, ordinary men in extraordinary circumstances, but traditional ones out of myth and tall tales. They are extraordinary men in ordinary circumstances made extraordinary by their presence there. We see this clearly when we compare Twain's heroes to models of heroes. Huck Finn fits thoroughly into the constructed outlines of the traditional hero drawn for us in Lord Raglan's *The Hero* and Otto Rank's *The Myth of the Birth of the Hero*. Hank Morgan looks very much like the hero in Joseph Campbell's *The Hero with a Thousand Faces*. But, even as heroes of the magnitude that fascinated Raglan, Rank, and Campbell, Hank Morgan and Huck Finn fail to perform as heroes in their realistic worlds. Although Twain built into both of them the superhumanity of the traditional hero, it proves too much for each. At the end of their novels, they betray our trust in their heroism and fail to make material the hopes their heroism leads us to invest in them. Each failure pushed Mark Twain to revise his concept of the hero and finally drove him to construct David Wilson, a different sort of hero, perhaps an existential one, who could survive the world he lives in.

These heroes do not fail under their own weight; they fail in context. *Adventures of Huckleberry Finn* starts in the northern Missouri river town of St. Petersburg and moves more deeply into the American South of the 1830s. That decade is the centerpiece of what many post-war historians have cast as an American idyll, Jacksonian Democracy, when the Jeffersonian ideal of a nation of free and equal men seemed, if not actual, at least within grasp. Huck Finn himself is a Jacksonian ideal: a spirit short on breeding and long on character, determined to do more than survive. He wants to thrive as an independent and natural man in a world of independent and natural men. This is the Huck Finn who vows to go to hell rather than turn in his friend Jim. Mark Twain, a student of history, knew Jacksonian Democracy to be a myth, knew it perhaps only with the benefit of hindsight, but knew it by his intimate experience with its reality. This marvelous era of human development existed, if it did at all, only by virtue of another institution: slavery. Huck faces and defeats the "sivilized" dragons which challenge his individual moral development, but the human horror of slavery, which generates the dragons and which as a system outlasts and outwits Huck's morality, keeps him ever on the edge of darkness. In the end, the darkness swallows him, just as the issue of slavery swallowed the high hopes of the 1830s and 1840s. To live at all among people, Huck must take part in their romantic fantasies about their world. Huck goes through a symbolic death to escape his father and avoid playing in any more of Tom Sawyer's moronic romances. But at the end of his book, he hopes to emulate his father's propensity to evil and he not only joins into Tom's game, but also becomes Tom Sawyer himself, at least in name. Instead of simply springing Jim and leaving, Huck bows to Tom and plays out the new romance to the hilt. And instead of ending the novel thriving, our hero ends tarnished and lost to us. Huck *had* to end this way, not because of his heroic character, but because of historical necessity. Slavery was the dark underside of a nation of free and equal men; slavery in the end defeats Huck. Twain cast Huck as a symbol of the Jacksonian Democratic ideal and, as the ideal fails, so must Huckleberry Finn.

In *A Connecticut Yankee in King Arthur's Court*, Mark Twain moves from the conflicts of his boyhood to those more immediate to him. Much more a psychological hero, according to Joseph Campbell's design, than Huck Finn, Hank Morgan starts his history by calling himself an American and then issues a boast which America itself could have made in the late 1880s:

> My father was a blacksmith, my uncle was a horse doctor, and I was both, along at first. Then I went over to the great arms factory and learned my real trade; learned all there was to it; learned to make everything: guns, revolvers, cannon, boilers, engines, all sorts of labor saving machinery. Why, I could make anything a body wanted, anything in the world, it didn't make any difference what; and if there wasn't a quick new-fangled way to make a thing, I could invent one. (4)

Like Hank, America made the best armaments and heavy machinery in the world and we were looking for ways to prove it. Hank Morgan gets the chance in sixth-century England, and he proves it conclusively: In a day and a half he owns half the country and lives at a level just below King Arthur. He dominates his world successfully. The Connecticut Yankee manipulates the world according to his own egotistical image.

In time, though, Arthur's world proves less malleable than the Yankee thought. It snaps back at him; even his most faithful aide tells him that the end "would have come on your own account, by and by." The Yankee responds to the attack against him with the same technology that prompted the attack, resentfully taking back all he has given and then destroying what is left. By the end, this man we cheered with abandon kills 25,000 people without remorse, without even a second thought. What Twain gives us in *A Connecticut Yankee* is a history of what America has repeated several times since in small and backward countries around the world, with the Indians as Twain grew up, in Mexico while Twain wrote the novel, and soon after in the Philippines. What Mark Twain saw, and why Hank Morgan too had to fail, was that Industrial America is also Imperialist America, and even a hero of Hank Morgan's proportions could not find a way out of that identity.

# Prologue

Huck Finn and Hank Morgan are both traditional heroes in what our historic imagination has taught us to think of as heroic times. But history is never simple, and neither are its symbols. As the heroic times failed us, in their undersides of horror and violence, so must the heroes who symbolize those times. This left Mark Twain with a problem: what kind of hero will not fail in the world as we know it? In the years after the publication of *A Connecticut Yankee*, Twain experimented with futuristic fiction, imagining impossible or faintly possible worlds.

He also wrote one more major novel. In it, he went not to the future but back to the territory he had mined with such sadly moving results in *Huckleberry Finn*. *Pudd'nhead Wilson* seems to take us back to the Mississippi River valley and the pre-Civil War South, but this world does not look or feel like the world we found in *Huckleberry Finn*. Its ironic and inactive hero appears heroic in terms the twentieth century understands much better than the nineteenth ever could.

David Wilson refuses the mold of the traditional hero. Nothing magical happens to him his entire life. He wears no disguises, creates no unusual occurrence, never leaves Dawson's Landing. The only significant action he takes—solving the murder of Judge Driscoll and revealing the true identity of the murderer—only serves to restore, not to change, the social order, albeit with him now at its head. At the novel's opening, Wilson arrives in an odd and in some ways magical world, where few people are what they seem and where "an invisible dog" barks disagreeably behind the facade of peaceful homes. Though unwelcome—an ironic joke the townsfolk do not understand casts him immediately as a pudd'n-head—he stays. For more than twenty years Wilson, trained as a lawyer, earns a little money from surveying and accounting and makes a life for himself by his interest "in every new thing that was born into the universe of ideas." Yet at the end of the novel he is "a made man for life," mayor of the town, successful lawyer, leading citizen.

The novel, however, sometimes published under the title *The Tragedy of Pudd'nhead Wilson*, does not leave readers cheering. Though David Wilson does not disappoint us in the way Huck and Hank do, he does not exactly satisfy us either. The townsfolk, who at the novel's start dubbed Wilson "Pudd'nhead," take on the title themselves at the end. Yes, David Wilson leads Dawson's Landing, but what sort of success can we call running a town full of idiots? A tragic one, Twain implies, but, tragic or not, it is the only sort of success the world allows. To make this point more painfully clear, Twain includes in his novel a traditional hero against whom we can compare David Wilson: Roxy. She constantly takes action against an unjust world: she switches her slave child for the master's, goes on a journey, engineers all her son's crimes which the novel gives us reason to believe are acts of retributive justice against the oppression of slavery. But Roxy ends like Huck and Hank, only worse; she is reduced from a "majestic" creature to a cringing hopeless one. Against this failure Twain sets David Wilson, who takes no action but socially acceptable ones, who patiently abides ridicule and obscurity, who creates for himself his own life with hair oil and bits of glass. His heroism is limited to understanding identity through fingerprints and to retaining his authenticity in a world unaccustomed to it.

Twain began with Huckleberry Finn, a traditional hero in an historically real world. In the isolation of the river his heroism inspires, but transferred to the real world it disgusts. Huck cannot fight Tom Sawyer's romantic visions, and he cannot compete with the system of oppression which that romance supports. He heads off to the territories, a failed hero. A turn to the present gave Twain no easier ride. Hank Morgan, less traditionally heroic but still a fine example of at least one model of the hero, seems capable of conquering a world. More than seems, he does conquer it; but he cannot govern it. He wants to change people at their roots and has only technology to help him. In the end, he has only technology to fall back on and only revenge as a motive. He destroys himself, the world he created, and very nearly the world he wanted to change. In David Wilson, Twain found a new sort of hero. Wilson promises nothing; anything he achieves makes us admire him. And what he achieves, aside from solving the mystery of Dawson's Landing, is simple survival. His world is absurd, a circus of Italian twins, dueling noblemen, human devils and imitation whites, and all Wilson need do to succeed in it is be himself. So: Huck Finn, a democratic hero, cannot survive the undemocratic world; an emblem of Jacksonian Democracy, he is destroyed by that which destroyed what he represents. Hank Morgan, a technological hero, cannot survive the untechnological world; an emblem of Industrial America, he is destroyed by ego, both his own and that which fueled our Gilded Age return to the childish exuberance of "Manifest Destiny." And David Wilson? An existential hero, a foreshadowing, perhaps, of a world Mark Twain never saw, except in his dark imagination.

*
**

Parts of this argument have been made elsewhere. The only full-length study of Mark Twain's heroes is *Unpromising Heroes: Mark Twain and His Characters*, by Robert Regan, which argues that the author repeatedly placed ordinary people in extraordinary circumstances, making heroes out of unpromising materials. The book does not argue any relationship among these surprising protagonists, nor does it take into account Rank's, Raglan's or Campbell's studies of the hero. Several books on Twain himself document his concern with politics, his anguish over slavery and American imperialism, and his knowledge of history. Most important among these are Roger B. Salomon's *Mark Twain and the Image of History*, Thomas Blues' *Mark Twain and the Community*, Philip Foner's *Mark Twain: Social Critic*, Bernard De Voto's *Mark Twain's America*, and James M. Cox's *Mark Twain: The Fate of Humor*.

I have not yet seen a book or article that shows how well Huck Finn fits into the traditional model of the hero, though several, such as "Huck Finn as Existential Hero" by Arthur Asa Berger and "Huckleberry Finn and the Tradition of the *Odyssey*" by Jack Solomon, touch on the subject. Several articles have noted the outlines of Jacksonian Democracy in Huck, and virtually everyone who has written on the novel has wrestled with the painfully unsatisfying ending. Nothing yet published, however, links these considerations. The fit between the story of Hank Morgan in *A Connecticut Yankee in King Arthur's Court* and the psychological model of the hero drawn by Joseph Campbell appears original with me. Many critics have seen the emblematic quality in the Yankee, for example Deborah Berger Turnbull in "Hank Morgan as American Individualist" and Lorne Fienberg in "Twain's Connecticut Yankee: The Entrepreneur as Daimonic Hero" come to mind. The political nature of the novel escapes few critics, but perhaps Nancy Oliver's "New Manifest Destiny in *A Connecticut Yankee in King Arthur's*

*Court*" states the connection I see between the Yankee and imperialism most succinctly. Henry Nash Smith's penetrating *Mark Twain's Fable of Progress: Political and Economic Ideas in "A Connecticut Yankee"* also addresses political issues. Much of the criticism on *Pudd'nhead Wilson* considers the dramatic problem of finding the locus of the novel's tragedy and the attendant problem of finding a hero. I have seen very little on David Wilson's existential qualities, though Forrest Robinson's *In Bad Faith* will lead scholars to more thorough consideration of existentialism in Twain. Critics have been much more responsive to Roxy's complex role as near-tragic near-hero than to David Wilson's heroics. The dark absurdity of Wilson's world and his resulting awkwardness have been described by Clark Griffith in "*Pudd'nhead Wilson* as Dark Comedy" and by George Spangler in "*Pudd'nhead Wilson*: A Parable of Property", among others.

Readers will notice that my critical slant differs from that which informs most Twain criticism. I have very consciously turned my back on biographical criticism, which has held on as the mainstay of scholarly writing about Mark Twain since De Voto's *Mark Twain's America* and Van Wyck Brooks' *The Ordeal of Mark Twain*. Perhaps this biographical list to the critical ship goes back earlier, to William Dean Howells' *My Mark Twain*, or even comes out of Twain's own remarkable popularity while he lived. I still find Mark Twain personally fascinating; my slant away from biographical criticism in no way rejects Twain, the significance of his authorship, or the intriguing connections so many scholars have excavated between the life and the work.

I have two reasons for withholding support for the biographical approach, in most cases. First, I believe that, because of it, Twain criticism has become stalled in the past decade. The line of inquiry has run dry. The image of Mark Twain gone West for half a life as Huck Finn and East for half as Tom Sawyer no longer stimulates the critical imagination. Twain's bifurcated self has been made to account for so much in Twain's fiction that the fiction itself risks being lost in this simplistic code. The skeleton key of "divided Twain" threatens to turn the wonder of entering the maze of Twain's work into a walk down a well-lit corridor. The books under consideration here still deliver a startling punch to first-time readers. Twain has been one of the best selling authors throughout the twentieth century. His books continue to resonate in subsequent readings. But much of the criticism seems to have gotten caught in a biographical trap which simply does not answer the fundamental question facing any critical inquiry: why does this phenomenon have so strong an effect? The "doubled-up-Twain" litany offers good answers, but not final ones. I have turned my back on this kind of criticism—not completely, but as much as I am able—because only by conscientiously exploring new critical lines might we come up with new answers.

My second point is that we read *from* a time, not *of* a time. Considering fiction as a primary document of the age in which it is written has proved tricky for historians, new and otherwise. Using a novel to understand history must of necessity produce as many difficulties as using history to understand a novel, looking at a piece of fiction as a sort of expression of the age in which it is written. We are hampered by distance: between our time and the author's, between the author and the time he or she writes of, and between the author and his or her own time. Biographical criticism attempts to fill that last chasm, but its information and efforts can never equal the task. As Twain himself said to introduce his autobiography, what someone does comprises only a tiny fraction of a life; what passes through a mind makes up the most of it, and that can never be fully recorded. Trying to place a work of fiction in the time from which it comes is a monumental and in my view mostly hopeless task. I frankly enjoy reading that sort of criticism, for its speculative value. Informed imagination can be tremendously satisfying. But the only historical position we can honestly take on a work of fiction is our own. We weren't with the writer when his ink hit the paper, nor were we alive when the books made their big splash. But we are alive now, and, when Mark Twain writes about the Mississippi Valley before the Civil War, we construct our image of the world he describes as much from the vision of that time and place that we have gained elsewhere as from Twain's own words. I can argue that David Wilson is an existential hero because readers of the book know what an existential hero is. A glance at a time line informs us Twain would not have known the word; but a reading of *Pudd'nhead Wilson* shows us he would recognize the ideas. Or even if he wouldn't, what difference does it make, if *we* understand the tale's workings that way? We read the book today. The book will be read tomorrow only if it has meaning for tomorrow's readers. Looking back to the time of the book's publication will help only if yesterday means something to tomorrow.

I neglect textual criticism in these pages, but I cannot withhold praise from the crew at The Mark Twain Project at the Bancroft Library at the University of California at Berkeley. Their magnificent editions become the standard the day they're published. These dedicated people also offer tremendous help to struggling scholars hoping to paw through Twain's letters, manuscripts, and memorabilia. I want to extend my special thanks to Victor Fischer and Robert Pack Browning, who bestowed their cordiality and assistance as though it honored them to do so.

This sort of criticism could be called anthropological or experiential. I am concerned with the shape and feel of the works in the context of conventional knowledge. Huck Finn leaves the impression as being something more special than what the rag-tag juvenile-delinquent pubescent objective description of him suggests. What contextual information contributes to the perception? Our knowledge of heroes and their powers, for one thing. I use Lord Raglan's *The Hero* not as an expression of truth about the hero but as a document of that knowledge, a true context for *Huckleberry Finn*. Why does the territory through which Huck takes his trip feel so historically real? Because our own histories of that time describe it just as Twain does. Is it just Hank Morgan's bouts of rage and egotism which make him seem to represent more of a generalized psyche than a real person? Joseph Campbell's *The Hero with a Thousand Faces* compiles the knowledge we have about heroes and the psyche; his perspective alerts us to the context in which we read Hank's story. My concern is thus both with the experience of reading and with the culture in which we read. The books under consideration here are both documents of contemporary culture and personal voyages for readers who enter them. My concern for the many contexts of the cultural experience of reading Mark Twain shares as much with Michel Foucault's *The Archaeology of Knowledge* as with Clifford Geertz's essays in *Local Knowledge* and *The Interpretation of Cultures*. Readers familiar with Geertz and Foucault will have no trouble spotting their influence on my work: in my insistent contextualizing of the fiction in the readers' paper trail we call criticism, and in my shifting of perspective when another offers a clearer view. I make no apology if you find the result personal and idiosyncratic. I only hope that you grow to share my idiosyncrasies through your personal experience with this critical rereading of the works of Mark Twain.

No, that's not true. I have another hope: that Twain—whether he is enjoying the climate in heaven or the company in hell—stamps this effort PAID IN FULL.

# Part I

❧

*Adventures of*
*Huckleberry Finn*

# 1

⋘⋙

# Huck's Heroism

Mark Twain's *Adventures of Huckleberry Finn* has left squadrons of uneasy critics. The novel's hero and the novel's ending seem so unsuited to one another that critics have been able to find no sure ground between them. Readers praising Huck Finn tremble at the formal confusion of *Huckleberry Finn*; readers moved by the novel's moral complexity doubt its hero's heroism. Understanding the novel as a whole, however, means seeing the hero in his story, and seeing him all the way through to the end, no matter how bitter. Few critics have demonstrated a comprehensive relationship between Huck and *Huck*, especially its ending. Early critics, such as Lionel Trilling and T. S. Eliot, lavished praise on Huck's courage in the face of a corrupt society, seeing him as a natural philosopher of the democratic virtues of equality and individualism. After Leo Marx knocked the stuffing out of this reading by pointing out in "Mr Trilling, Mr. Eliot, and *Huckleberry Finn*" that the last fifth of the novel was wholly inconsistent with it, modern critics looked for a moral structure for the novel which included the evasion sequence. George C. Carrington made the best and most comprehensive attempt in his *Dramatic Unity in "Huckleberry Finn."* He writes, "The highest meaning of the novel lies in the reader's outraged response to it, the central part of that response being the usual resentment of the ending. Without committing himself or forcing us, Twain allows us to identify contentedly with Huck; then he disillusions us, and we howl" (122). Carrington wisely reads the ethic of the novel as situational and Huck's growth not as moral development but as increased expertise in influencing the small dramas in which the situational ethic obtains. Like most later critics, Carrington gives Huck's heroism no quarter. Huck's moral heroism,

3

like the "masochistic interest in Jim, is [the reader's] own creation, not Huck's" (123). Carrington finds a unity in *Huckleberry Finn* in part by denying Huck the kind of heroism most readers experience in the text.

I believe we can find this unity between the book and its narrator even closer to our experiential knowledge of the novel by looking first at Huck as hero. In the following chapters I will argue that we experience Huck as a hero in the novel because his story closely resembles models of traditional heroism. Other interpretations of Huck's heroism—as existential hero, as romantic hero, as nonhero—illustrate aspects of Huck's function in his world, but few account for both his character and behavior. Huck's traditional heroism is masked slightly by the transformations of oral story-telling literature makes—the transformation of royalty into rapscallions, for example—but reading Huck's story in the context of inherited tales makes the correspondence between the two startling. Huck closely fits our expectations of the traditional hero. This discovery answers one question for us and suggests an answer for the second: we see now why we view Huck as a hero, among the greatest creations of American literature, despite his failure at the end; and we begin to see why Huck has to fail. Twain has taken a traditional hero, a creature of oral tale-telling, by nature ahistorical, and put him in a fiction wholly unsuited to him. The context distorts and defrocks Huck as hero. He looks either foolishly romantic or helplessly unheroic, his heroic powers diminished, perhaps completely sapped, by his surroundings. It is at this point of dissonance that we find Carrington's "highest meaning of the novel," a juxtaposition poignant and disappointing. Mark Twain has created a comprehensive traditional hero and placed him in a world where his heroism cannot function, where the magic, the idealism, the integrity of the traditional hero have no power.

In the next chapter I will examine the sort of world the novel creates, a world which has the power to defeat a hero's magic. Finding this world poses as many difficulties and perhaps fewer rewards than Columbus' explorations. We must navigate Huck Finn's language to get to it, and Huck's talk resists the application of most critical tools beyond simple appreciation. Tense confusion makes separating Huck-the-writer from Huck-the-written-about nearly impossible. Diction and a flexible irony make separating Huck and Twain a matter of assertion, not proof. Huck's studied ignorance makes the readers' complicity in the novel's construction an integral part of the fiction. Huck's language creates of *Huckleberry Finn* a text impervious to deconstruction, a sort of fun-house whose construction resists any understanding of its construction from within. To comprehend, critics must get above and look down into the novel. This movement reveals in the novel a special sort of reality, one based on a confluence of time and writing. Time—the measure of time, that is—and writing create history, and the world of the novel is an historically conceived one. Further, they defeat tradition, particularly the oral one where heroes exist out of time and where the rules of the world of experience no longer apply. Huck's heroism loses in the novel's end to nothing more—or less—than history.

That history, though, is not simply abstract. The history in *Huckleberry Finn* particularly concerns Jacksonian America. Huck is made to be more than a traditional hero; he is the hero of the age. Using the work of historians of the period, the third chapter reveals Huck as the emblem of the Jacksonian cultural goals of Nature, Providence and Will and the Jacksonian socio-political goals of equality, democracy and individualism. More, we see in looking into the journals and travelogues of the day just what everyday Jacksonian America looked like and find it looks exactly like the world the novel presents us. The tensions in the novel exist not only between an oral hero in a written world, the ahistorical powers of magic against the unstoppable flow of time and writing that is history, but also between the ideals of an age and its reality. Jacksonian Democracy braced itself with the twin concepts of individual freedom and political equality, but it stood on the twin abuses of slavery and Indian resettlement. The novel begins where *Tom Sawyer* ends, with Huck and Tom recapturing the money Injun Joe stole. It ends, as critics have always noted, in moral disarray, our hero's efforts to free Jim decimated by a culturally based romantic idealism, the last piece of Huck's crusade blown away by the unexplained whimsy of Miss Watson's death-bed manumission. This confluence of heroes and history, of Jacksonian ideals and Jacksonian life, produces new flashes of meaning in *Huckleberry Finn*.

Let us begin by clarifying the nature of Huck's heroism. Many critics argue for Huck's complete lack of heroism. Lawrence Scanlon's "Unheroic Huck," for example, finds a host of opportunities to make of Huck a traditional hero, opportunities Twain sets up and rejects to prove Huck's lack of heroism. Scanlon finds the novel's initial cave and barrel imagery reminiscent of the womb and writes, "Usually when womb imagery appears in literature, it is preparatory to the rebirth of the hero" (100), but in the novel Huck is not reborn from those wombs; he just surrenders himself to the Mississippi. For Scanlon, Huck's predeliction for passivity is the fundamental aspect of his character. The raft, controlled only by the river's flow, matches perfectly the nature of its inhabitant, and that is why Huck finds happiness on it. Huck's "lack of purposive action" (107) continues to the novel's conclusion where readers at last get frustrated with Huck. "By prefering passivity to action, fantasied death to active life, Huck turns the conventional notion of the hero upside down" (111). In making him a nonhero, Twain shows "that all forms of response to society as it presently constituted are alike impossible, if not insane" (113).

Scanlon's argument invites two fundamental questions. First, exactly what society has Huck refused participation in? Apart from the occasional manhandling by the King and Duke, characters his own actions brought into his life, nothing induces Huck to leave the river. Huck visits Mrs. Loftus because "it was getting slow and dull, and I wanted to get a stirring up, some way" (66). He begins the final portion of the novel with an extremely purposive action: "For a starter, I would go to work and steal Jim from slavery again; and if I could think up anything worse, I would do that too" (271). Even though Tom Sawyer dominates the evasion, Huck's actions form a necessary part of it. If Huck were an absolute devotee of inaction, there would be no book; he would never write one. Huck's conflicts with society come not from his attempts to escape its domination of him, but from his persistent will to self-determination when within society, a will that drives him to perform actions he knows society cannot approve. Taken from Huck's point of view, society is any group structure which disallows his freedom; a calculated lack of response to this society is impossible because the society itself only exists in contradistinction to his own actions.

Second, taking Scanlon's arguments on its own terms, what distinguishes a nonhero from a hero of a more definable sort? Scanlon writes, "If in this context a hero is defined as one who acts bravely and purposely on behalf of himself and others, a whole culture possibly, and an anti-hero one who acts similarly to destroy himself or his society, the non-hero does not act at all. His primary, and sometimes all-embracing, feature is passivity" (111). This passivity is not powerlessness, Scanlon insists. "Mark Twain through Huck's passivity has rendered an even more telling judgment on society than he could have with a frontal assault" (113). Other critics give other names to heroes performing the functions Scanlon ascribes to Huck. In "Huck Finn as Existential Hero: Making Sense of Absurdity," Arthur Asa Berger argues that "Huck functions as a *fool*," making "use of the humor of pattern and exaggeration, techniques used throughout the book" (13). A fool, Berger leaves his reader to gather, points out his own wisdom by exaggerating the patterned idiocy of society at large. Huck achieves this primarily through his pragmatism, that fundamental American characteristic. We first see Huck's pragmatism in his unsuccessful prayers for fish hooks; it reaches its peak in his subtle ridiculing of Tom by "letting on" picks and stairs are case knives and lightning rods, as long as Tom's plan will eventually free Jim. He tells Tom, "When I start in to steal a nigger, or a watermelon, or a Sunday school book, I ain't no ways particular how it's done, so it's done. . . . I don't give a dead rat what the authorities thinks about it, nuther" (307). According to Berger, Huck "is his own authority" (14). Counter to Scanlon's argument, Berger notes that, as a fool, Huck is not expected to act, only to represent. "Huck symbolizes man's possibilities for goodness and Huck's moral development is a demonstration of man's potentialities being realized" (15). At the same time, Berger's argument goes, Huck's alienation from society and his frequent adoption of other identities to cope with the alienation establishes Huck as an existential hero. "Huck Finn suggests . . . what might be called an awareness of the possibility of error. This is important, for if we are aware of error then we can try to correct it" (17). Huck's heroism is of a moral nature, Berger implies; his inaction matters less than his ridicule of society on one hand and his moral awareness on the other. Being who he is, knowing what he knows, is Huck's heroic action. The whole book serves as prelude, Berger asserts, to Huck's final action, the mythic initiation of lighting out for the territory, a new land, which Berger equates with Mircea Eliade's Center of the World.

This somewhat incoherent presentation of Huck's heroism appears a bit closer to the Huck we experience in reading *Adventures of Huckleberry Finn* than Lawrence Scanlon's, but there remain several gaps and problems. First, Huck reaches his moral peak in famous Chapter 31, when he consigns himself to hell for his willingness to save Jim from further enslavement. Leo Marx points out in the influential essay "Mr. Eliot, Mr. Trilling, and *Huckleberry Finn*" that, while Huck does represent "the redemptive possibilities of the human race" (437), those possibilities remain only that. The failure of the novel's ending is the failure of Huck himself to make good on his moral promises. When he lights out for the territory ahead of the rest he leaves his betrayed readers' hearts behind. If this move west proves "Huck's authenticity," as Berger contends, then the move ought to elicit a sympathy for Huck's quest, not the coldness we do feel after 80 pages of Huck's participation as the erstwhile Tom Sawyer in the torture of his friend Jim.

Further, the very moral integrity upon which Berger bases his argument is suspect. A close look at Chapter 31 reveals an acceptance of society, not a refusal of it. Huck has "got to decide, forever, betwixt two things, and I knowed it" (270): between following law and morality by returning Jim to Miss Watson, or breaking law and morality by freeing him. Huck perceives his choices as two: being socially acceptable, like Tom Sawyer or the Widow Douglas, or being socially unacceptable, like Pap or the King and Duke. Huck chooses to join his father and the royalty in hell, a choice he makes in the very first chapter in response to Miss Watson: "She told me about the bad place, and I said I wished I was there" (3). All Huck's experiences have simply served to refine his determination to spend eternity with the Devil. His first-chapter assertion grows out of his desire to "go somewheres, all I wanted was a change, I warn't particular" (4), granting the moral plane the same boundless feel as the West's Great Plains. By the peak of his moral crisis, however, the range of possibility has narrowed to a choice between social convention and hell. In case we miss the point Huck repeats his claims to be "lowdown," "born to wickedness" and so on. Huck's alienation from society is only an alienation from a part of it, the society implied by the term 'society pages.' Huck identifies himself with Pap's class, with Pap himself and with Pap's wholesale acceptance of the institutional immorality we find in his "Call this a govment" speech (33–34), an institutional immorality against which we deeply want Huck to rebel.

Second, though Berger claims for Huck some traditional heroic qualities, he does not make himself specific. Huck is cast as fool, he says, but in the book itself Jim plays the fool in Huck's court; the conversations about Solomon and the French language in Chapter 14 will prove that. Berger alludes to the continuing death and rebirth of Huck but does not fit these heroic attributes into a heroic model. His consideration of Huck's traditional heroism is left at the level of allusion.

Several cogent arguments about the nature of Huck's traditional heroism have appeared. The premier one, from Robert Regan's *Unpromising Heroes*, examines Huck against the background of the well-articulated, folktale-based type of the title. Regan finds in Mark Twain a pattern of heroism stemming from youngest-child folktales. In these stories, stronger but ill-willed older brothers serve themselves instead of their ailing fathers, mothers or lovers. The disenfranchised, disdained, and dispossessed younger brother performs the needed service, usually through a combination of cunning, kindness, and magic, but is temporarily denied reward by the actions of his jealous siblings. In time, though, he rises to kingship either through marriage to a princess or inheritance of his father's throne, again achieved through this same combination of cunning, kindness, and magic. Regan maintains that this unpromising or unlikely hero theme underlies most of Twain's heroes, Tom Sawyer, Hank Morgan, and David Wilson most notably. Only rarely "Mark Twain could, by special effort, escape the narrow confines of his most persistent theme, and produce, albeit painfully, as in *Adventures of Huckleberry Finn*, a hero who is motivated by impulses more exalted than the dream of glory" (14). Regan argues that Huck's character, and not plot exigencies, directs the novel in the end to pit Tom, Twain's conventional hero type, against Huck. Regan sees Huck's character much as Berger does, as a moral force for disengagement, a Bartleby on a raft, always prefering absolute inaction to social conformity and corruption. When forced to action by the strength of his conviction he discovers just how much trouble bravery and higher purpose can be. Tom, "still motivated in all he does by a neurotic impulse to make himself a hero" (158), Regan writes, "provides a conclusive dramatization of Huck's election of the anti-heroic—the genuinely heroic—life" (159). Temporarily tempted by Tom, Huck agrees in the novel's final fifth to an uneasy peace with his past, the romantic and artificial world of Tom and St. Petersburg. The compromise is rife with tension, though, and Regan sees the outcome of this conflict as beautifully represented by the question of identities: Huck only seems to become Tom, but "Huck of course never quite forgets his true identity" (160), the security of identity itself being Huck's only true claim to heroism.

Regan reads Huck convincingly. Sadly Huck lies outside the province of his study; Regan does not turn his folkloric eye on Huck himself and instead sees him only as a counter to his other, well-argued traditional type. He defines Huck primarily as not-Tom: antiromantic, inactive, inward-directed, asocial. Unfortunately he leaves a particular reversal unexplored, a reversal I will myself explore later: the picture of Huck Finn as a Promising Un-hero, a positive definition of Huck's traditional heroism gone down in failure at the novel's end.

Other critics have found traditional heroic characteristics in Huck, many of which run counter to Regan's portrait-by-negation. Daniel Hoffman, in his classic *Form and Fable in American Fiction*, sees Huck's "moral eminence" in his stark contrast to Tom's romantic visions. Huck resists the bookish artifice of Tom and the con-men Duke and King, whom Hoffman sees in moral alliance with Tom, and instead goes to school with Jim, where he learns the hidden powers of Nature. Jim is more than Huck's fool, more than the traditional hero's also traditional strong and stout-hearted friend. For Hoffman, "If the river is a god, Jim is its priest. . . . Only when Jim is alone with Huck on the river island or drifting on the current is he so free from the corruption of civilization that he can partake of the river god's dark power" (335). Learn as he might, Huck's powers have boundaries. While in his easy assumption of alternative identities he "seems to remain true to the American folk concept of the metamorphic hero" (343), his "powers of transformation are not . . . illimitably protean" (346). His attempts to be like Tom only increase the danger to himself and Jim. Huck can survive "the threats to his identity of the retrograde Pap, of the avaricious slave-hunters, of the feuders with their courtly savagery and the lynch mob with its cowardly passions" (348), but among the quality against whom these vermin define themselves, a quality among whom Tom's artifice works superbly, Huck has no power and must flee. Huck's "classical pattern of death and rebirth of the hero" (343) places him outside of the real world's realm. In the real world, when operating smoothly at its most corrupt, Huck's powers do not work. The magical pairing of Huck and Jim does not represent a homoerotic deathwish, as Leslie Fiedler maintains in *Love and Death in the American Novel*. Instead, Daniel Hoffman writes, "the two themes" the regular pairing of white and nonwhite in American literature "exemplify are primitivism and egalitarianism" (349). In this sense, we can construe Huck's heroism as fitting a part of Scanlon's earlier definition of the hero: Huck represents virtue for the whole culture.

Some critics disagree with aspects of Hoffman's view of Huck. Warren Beck in his seminal "Huck Finn at Phelps Farm," the first extended attempt to resolve the conflict over the ending of the novel, writes that "Mark's conception of Huck was not superficially romantic but genuinely and deeply so. Huck is not a noble savage, existing with naive aplomb in an unmodified innocence; he transcends ignorance, step by slow step, as any man must, by taking upon his own shoulders the knowledge of good and evil" (27). More than a decade later, Alan Ostrom made Beck's "knowledge" more specific: "The sole continuing conflict in the novel, in fact, a conflict made manifest in every incident, every episode, is the conflict between the person-as-individual and the person-as-member-of-society. For if Huck is a Romantic youth figure, he is *not* a noble savage" (164). Individualism marks this romantic character. The contrast between Huck and Tom in the novel's end is not between socially approved and sophisticated romance and elitism on one hand and antisocial primitivism and egalitarianism on the other, these critics imply, but between a false, book-based romanticism and a true, self-based one. Following this, Neil Sapper views Huck as a Tocquevillian individualist. "Tocqueville has provided an archetypal image of Huck Finn" (37), Sapper claims, by defining individualism as "a calm and considered feeling which disposes each citizen to isolate himself from the mass of his fellows and withdraw into the circle of family and friends; with this little society formed to his taste, he gladly leaves the greater society to look after itself" (Tocqueville, *Democracy in America*, 506). As many critics have pointed out, most notably Robert Shulman in "Fathers, Brothers, and 'the Diseased': The Family, Individualism, and American Society in *Huckleberry Finn*," Huck and Jim form a family which "suggests the possibility of an individualism not at odds with the community" (327). It is in this family, most critics agree with Hoffman, that Huck acquires the knowledge that makes him a heroic force. Few critics have solved the problem of what transforms his heroism into a spent force when Huck reaches the Phelps plantation.

Two things remain consistent in these inconsistent critical appraisals of Huck Finn's heroism: Huck's heroism has traditional qualities; and no matter what form that heroism seems to take prior to Chapter 31, it comes out bruised and tarnished between that point and the end of the novel. I began this review of critical thinking on Huck's heroism with the comment that these two common observations remain insufficiently linked. The slippage between Huck's traditional heroism and his failure to act heroically (or between Huck as hero when alone and Huck as failure in society) invites deconstruction. But before I turn my attention to Huck Finn's language, which provides our best clue in solving this disjuncture, we must clarify our conception of these divided parts.

The nature of Huck's failure at the Phelps' farm seems clear: the pressure of this world prevents him from making good on the heroism promised earlier. This is why we find critics arguing first that Huck is a hero and then that he is not, or arguing that he is a noble savage or a romantic youth figure and then not. This formulation of the problem advances us towards a solution in the following way. Rather than assuming that the failure of Huck's heroism is narrative—that is, that Huck himself changes his character in the course of the book, or that Twain failed in keeping Huck consistent—this construct assumes that the book is *about* the failure of a hero. Other narratives of failed heroism must be told from the third person, because the hero dies, or involve comically small achievements, such as the failure of the hero in John Barth's *The Floating Opera* to kill himself. In *Huckleberry Finn* we have instead a true hero with worthy goals who, unaware of his failure or his heroism, tells his own tale. While the perspectives discussed above grasp aspects of Huck's heroism, none has laid hold of that heroism's very nature, something we must do in order to comprehend its failure. And as an expression of contemporary knowledge of the nature of heroism in fiction I know no better book than Lord Raglan's *The Hero*.

Not that Raglan's treatise comes without objection. In the fifty years since its publication, *The Hero* has sustained a nearly endless barrage of criticism. Almost all the resistance to the book comes down to its lack of rigor. *The Hero* in no way meets contemporary criteria for critical validity: Raglan was an amateur; he did most of his research in his own library; he often appears more concerned with wit than substance in his arguments. His choice as to what to include both in his book as a whole and in his particular construction of the hero's life seems purely arbitrary. His work reads more like pleasant fireside chat, fascinating but aimless, than a serious inquiry into important matters, a particularly painful scratch to dedicated scholars of folklore hoping to get their long-neglected discipline some deserved respect. Further, one significant point relies on the long-discredited premise that all folktales derive from a single point, an Ur-form.

But I do not use *The Hero* as I have used the Twain critics I have mentioned thus far. Criticism is secondary material; Raglan's work, whatever its flaws of rigor, is a kind of primary document. Whether or not what he writes meets disciplinary criteria for criticism matters less in this context than the text's expression of a cogent and popularly acceptable notion of the traditional hero. The book's continuation in print over more than half a century of critical disrepute indicates its wide use for just this purpose. I do not mean my use of it here to be an indication that either I or readers generally accept Raglan's premise that all the heroes which concern him derived from a single ritual drama performed in the lost past; our wider knowledge of history does not render Gibbon's *Decline and Fall of the Roman Empire* useless, but rather only qualifiedly useful. I do not mean Raglan to be taken as the complete or final expression of the hero. His arbitrary partiality does leave gaps, but that does not prove that what he does include is incorrect. And Lord Raglan's charm and humor has given his book and ideas a much longer life than more rigorous and less interesting scholars might have achieved.

Raglan attempts to prove in his classic work that the roots even of literate fiction lay in ancient ritual drama. In ritual drama, Raglan says, myth and ritual combine in a religious ceremony; a story of magical import is told and acted by the tribal kings and leaders as a sop to the gods or a satisfaction of some lost tribal need. In time the myth and the ritual become separate. Raglan does not say why; perhaps because the teller of the tale finds some benefit in telling his stories nonritually or because other raconteurs in the group appropriate aspects of ritual telling to their secular purposes—explanations of the tribal past, simple entertainment, what-ever. The myths persist, coming down to literate culture as history or as fiction.

The view of myth as history grows from the belief that, within even the most outlandish and supernatural events of myth, there resides a kernel of historical fact. So: Hercules might not have swept out the stable, but he was a very great king, of massive strength, who came to rule by overcoming tremendous adversity. The savageness of the wise humor with which Raglan ridicules it testifies to how recently this view became discredited. Stories are not based on fact; instead, stories transform fact into a fiction that audiences find more believable. A preliterate culture, having a past but no history, tells its stories with more concern for truth than facts; facts cannot be verified without records, but truth relies only on the agreement of the audience. Raglan demonstrates how this habit of telling tales which transform facts survives the coming of writing. The differences between literate and preliterate cultures encourage the misappropriation of stories told in a lost context. For example, discussing the mythification of Henry V, Raglan writes that "those who composed the traditional stories about Prince Henry applied to him, in a more or less modified form, stories they had heard in a different but not dissimilar connection" (212). This fictionalization of history requires its Henry to have a riotous youth and a near indecent association with a man like Falstaff. "To Shake-speare's audiences the proper way for a budding hero to behave was to roister with a drunken buffoon" (213).

This willful neglect of the historical Henry, almost dour and rather staid as a prince, points to the limited interest storytellers or their audiences have in historical reality when creating a mythical hero. Literate peoples attribute mythical proportions to recent his-torical or even contemporary figures, as I will indicate later in re-gard to Andrew Jackson.

Heroes connected to history by invention rather than fact— for example the creations of modern fiction—have much less re-straining their fulfillment of the traditional requirements of the hero. We would expect to find, then, a correlation between the at-tributes of a traditional hero and characters from contemporary fiction. But literate culture moves against the employment of types in its storytelling. Preliterate cultures have few ways to store knowl-edge; the apparent repetition of stories and types serves this end. I say apparent because pure repetition, repetition without variation, is impossible without the very tools that make a culture literate. This variation goes unnoticed—or if noticed is denied—by the members of the concerned tribe. These changes reflect the changing knowledge of the audience's world, but the audience's insistence that the story is pure repetition expresses the need to have a cultural link to the common knowledge which makes the audience a unified group. A culture of books and libraries, archives and museums, has no need to tie itself to its past; those ties are strong enough. Such a culture needs instead to differentiate itself from its past, to fight its past to achieve its needed change. The very notion of a supernaturally empowered hero contradicts literary tradition: the supernatural takes place out of time and is therefore highly resistant to the sort of change literature documents. Literary tradition seems to prefer heroes who are ordinary people in extraordinary circumstances; a thorough investigation of the heroes of this past century's fiction will produce few that follow Raglan's model of the traditional hero. Literate culture constantly develops new heroic patterns for its fiction; the existence of other hero types, such as the anti-hero, shows this. A quick review of Raglan's hero shows broad areas where the design of the traditional hero jars modern sensibility. Royal birth is, for the most part, out of the question in contemporary fiction. The mysticism and religiosity of the last eight points—the remarkable fit between this standard recitation of the traditional hero's death and the last days of Christ should both give pause to believers in Christ's historicity and proof to my point—appear awkward in the imagination of a scientific age. One part fits literate fiction; Raglan himself points out that the tradition of romance is "based on the central part of the myth" (191). That accounts only for points 10 through 13 in the Raglan's following model:

1. The hero's mother is a royal virgin;
2. His father is a king, and
3. Often a near relative of his mother, but
4. The circumstances of his conception are unusual and
5. He is also reputed to be the son of a god.
6. At birth an attempt is made, usually by his father or his maternal grandfather, to kill him, but
7. He is spirited away, and
8. Reared by foster-parents in a far country.

9. We are told nothing of his childhood, but
10. On reaching manhood he returns or goes to his future kingdom.
11. After a victory over the king and/or giant, dragon or wild beast,
12. He marries a princess, often the daughter of his predecessor and
13. Becomes king.
14. For a time he rules uneventfully, and
15. Prescribes laws, but
16. Later he loses favor with the gods and/or his subjects, and
17. Is driven from the throne and city, after which
18. He meets with a mysterious death,
19. Often at the top of a hill.
20. His children, if any, do not succeed him.
21. His body is not buried, but nonetheless
22. He has one or more holy sepulchres. (179–80)

A quick review of this sequence shows a tripartite structure. Points 1 through 8 recount the birth of the hero; 9 marks the sharp division between that story and the traditional romance of points 10 through 13. Point 14 establishes another break before the final third, the death of the hero. These three stories—birth, ascension to power and marriage, and death—are slung together to create a semblance of a whole life. These periods of dormancy are as telling for the traditional hero as the stories they link: it is almost as though the hero does not exist except when fulfilling the active requirements of heroism.

Despite the winds blowing against the possibility of a hero of modern fiction fitting into Raglan's heroic scheme, Huck Finn fits remarkably well. Without interpretive stretching, Huck fits half the provisions of the hero; interpretations modifying Raglan's scheme for modern American readers add several points of correspondence. The sequence of Huck's heroic acts does not match Raglan's, but, as I have noted, literariness encourages transformations of tradition. We do find in *Huckleberry Finn*, however, what Raglan found in his examination of traditional myth heroes: the same elements, though disordered. Because a written text needs to distinguish itself from previous written texts in ways unnecessary and unthought-of for oral tales, and because of the circumstantial need for variation in both oral and written cultures, we must expect many changes in contemporary renditions of traditional story-telling elements. These elements can be quite small, such as the national origin of adversaries, which in American war movies have changed from Japanese and German to Arab and Russian, or, as we see in *Huckleberry Finn*, quite large. Raglan writes that these elements change to suit the audiences' capacity for belief. We therefore cannot simply launch into an attempt to correlated Huck Finn and Raglan's construction of the hero. We must first explore how several modern readerly beliefs have affected the representation of traditional heroic actions.

I would like to review three aspects of the traditional hero and their transformations in *Huckleberry Finn*: the impermanence of death; the existence of kings; and the involvement divinity or magic in real life. Contemporary America has an egalitarian, scientific ideology which allows little or no room for palingenesis, royalty or the supernatural, and yet these are vital ingredients in traditional popular stories. The democratic drive to include tales from the people in works of literature, perhaps best represented in the nineteenth century by Mark Twain, stems from the same ideology which actually makes aspects of those tales acceptable only as folklore, not as literature. To escape the identification of folktales with the quaint and arcane, storytellers must either transform these traditional elements or abandon them entirely.

Though Raglan does not explicitly include a round trip to the underworld in his hero pattern, he finds the Orpheus myth repeated and transformed for many heroes of tradition. Modern concepts of death preclude a true return from afterlife except in certain forms of reincarnation, but those beliefs have not eliminated the presence of palingenetic archetypes in contemporary fiction. Modern gothics often substitute coma for death, with the hero-victim often returning evilly empowered; Raglan notes that Christian-era holdovers from ritual drama play under the auspices of the Devil and that, in these holdovers, supernatural heroes become supernatural villains. Film, halfway between the elite novel and the gothic romance for realism, plays this theme often. Paddy Chayeffsky's and Ken Russell's 1980 film *Altered States* has its scientist-hero reach into the underworld of our genetic past and return, again evilly transformed. American fiction of this century has used this theme in many forms. John Barth's *The End of the Road* opens with its protagonist in a deathlike trance; he is analyzed and cured by a scientist. The planned confusion between characters named Quentin in William Faulkner's *The Sound and the Fury* creates the effect of death and return. In "The Aspern Papers" Henry James sends his unnamed narrator into the dusty death of the past and brings him back again. All of these renditions of the Orpheus myth of death and return work by transfiguring the nature of the death involved.

Sufficient critical attention has been paid to the presence of this theme in *Adventures of Huckleberry Finn*. No reader can help but notice the endless comparisons with and invocations of death in the novel. To bring Orpheus to bear in this book, Twain chooses a simpler solution than did his successors: he has his hero fake death. This simple solution meets the necessary criteria of creating out of something as incredible as palingenesis something more credible than the bungled romance of the evasion. It also provides opportunity for humor and elegance. Huck rigs his own death to escape Pap. For the next several chapters we receive pointed reminders of Huck's ambiguous position among the living: he witnesses attempts to find his body; he encounters Jim who, like everyone else, believes him to be dead; Mrs. Loftus speaks to Huck matter-of-factly about his murder. Chapter by chapter death appears. Before his own death, Huck "don't take no stock in dead people" (2) and he can not hide his disgust that Tom Sawyer's Gang "hadn't killed any people, but only just pretended" (14). But after Huck fakes his own death real death is everywhere: with the murderous bandits aboard the *Walter Scott*, in the floating house, at the Grangerford-Shepardson feud. Between acts leading to death, in moments of relative peace, Huck is so lonesome he wishes for death, or is imperiled by the elements, or takes on the identity of the mysterious dead baby Charles William Albright. His first encounter at the Phelps farm reminds us of the underworld nature of his journey. "I heard the dim hum of a spinning wheel wailing along up and sinking along down again: and then I knowed for certain I wished I was dead—for that *is* the lonesomest sound in the whole world" (277). When Huck is mistaken for Tom Sawyer "it was like being born again, I was so glad to find out who I was" (282). For the whole of the evasion Huck lives in the twilight world between life and death; being Tom is only *like* being born again. Only when Huck recovers his identity with the reappearance of Aunt Polly can he be said to reenter the living world completely. Like so much in

*Huckleberry Finn*, death is more a matter of appearance than reality. Huck's death at his father's cabin convinces the good people of St. Petersburg; on the symbolic plane it convinces readers. The novel manages to incorporate the mystical qualities of palingenesis without straining contemporary readers' credulity.

Raglan believes traditional heroes of folktales are kings because the central figure in ritual drama was a king whose primary kingly responsibility was the ritual drama. "If folktales were really composed by the folk, we should expect them to deal with subjects with which the folk are familiar—matters of village courtship and marriage, of quarrels and revenges, of seedtime and harvest, of plenty and dearth, of hunting and fishing—. . . but we should be disappointed. It is very seldom that peasants appear in the tales at all" (139). Instead, folktales concern either royalty or talking animals, which are in Raglan's view disguised royalty. In America, this presents a problem: we have no royalty. American fictions have solved this lack by replacing royalty with the rich and powerful. Prime-time soap operas dwell interminably on this class, as do movies; even the extraordinary *Ordinary People* documents a very well-to-do family. We interpret the determination not to write about royal-equivalents as political, as in the works of Richard Price or Marge Piercy. Earlier writers of the lives of plain folk have had to defend their choices with political or aesthetic manifestos: Norris and Dreiser championed naturalism, Dos Passos and Steinbeck a whole America. But lives of the socially advantaged do not require a political or aesthetic philosophy to be written: James and Fitzgerald wrote of almost no one else.

Not so Mark Twain. *Huckleberry Finn*'s low-life sensibility so offended high-brow Concord that the town banned it from their library. Though the novel contains little of the cultural elite, it is almost overloaded with a certain sort of royalty: the Duke and the King. After noting that "All kings is mostly rapscallions," Huck says "Sometimes I wish we could hear of a country that's out of kings" (201). America might be out of inherited royalty, but in Twain's construction we have picked up another kind. America's kings, like Huck's and Jim's unwelcome companions, get their crowns by bilking the public. This is a sort of back-handed praise of America: we invert the traditional political hierarchy, putting the people on top and the royalty on the bottom. So long as the King and Duke and Pap and others of "his kind of people" (165) remain inversions of the social code, they will rule their particular underworld. Royalty dominates *Adventures of Huckleberry Finn*, the story of two unfortunates on the outs with conventional society. Huck, born into this inverted royalty, at first rejects it but later apprentices and becomes a "valley" to it. In his paradoxically moral stand of freeing Jim and going to hell, Huck rejoins the class to which his blood entitles him membership. He sets himself, as did the King and Duke and Pap, against society from within it, not from outside it. Twain has found a place for royalty in America, logically in opposition to the conventions of their democratic world.

Magic plays a fundamental role in the life of the hero. "Against the hero with the magic weapons the monster is powerless; he falls at the first blow. That is because the hero is a ritual personage using ritual weapons to deliver a ritual blow" (147). Magic acts play like miracles in drama, Raglan argues, and miracles have the following traits: they are performed by superhumans, their results are appropriate for superhuman acts, and they can only come out of ritual acts. In *The Tempest*, he writes, Ariel can appear and disappear miraculously, but in the plays of Prince Henry, Falstaff cannot. The relative positions of the hero and fool are the same in these plays, but the audience's acceptance of the miraculous has changed because of the conditions of the drama. Conditions in modern America disallow the miraculous. As a rule, narrative miracles need to be couched as science, as in science fiction, presented as the conscious deception of a public on the part of a confidence man, or imagined in metaphor, the magic of words. In Hemingway, for example, miracles become metaphors, plain and obvious symbols, such as the diverging railroad tracks in "Hills Like White Elephants." In this construction of the miraculous, the author himself becomes the supernatural force determining the shape of the fictive universe; this sort of magical transformation forms the core of metafiction. Con artists gratify the need for the supernatural by the creation of alternative realities; when we read fictions about them we see and accept both the narrative reality and the artificial ones they create within it. And science fiction allows anything to happen, especially the supernatural, so long as it is accompanied by an explanation that has the look and feel of science. Twentieth-century America looks askance at miracles and shapeshifting. It demands in their place the power of metaphor, the dodge of science fiction or the artifice of con artistry.

Twain himself, often called the father of American Realism, resists the miraculous. In his hilarious dismemberment "Fenimore Cooper's Literary Offences," Twain writes that one of the "nineteen rules governing literary art in the domain of romantic fiction" requires "that the personages in a tale shall confine themselves to possibilities and let miracles alone; or, if they venture a miracle, the author must so plausibly set it forth as to make it look possible and reasonable" (*Unabridged*, 1242). In *Huckleberry Finn* he observes the rules of realism by rendering the miraculous commonplace. Conventional religion, the common residence for modern-day belief in the miraculous, is usurped from the first chapter on: Miss Watson's description of heaven only makes us laugh; the feuding families are called Shepherdson and Grangerford; the King milks religious sentiment at a revival meeting. Religion has no magic powers in the novel except in limited metaphors: we hear of "Moses and the Bulrushers" only to illuminate Huck's role as liberator. If we are looking for magic and miracles in *Huckleberry Finn* we will have to look outside conventional religion.

Outside religion we find superstition, the term we give substandard beliefs. Before Huck ventures into the underworld, superstition afflicts everyone in the novel, but most particularly Huck and Jim. Twain ridicules these beliefs more savagely than he ridicules conventional religion, showing us that Jim's "superstitions, like the hagiolatry of the ignorant peasants in *The Innocents Abroad*, are the manacles upon his soul" (Hoffman, 331). Jim's transformation of Tom Sawyer's prank in Chapter 2 into world-wide witch travel derides both Jim and superstition. But then, on Jackson's Island, "the nature of Jim's superstitious belief undergoes a change" (Hoffman, 332). Jim reads rain in the birds and the future in almost anything. He becomes a magus of Nature, and the satire of superstition transforms itself into a sort of respect. Granted Huck believes Jim only skeptically, and granted too that Huck's river-rat ignorance allows the reader to retain some distance from even that skeptical belief, but still, the early chapters' ridicule has become something closer to wonder. The belief in superstition gains some authority by the novel's end. Jim says "Signs is *signs*, mine I tell you; en I knowed jis' s well 'at I 'uz gwineter be rich agin as I's a stannin' heah dis minute!" (361) He predicted when on Jackson's Island that he would be rich and he is: not only with Tom's forty dollars, but with himself—a discovery he also made on the island.

In place of the more traditional shapeshifting, the novel gives us artifice, which also grows in power and value in the course of the book. In the initial chapters, before Huck's death, Tom, the master of artifice, receives nothing but mockery for his creations, not only from Twain but in time from Huck too. Huck, it seems, has even less patience than the reader for Tom's vision of Sunday School children as bewitched Arabs. But Huck enters the underworld via Tom's sort of artifice and once in the underworld not only indulges in artifice with astonishing regularity but also sees Tom's expertise at it as praiseworthy. His first thought after his faked murder is of Tom: "I did wish Tom Sawyer was there, I knowed he would take an interest in this kind of business, and throw in the fancy touches. Nobody could spread himself like Tom Sawyer in such a thing as that" (41). Huck's hedged enthusiasm in that passage —I find it easy to read ironically—gives way in the course of the novel to a less grudging version. Huck goes from derision of artifice with Tom Sawyer's gang to wholehearted practice of it as he adopts new life after new life, becoming in the end Tom himself. The presence of the Duke and King remind us that Huck is not employing any magic to achieve his shapeshifting; Huck just practices the con-artists' game.

We can see in these contextual considerations of Huck's traditional heroism the clear retention of myth. Without straining our credulity, Twain includes magic, royalty and palingenesis. We learn to expect a hero who can employ the powers of this transformed tradition, who needs the help of Jim, the traditional wise-fool sidekick, who has the vision to see a quest in the random events witnessed and experienced by two outcasts floating down a river on a raft. We get Huck Finn, a hero whose story runs surprisingly close to Raglan's 22-point model.

Even if we include knowledge gained from *The Adventure of Tom Sawyer*, a questionable practice made allowable by the reference to the earlier novel in the latter's first chapter, we can still say nothing to several of Raglan's points, such as 1) the hero's mother is a royal virgin, 3) often a near relative of the (father), or 4) the unusual circumstances of conception. In the special way noted above, though, 2) Pap is a king. If, as Daniel Hoffman says, the river is a god, simple metaphor makes 5) Huck the son of a god: the river gives him birth in too many metaphorical ways to index here. We can give Huck half a point for his supernatural origins.

6) His father does attempt to kill him, though not at birth, and 7) he is spirited away, and 8) reared by foster parents. Whether or not the widow's place in St. Petersburg can be considered "a far country" from Pap can be debated; Pap, not Huck, has gone away. But the distance between Pap and proper society, the very distance that makes a certain sort of king of him, is immeasurable, being simply the same as the distance between two sides of a single coin. 9) We are told nothing of his childhood.

10) On reaching his manhood he goes to his future kingdom. With this point we enter the romance part of the traditional hero's narrative and for Huck the essence of his story, which is in formal terms a picaresque *Bildungsroman*. Huck's escape from his father through death is his entry to manhood, and the idyllic colors in which he paints Jackson's Island leave little doubt that the island is his kingdom. It takes Huck most of the novel to achieve his 11) victory over the king, in this case the King and Duke, who stand in for Pap. Unless we want to accept Leslie Fiedler's thesis on the submerged homosexuality between Huck and Jim, I can find no candidate for 12) the princess he marries, except Mary Jane Wilks. In the artifice the King has created, Mary Jane, though not his daughter, is the King's niece. Huck writes of her:

> In my opinion she had more sand in her than any girl I ever see; in my opinion she was just full of sand. It sounds like flattery, but it ain't no flattery. And when it comes to beauty—and goodness too—she lays over them all. I hain't never seen her since that time that I see her go out that door; no, I hain't ever seen her since; but I reckon I've thought of her a many and a many million times, and of her saying she would pray for me; and if ever I'd a thought it would do any good for me to pray for *her*, blamed if I wouldn't have done it or bust. (244)

There is no marriage here, but Huck and Mary Jane cry together and have an emotional future, at least in Huck. This is worth a remark, but not worth a point. I have already noted the ways in which Huck 13) becomes king in his morally ambiguous stand on freeing Jim. It is by this act that he finally accepts of himself that he is one of Pap's people, and we never see him drop this self-interpretation the remainder of the book.

Raglan acknowledges that "every literary community has certain types of story outside which none but exceptional geniuses can venture" (143). I have no need to argue for Twain's exceptional genius; the very existence of this study and the hundreds like it give testimony. I must note that Twain's manipulation of the hero-pattern's death sequence in *Adventures of Huckleberry Finn* adds to his reputation for genius. As should be clear from the earlier discussion of death and return in the novel, Twain lays the final third of the hero's life over the whole of the story. The death of the hero occurs simultaneously with his life. Huck Finn's death does not come at the end of his reign as king but rather throughout his entire narration, and Huck's continued reference to death not only reminds us that we are reading his journey through the underworld but also outlines for us the experience of death. This experience chills us and we fear for Huck's life, paradoxically, of course, because we know emphatically that Huck will not die: Huck is telling the story. The novel splinters the story of the hero. Huck knows he is telling us the romance; he does not know he is telling us his death. This is possible because we actually experience two Hucks: Huck-the-written-about and Huck-the-writer. We do not actually hear from Huck-the-written-about; everything we know about him comes to us through the recollections of Huck-the-writer. Huck-the-writer makes clear throughout the book he knows he is telling us a story, the subject of which is the romantic history of an earlier version of himself. The framing presence of Twain enables us to recognize that, while Huck-the-writer tells about the other Huck, he also tells a story about himself of which he has no consciousness, the story of his death and rebirth.

In the next chapter I will explore the relationships between the two Hucks, Twain and the reader more fully. For the purpose of seeing how Huck fits the model of the traditional hero, knowledge of this division between the teller and the told of is sufficient. This interpretive tool makes Twain's genius manifest: Huck 14) for a time reigns uneventfully while he composes the book we read. The equivalence of writing to 15) prescribing laws is too obvious to dwell on. Readers of novels are both its subjects and gods, with whom Huck 16) loses favor as Huck-the-written-about participates in the torture of Jim and Huck-the-writer allows Tom to dominate his story. Attempts to "sivilize" Huck 17) drive him from his kingdom, which is to say outside of the society entirely, as opposed to his royal position in it but against it. His 18) death, suspended as it is over nearly the whole length of the novel, is mysterious. Huck-the-writer dies like any narrator, when he has written his last word. This takes place at the Phelps farm, which while not described explicitly as occupying 19) the top of a hill leaves that impression; a quick look at E. W. Kemble's drawing to head Chapter 32 (276) confirms that. 21) Huck's body does not get buried, because Huck-the-writer has no corporeal form. 22) He has an uncountable number of holy sepulchres: every copy of *Huckleberry Finn*, "a trouble to make" but an enduring temple to his status as mythic hero.

Huck Finn's heroism plainly suits the traditional model; the points of correspondence between his story and the model often exceed the number found between the model and the heroes Raglan used to assemble it. This discovery in part answers why readers sympathize so strongly with Huck. We construct our heroes to carry our hopes for us, and I will explore what hopes we ask Huck to carry later. But just from the argument above, we see that Huck's heroic shoulders ought to be strong enough to carry whatever burden we place on them. They are not, of course: Huck ceases to be a hero, traditional or otherwise, when we reach the novel's end. The evasion seems to readers too long, too showy, too baroque, too burlesque, and all this it may be. But if Huck is a hero of traditional power the world that defeats him will need something equally powerful to overmatch him. Complaints aside, we must all agree the evasion does overmatch Huck, both in his morally questionable participation in what amounts to Jim's long torture and in his narratively questionable retirement to the position of Tom Sawyer's comrade. The next chapter will investigate the power that allows *Huck* to defeat Huck.

# 2

❧❧❧

# Huck's Talk, Twain's History

The goal of this chapter is to place Huck Finn as hero in his own work. As I noted at the beginning of the last chapter, past efforts to do this have either rejected the work, especially its ending, or rejected Huck's heroism, especially its traditional form. But since both these elements are fundamental to the experience of reading *Adventures of Huckleberry Finn*, we must establish a construct for the novel which can embrace them both. The last chapter detailed Huck's heroism; this one will describe Huck's world. The tension between these two has made their critical melding difficult. Yet this tension is itself the heart of *Huckleberry Finn* and in order to get to this heart, we must pass through Huck's language, because only through his words can we see his world. But Huck's language is difficult to pass through. Like thick glass, it distorts, only slightly, what is behind it and prevents direct access. To get to Huck's world and the tension between it and him, we must do more than attempt to pass through the language, give up as hopeless, and then just describe what we see through it. Rather we must confront the language itself, comprehend its distortions, and then refigure what we see. In short, we must pass through what Huck says without destroying it.

Huck's language comes to us rife with deceptions. Lee Clark Mitchell writes in "'Nobody But Our Gang Warn't Around'" that *Huckleberry Finn*

> develops not according to the linear progression of history, but out of a repetitive, recollective motion that seems to abrogate time—a narrative motion best exemplified in the self-circling pattern of Tom's cruel attempt to 'set a free nigger free.' By re-

peatedly turning back on itself . . . the novel further exposes an authoring Huck who does not quite succeed in disguising discourse in story. (97)

Mitchell in this argument touches on the primary obstacle to analysis of Huck's language, an obstacle in the end absolute. The novel hides its speaker in plain sight, present but inaccessible. We find in reading *Huckleberry Finn* not simply the recollected adventures of a good-hearted river-rat, but also a chorus of voices so dependent on each other that no reader can completely separate Huck Finn, Mark Twain or even him- or herself from the others.

I concluded the discussion of Huck's heroism with the separation of Huck-the-writer from Huck-the-written-about. We found such a separation necessary to understand Huck's character; after all, that dual presence forms the essence of Huck's performance within the book. But just as human beings who are said to have two different sides—Mark Twain/Sam Clemens, for example—remain one in fact, so these two Hucks remain one in our reading experience. They are projections of one another, distinguishable but inseparable. We see this paradox in the prose itself. The book's famous opening establishes the difficulty. In "Language and Identity in *Adventures of Huckleberry Finn*" Brook Thomas remarks, "In the first paragraph Huck acknowledges his existence as a character in another work of fiction, names the book's author, and most important reminds us that any work of fiction necessarily includes a few 'stretchers' " (7). Thomas goes on to note what is truly most important: that, the whole world of the novel being a world of lies, readers can only differentiate between good and bad lies "by relying on another lie. This lie that gives meaning to all the other lies is the book itself: a self-conscious work of fiction" (9). According to this principle, Huck authors himself. As author he creates a lie: a boy named Huck who escapes both civilization and anticivilization to find freedom and friendship and terror on the Mississippi river. This interpretation divorces Huck-the-writer from Huck-the-written-about: Huck-the-written-about is a put-up job, a con of the reader by Huck-the-writer, an interpretation which makes the authoring Huck the novel's only real subject. This critical assertion, whether true or not, at least has the benefit of providing access to the novel through its language. By this, the real Huck, Huck-the-writer, refuses his own traditional heroism and slips all the way past picaro into con man. Huck authors a facade and dupes us as successfully as the King dupes Pokeville.

Laurence B. Holland makes this point again in specific reference to an event in the novel. Huck-the-writer,

> when he looks back and remembers the incident on the raft when he tore up the letter to Miss Watson, now knows that Jim has already been freed. But to reenact the drama which constitutes his heroism, to recreate it in its vividness and moral urgency, Huck must in memory keep to the lies of silence. (83)

Even at his point of greatest moral integrity, Huck's slip shows. He is a posturing liar, Holland asserts, making the writing and destruction of the letter to Miss Watson into "something more." "Created in the lie," he writes, "is the will to make the action convincingly seem, and in the language to be, a commitment of the moral imagination beyond what Twain knows it was then in fact" (84). This separation of Huck-the-writer from Huck-the-written-about necessarily gives primacy to Huck-the-writer: all the language in the book is his. The novel then becomes a trick, something closer to Vladimir Nabokov's *Pale Fire*, but without the integrity of having the narrator's artificiality itself comment on the book's intended subject, art. Huck becomes the final authority on his world, as the insane Kinbote does on his, but his authority is more an anti-authority: you can trust nothing he says. Huck becomes Tom Sawyer in fact and we become Huck at the Phelps farm, giving grudging acceptance to his artifice.

This interpretation has real value, but unfortunately runs counter to most readers' experience with the novel. The first and last paragraphs of the novel push the certainty of its being written. This awareness helps us see the simultaneity of two Hucks' tales, the one of the hero's romance and the other of his death. But the reminder of the story's writtenness does not make us forget either that "Mr. Mark Twain" is behind Huck-the-writer, or that Huck-the-written-about—in the end no more or less obviously fictional than the authoring Huck—is most prominently before us. George Carrington wisely notes:

> The novel begins with such subtlety that it is almost impossible, especially in normal non-critical reading, to realize the shift from

reflection and summary to the actual narrative itself. After commenting on *The Adventures of Tom Sawyer* in the first paragraph, Huck summarizes its ending in the second paragraph, and then, in the third, begins to summarize the post-*Tom Sawyer* events—that is, the events of *Huckleberry Finn*—in such a way that no one who had not read *Tom Sawyer* could tell which events are which. (114)

The fourth paragraph begins a specific story of Huck's life at the widow's and so "without warning and thus without thought we have moved from the static general past to the dynamic immediate present, the present of fiction, in which the book remains until the last paragraph of Chapter the Last" (114). Carrington here ignores the novel's occasional intrusions of Huck-the-writer into the text—"I've noticed that thing plenty of times since" in Chapter 2, for example, and Huck's fond remembrance of Mary Jane Wilks quoted above—but elsewhere cites "clear glimpses of Huck as external maker of the book."

These appearances do not alter Carrington's main point: that we experience Huck-the-written-about as the novel's focus. This is not because Huck-the-writer erects him as a con, but rather for two other reasons. First, the novel's compelling conflicts involve Huck-the-written-about, not Huck-the-writer. Unlike Pip in Dickens' *Great Expectations*, for example, we find no disjuncture between the Huck writing the book and the Huck in the midst of the book's adventures, and neither does Huck himself. Huck ends the novel pretty much as he begins, turning his back on a civilization he just can't stand. Between his first lighting out and his second, only his experience changes. We can only speculate on the changes in Huck from the beginning of the book to the end: he probably will not pray for fish hooks anymore; but then he probably will not pray at all, just as he probably would never have tried it if the widow had never gotten hold of him. The changed Huck does not concern us. The Huck who watched Buck Grangerford's murder, the Wilks sisters' bilking, the King's and Duke's tar-and-feathering, the Huck who learned Jim's magical wisdom on the river, who humbled himself to a slave, who found you couldn't pray a lie—or write one, he would probably say: he destroys the false letter—*his* dangers hold most of our interest. The difficulties facing Huck-the-writer as he interprets his experience compel us less.

Second, and a greater difficulty to the con-man interpretation, is that Huck-the-writer and Huck-the-written-about cannot be split in any thorough enough way to support the argument. The premise of two distinguishable Hucks allows us to solve the novel's troublesome ending—we are disappointed because we find we have been duped—but no matter how useful the construct, its premise remains flawed at the point where most critical adherents hang their argument: Huck's language. Janet Holmgren McKay's stylistic analysis in "'An Art So High'" provides a special insight into the evidence. She writes that

> The kinds of errors that Huck makes are by no means haphazard: Twain carefully placed them to suggest Huck's basic illiteracy but not to overwhelm the reader. Nonstandard verb forms constitute Huck's most typical mistakes. He often uses the present form or past participle for the simple past tense, for example, *see* or *seen* for *saw*; his verbs frequently do not agree with his subjects in number and person; and he often shifts tense within the same sequence. (64)

A move from McKay's exclusively stylistic concerns to the present problem of the degree of distinguishability between the two Hucks proves enlightening.

The misuse of present or past participle for simple past does more than create the impression of vernacular: It scrambles time. In order to keep Huck-the-writer distinct from the other Huck, we must realize that he is composing long after the events he describes, but the substitution of tenses "takes his experiences and generalizes them to the habitual present" (McKay, "Art," 64), obscuring the time shift which is the only real tool for distinguishing between Huck-the-writer and Huck-the-written-about. This habitual present is occupied by both Hucks. Time becomes ritual, in some ways; not historical time, where one event leads on to the next in a fashion suggesting inevitability, but ahistorical time, where the events of the composing present mix undistinguished with the events of the composed past.

The disagreement between subject and verb also rattles our conception of agency. If we cannot with security assign responsibility for an action to one Huck or another, we cannot keep them separate. The easy slips from past to present result in so close a relationship between Huck-the-written-about and Huck-the-writer that we mostly experience them as a single character. For example, when the Duke tries to remember Hamlet's soliloquy Huck writes:

> By and by he got it. He told us to give attention. Then he strikes a most noble attitude, with one leg shoved forwards, and his arms stretched away up, and his head tilted back, looking up at the sky; and then he begins to rip and rave and grit his teeth; and after that, all through the speech he howled, and spread around, and swelled up his chest, and just knocked the spots out of any acting ever *I* see before. (179)

The verb use in this relatively typical passage makes distinguishing between Hucks nearly impossible. If the writing Huck simply gets so excited as to fall into the present tense with 'strikes' and 'begins', why is he not excited into the present tense for 'howled', 'swelled', and 'knocked'? If we agree that Twain's use of verb tense is not haphazard, we have to see that one of the aims of this admixture is to indicate an identity between the narrating Huck and the narrated one.

The con-man thesis depends on the clear distiguishability of the two Hucks. For this thesis to be true, we must constantly be able to spot the seam between the artificial Huck and the real, authoring one. But there are in fact places where the seam disappears, linking the Hucks into a common entity. Alternatively, for this interpretation to bear meaning, there must be a discoverable pattern to the places in the novel in which the two supposedly separate Hucks are corporate. There does not seem to be such a pattern; the point can only be that the tale's telling discourages the interpretive division between the two Hucks. Interpretations of the novel or of its main character which use the distinction between Huck-the-writer and Huck-the-written-about must also respect the integrity of the two Hucks. The outline I made above of Huck's heroism does this.

Interpretations depending on similar divisions in the novel's narrative will find similar difficulties. The character we identify as our hero cannot be fully separated from the character who writes him; the writing Huck cannot be fully separated from Mark Twain; the reader cannot be fully separated from the book. The configuration of these inseparable parts—shapes made by the distortions of Huck's language—informs us as to the shape of the world of the novel.

We can understand this in part through the relationship between Huck Finn and Mark Twain. The arguments for this equivalence have lived long and prospered. They start both from biography and criticism; a brief recounting of this well-worn ground will demonstrate the equivalence. Biographical critics have made axiomatic the observation that Huck Finn's voice is Twain's best self-expression. Huck cannot speak alone as Twain's complete fictional self; he needs to be paired with Tom Sawyer, as we find Twain having done in so many manuscripts, to give us a rounded view of the author's living mind. Twain himself headed for the Territory when the Civil War proved more than he could stand, though the West he went to had been much defiled since the time of Huck's supposed move. Twain spent several rough-and-tumble years among the pioneers before settling down to an Eastern af-fluence gained through Tom Sawyerish romantic fictionalizing. Twain's Huck Finn Western experience was always close at hand—in his travels, his rough language and his tastelessness—to ease the chafing of establishment restraint.

The literary arguments are more interesting to detail here, and more important for demonstrating an equivalence in the novel between Huck and Twain. In other literary presentations of self, notably *Roughing It*, Twain paints the same sorts of word pictures of nature we receive from Huck, such as the storm on Jackson's Island (59–60) or the sunrise over the Mississippi (156–57). Several incidents in the novel seem to render Huck a transparent mouthpiece for Mark Twain. The raftsmen's passage of Chapter 16 appeared first in *Life on the Mississippi* in Twain's own voice. Its transfer to Huck's voice required minimal changes, except in its frame. Huck's periodic expressions of abstract pragmatism, scepti-cism, and ideological tolerance seem pure Twain. In such state-ments Huck becomes so transparent he is difficult to see. Only the talk is left behind; the rest of Huck has vanished.

In many other passages, distinguishing Huck from Twain ap-pears easy, but in fact the complexity of the relationship escalates. Critics have often noted that the satirical rendition of Emmeline Grangerford's art and poetry shows Twain's controlling hand. The tribute to Stephen Bots, we feel, is not by some fictional but de-

ceased character named Emmeline Grangerford, but rather by
Twain in ridicule of a type of writing by entirely-too-many, entirely-
too-active sentimentalists. Even today obituary pages overflow with
the stuff. Huck's admiration for Emmeline's creative genius, on the
other hand, appears genuine; he believes that, if she "could make
poetry like that before she was fourteen, there ain't no telling what
she could a done by and by" (140). In this incident, and in the
Duke's fracturing of Shakespeare and Huck's admiration of its rendition quoted above, the novel presents a complex relationship between Huck and Twain, between narrator and author. Both are
plainly visible, each as present in the text as the other, but Huck is
there only as Twain's foil. The power of Twain's authority turns
Huck into a vehicle for comic irony. In these passages, Huck does
not stand in for Twain; he is no transparent mouthpiece for his
master's voice. Twain is transformed in the text from the simple
voice in Huck's words into a second presence which only reduces
Huck to the author's other, his ironic anti-authority.

This is a simple irony compared with another, more common
sort we find in *Huckleberry Finn*, in which we do not have direct
evidence of Twain's presence in the novel, only evidence of his
having shown himself. This form of ironical relationship appears
throughout the book in Huck's naivete. Perhaps the Grangerford
episode shows Huck's distance from a near-invisible author most
clearly. Twain is present as only a bare outline for much of what
happens during this sequence. Huck is left on his own, just the
teenage son of a Mississippi town drunk, with no more sense—
moral, aesthetic or otherwise—than a raft. With absolute sincerity,
Huck praises the somber beauty and stateliness of the Grangerford
home, an icon to Southern gentility Twain would demolish. If
Huck regards the feud itself as something immoral, he does not
show it. When, immediately following his description of the Grangerford clan in Chapter 18, Huck finds himself witness to Buck's
attempt on Harney Shepherdson, he questions Buck but offers no
judgment. Huck objects to his Sunday church-going not because of
the Grangerfords' hypocrisy, obvious to us and to Twain, but because it was full of "tiresomeness." The Grangerfords "had such a
powerful lot to say about faith, and good works, and free grace,
and preforeordestination, and I don't know what all, that it did
seem to me to be one of the roughest Sundays I had run across yet"
(147). Though it can be argued that part of this antireligious sen-

timent comes from Twain, Huck's ignorance of the moral duplicity of "the quality" places him at a distance from his author. While it is possible to conjecture that Twain is laughing off-stage, while we might say Twain set Huck up to ridicule him in front of his readership, we cannot lose track of the fact of the difference in Twain's ironical use of Huck concerning Emmeline's poetry and his use of Huck in most of the feud episode. Twain's presence in the text varies and therefore so does the distance between author and narrator.

The book also presents situations where Twain can be seen only in the faintest outline in the text, even where he seems to disappear completely. By the Wilks episode, Huck appears to have developed sufficient moral sense to stand in for Twain on his own. Twain's equivalence with Huck when the King first bamboozles the girls and the town seems obvious. Referring to the King's slobbering and indirected reported speech, which ends, Huck says, with a "pious, goody-goody Amen" (213), one critic writes, "*Goody-goody* seems to be Huck's; *pious* is Twain's added lick" (McKay, *Narration*, 138). But after that, Huck is on his own. He bumbles his own way through his conversation with Joanna. Is Twain laughing somewhere out of view? We can not see him in the text. Huck hatches his own plan to save himself and the Wilks girls, and, unlike any other purposefully entered adventure in the novel, Huck develops this one without a worshipful invocation of Tom Sawyer, Twain's other alter ego. Twain disappears and Huck becomes opaque, an independent force determining his own story. At the end of the episode Huck escapes "the most awful trouble and the most dangersome" (257) and momentarily rids himself of the King and Duke too. The disappointment we feel as readers when the false royalty returns comes from several sources: Huck's own feelings about their return; the rekindling of evil in the novel; and the two-sided loss of Huck's independence, his freedom to run his own life and his freedom to tell his own story. The intrusion of the King and Duke into the book—an intrusion that occupies a third of the novel—reminds us of Twain's intrusion into the life of our hero.

The relationship between Twain and Huck reaches its pinnacle of complexity in Chapters 21 and 22, the twinned incidents of Boggs-Sherburn and the circus. Chapters 21 and 22 show off the complexity of relationship between Huck and Twain unlike any others. Each sentence forces us to question its authorship and authenticity. One passage is near-pure Twain, the next near-pure Huck; throughout, Huck stands at varying ironical distances from Twain. We have almost no luck in trying to determine the source of the words we read. For example, we see Twain's hand in Hamlet's tortured soliloquy. Huck excuses his remembering the speech months later by saying that he "learned it, easy enough, while he was learning it to the king" (179). On the next page, Huck introduces the Shakespeare bills "They read like this," but he gives no reason for us to believe in the accuracy of his rendition. Does Twain supply the words, did Huck have a copy with him as he wrote, or do we just have to trust Huck's memory? Though we can argue that we must take Huck's word on all his adventures, few of them come with documents which could prove the case one way or another. But still, even in this case, we must leave the problem undecided. If we can not decide the source of the Shakespeare bill, even with its possibility of concrete proof, how can we accept that the fractured Hamlet comes to us cleanly from Twain through Huck's memory, with far less evidence? My point is simple: these two bits of information from undecidable sources set up the confusion of authority and authenticity we find in the following fifteen pages.

From the Shakespeare bill, Huck/Twain launches with barely a transition into a description of Bricksville, a savage index of valley low-life. Huck describes the residents as "a mighty ornery lot" who "talked lazy and drawly, and used considerable many cuss-words. There was as many as one loafer leaning up against every awning-post, and he most always had his hands in his britches pockets, except when he fetched them out to lend a chaw of tobacco or scratch" (181). What is the relative position of Huck and Twain here? Huck's voice gives us the description through the murder of Boggs, a voice capable of only limited judgment even of the wretched cruelty the townies show by "putting turpentine on a stray dog and setting fire to him, or tying a tin pan to his tail and see him run himself to death" (183). But the passage clearly contains Twain as well, who backs up Huck's distaste for Bricksville with a strong indictment. Twain echoes in the word choice—'concerns' and 'white-domestic'—and the humor—the sow "as happy as if she was on salary" (183). In the last sentence of the description, Twain at last reveals his presence: "Such a town as that has to be constantly moving back, and back, and back, the river's always gnawing at it" (183). Twain, not Huck, has given the river this symbolic power. This is not irony: Huck is not blind to the town's faults as he was to the Grangerford's overblown gimcrackery; he and Twain both condemn the town, but in different keys. In the two-page description of Bricksville we read Huck, in language almost all his own, and hear Huck; but, because we have had to leave undecided the sources of two long passages just before it, we are primed to hear Twain too, so the description echoes both voices. The mysterious absence of the King and the Duke—characters we devoutly wish to rid ourselves of and cannot—here provides Twain with a hole in the text he promptly fills with himself. We will see this whisper of equivalence between the Twain himself and the con men again later.

The positions of author and narrator undergo a change with the appearance of Boggs. The townspeople show themselves capable of humor and compassion, easing the hostile glare of the earlier pages, and Huck takes a step away from Twain. Huck is frightened by the drunken horseman, a fear we laugh at because we believe the man who says of Boggs, "He don't mean nothing; he's always carryin' on like that, when he's drunk. He's the best-naturedest old fool in Arkansaw—never hurt nobody, drunk nor sober" (184). But Huck's fear seems to have scared Twain out of his language. There are no telltale signs of Twain in Huck's words to the end of Chapter 21: no choice from outside Huck's verbal range and no humor at all. We see Twain behind the text only in his role as creator of symbol. He is the one who has Boggs embalmed between two Bibles; he sends in the "long lanky man, with long hair and a big white fur stove-pipe hat on the back of his head, and a crooked handled cane" (187) to recreate the shooting. The distance between narrator and author has widened: Huck no longer speaks Twain's words; he just describes what he sees. Unlike the image of the river gnawing at the town, a speculative generalization which puts Twain squarely in Huck's mouth, Twain has only left a signature on the concrete events Huck describes.

The next chapter begins much as the last one ended, but Twain shows himself stronger and stronger as the action leads up to Sherburn's speech. Huck reports on the slave "bucks and wenches" who "break and skaddle back out of reach" (189), but it is a conspiracy between Twain and the reader to allow us to recognize in their actions the slaves' fear of being lynched by the mob. The mob is described as a wave in the next paragraph; where would fresh-water Huck get the image? By the appearance of the simile "like eating bread that's got sand in it" just before the speech, we hear Twain's voice. But in whose voice is Sherburn's speech itself? Compare it with the opening of Huck's 'speech', the novel itself. "You don't know me without . . . "Huck says; Sherburn says, "Do I know you? I know you clear through." Obviously the 'you' refers differently in each case, to the reader in one, to the mob in the other. But Sherburn names one of the crowd, Buck Harkness, and calls him half a man. We cannot have forgotten the book's earlier Buck, the Huck-equivalent Buck Grangerford—himself, like Huck, half a man, an adolescent. Sherburn finishes "and take your half-a-man with you" and Huck writes "Buck Harkness he heeled it after them, looking tolerable cheap. I could a staid, if I'd a wanted to, but I didn't want to" (191), sounding like the townspeople talking about tobacco earlier. Without stretching the novel we can see Huck as the specific audience of the Colonel's speech, just as we are the audience of his own. Set up by our earlier undecidedness, this speech, the accurate repetition of which we might have otherwise attributed to Huck's phenomenal memory, seems to come directly from Twain. Twain, in the guise of Colonel Sherburn, addresses Huck, a position between author and narrator we do not find elsewhere in the novel. I leave interpretations of this unique event aside; I wish only to demonstrate the variety and complexity of relationship between Huck and Twain, especially here at the physical center of the novel. We cannot separate Huck from Twain, because everywhere we look we get echoes of Twain and echoes of Huck, shadowy replications erected by the holographic magic of language.

Without transition, Huck takes us to the circus. This last section of these chapters suddenly changes the position of Twain in the text, a change that provides three insights into the relationship between Huck and Twain. First, Huck becomes grossly naive in the breath between the Sherburn episode and the circus. After admiring the stunt riders with boyish wonder, Huck gives a one sentence description of the clown, ending "how he *ever* could think of so many [funny things], and so sudden and so pat, was what I could in no way understand" (192). We supply the obvious answer: the funny things were written down before, or repeated often enough to be remembered, like the Duke's Hamlet. That Huck, our novel's writer, could not comprehend that perfectly exposes him here as

Twain's ironic foil. But Huck's ignorance comes in at least two kinds: his naivete about the world within the novel, an ignorance in part remedied by his adventures; and an ignorance of the symbolic content of his own experience. Huck cannot make connections between his adventures. Huck does not recognize the ringmaster's reaction to the drunken rider as a planned part of the show, an example of his first sort of ignorance. But he also does not realize that the rider retraces Boggs' last drunk just as surely as the white-hatted stranger did. Huck's ignorance gains resonance by this doubling: he is not only Twain's ironic foil but also Twain's sincere messenger, sincere because he does not know enough to interfere with the message. We see this sincerity in Huck's final statement about the circus: "There may be bullier circuses than what that one was, but I never struck them yet" (194). That Huck sees no better circuses between the one in Bricksville and writing about it no more than two months later is no surprise; it is unlikely he saw any. That statement comes from Mark Twain or perhaps just some part of Twain that is Huck Finn grown up.

We can see from all this just how fruitless a critical attempt to separate Huck from Twain becomes. The language of *Huckleberry Finn* binds them together. Any attempt to pass through the language to the heart of the novel by finding the seams between the author and the narrator begins with an impossible task. The same can be said of an attempt to find the seam between the text and the reader. If a successful wedge could be placed between the reader and the text, one could argue that the novel has been constructed as a game, something along the lines of a mystery. We could then say that Twain makes a cryptic proclamation of the mystery's goal in his famous introductory notice: he does not say there is no motive, moral or plot in *Huckleberry Finn*; he only threatens anyone attempting to find them. An ability to isolate the text from the reader would greatly simplify the effort of solving any of the mysteries.

But a clean separation is as impossible between reader and text as between Huck and Twain or the authoring and authored Huck. Huck's escape from the slave hunters in Chapter 16 serves as a perfect model of the reader's complicity. Huck never says his fictive father has small-pox; the hunters themselves supply the presumption. Huck has just told his story in such a way that the men leap ahead to their own conclusion. Twain had no reason not to make the small-pox part of Huck's new fiction from the start, except to demonstrate the complicity between a tale's teller and its hearer. The same experience happens again and again in the novel; for example, Mrs. Loftus supplies Huck with a back-up fiction when his first one fails. By the end of the book, Huck does not even need to make anything up, because people just give him fictional identities when he needs them.

We find this pattern in our own relationship with the novel. It begins in the language, of course. Huck's talk overflows with convolutions, second-level confusions of intent. We think we know exactly what Huck means when he says "I was stealing a poor old woman's nigger that hadn't ever done me no harm" or "when nobody but our gang warn't around," but these and the dozen other crucial phrases in the book do not in fact say what we believe Huck wants said. Often as not they say the exact opposite. Only through the reader's intervention do the words of the novel themselves and their apparent intended meaning coincide. Forrest G. Robinson in "The Silences in *Huckleberry Finn*," A. E. Dyson in "Huckleberry Finn and the Whole Truth," and Louis D. Rubin in "Mark Twain and the Language of Experience" all make cogent arguments that the essential disjuncture between what the novel says and its assumed intention affects the novel's action as much as its language.

The inconsistent seams between its constituent parts restrains the use of some interpretive tools which might otherwise be brought to bear on the novel. Most notably, I would say, the preceding discussion demonstrates that *Huckleberry Finn* resists deconstruction. The language of the novel so tightly integrates the narrated Huck with the narrator Huck, Huck with Twain and the reader with the novel itself that any consistent textual gap capable of taking the deconstructive wedge proves near impossible to find. I do not want to argue that we cannot increase our comprehension of the novel by a deconstructive reading; I only mean that the novel itself discourages the attempt. It is equally unlikely that biographical criticism will render more than a partial insight into the novel. By privileging only one of the several clearly interdependent parts of the novel, the interpretation of it will be dangerously skewed. Especially since the effort here is to encounter the work holistically, to investigate what appears to be the central conflict in the novel by examining how the whole novel contributes to it, we must discount a method directed to only a part of the work.

It seems that *Huckleberry Finn* encourages a kind of madcap impressionism in critics. The fundamental complicity of all its parts transforms a critical investigation of the text into a visit to a house of mirrors. No matter where a critic stands in the frame of the novel—with Huck-the-written-about as he goes from wise youth to Mark Twain's clown, with Huck-the-writer as he goes from impassioned confessor to dissembling con man, or with Twain himself as he blithely appears and then disappears from the text—the mirrors replicate his or her patterned inability to securely assign the novel's words and actions a source. This inability renders the enterprise of uncovering morals, plots, or motives in the book more futile than, as the initial warning implies, dangerous. And in the realm of criticism—in any realm, actually—futility defeats danger every time.

So the question remains: how to get at *Huckleberry Finn*? If we see the novel as a house of mirrors, our path of attempt should be clear, though not simple: we must step out of the novel itself, above it if possible, and look in from there to see how the system of reflections and refractions work. The essential pleasure of a house of mirrors comes from being within it, victim of its programmed attempt to hamper our ability to distinguish reality from images of reality; this is the essential terror of the experience too. *Huckleberry Finn* presents us with both pleasure and terror whenever we try to sort out the experience of the text from within it.

I want to avoid a protracted discussion of reality and images of it in the novel. As should be clear, such a discussion will keep us trapped in the house of mirrors, turning forever in on ourselves. It is enough to note that *Huckleberry Finn* acknowledges its own mirror-house theme by its constant repetition: Huck constantly assumes disguises and identities, very little is as it appears, truth remains elusive. Look at the downfall of the King and Duke at the Wilkses: we never know whether or not the second set of brothers are simply more genuine humbugs, as Allison Ensor notes in "The 'Opposition Line' to the King and the Duke in *Huckleberry Finn*." So many episodes work by a confusion of reality with its images that the novel presses epistemology as its central problem, and it is in some ways. The point of this confusion is not to demand that the reader sort image from reality in the novel; that would be simply a version of the game interpretation, a relative of the con-man interpretation. Such an effort is not only theoretically unsound, but also futile; the novel confuses its own reality so hopelessly that sorting it from its images becomes impossible. The better approach to the confusion of the fictive reality and the false images of it is to get above the maze of mirrors and glass in order to discover their pattern. That is the reality which truly concerns us and the one from which we might reap true rewards.

Before going on, we must separate three terms: realism, realistic, and reality. 'Realism' refers to a literary movement; 'realistic' to a style; I am using 'reality' to suit my purpose here. Twain's place as father of American realism is axiomatic, and like all axioms tautological. Michael Davitt Bell fashions a convincing argument against raising a monument to this paternity in "Mark Twain, 'Realism', and *Huckleberry Finn*." Whether or not Twain followed or founded American realism has only tangential relevance to the question of whether or not we can term his writing realistic. All fiction hopes to represent reality, even surrealist fiction; but what we mean when we say a particular fiction is realistic is that it attempts to portray common experience. Common experience is a relative term though, and what a certain people at a certain time maintain it to be will not be shared by other peoples at other times. We believe now, for example, that episodic fictions presented in a written form meant as imitation of speech and containing no events impossible outside the natural world—itself a relative concept—are realistic. *Huckleberry Finn* suits these criteria, as do countless other novels. The question of reality and its images in the novel has little to do with either realism or realistic fiction. It has to do with fictive vision, the specific world the novel creates. We are now looking for *Huckleberry Finn*'s reality, and for that we must go beyond Huck Finn's reality, Twain's reality, literary reality and reader reality, because the reality of this miraculous text is larger than all those.

Two critics have developed exceptionally thorough readings of the world Huck Finn occupies, comprehending the experience of Huck's world through metaphors of literature. Jane Johnson Benardete and George Carrington present the novel's reality in strikingly similar ways; Carrington's reading can be seen as a complement to Benardete's, but with more detail and finer resolution. Though I do not agree wholly with either's notion of the text, their arguments offer the most comprehensive theoretical structures extant for understanding the world of *Huckleberry Finn*. I synopsize them here because their structures lend crucial support to any further understanding of the novel.

Benardete maintains in "*Huckleberry Finn* and the Nature of Fiction" that the novel invites a metafictional reading. She argues

> that *Huckleberry Finn* is a book about the nature of fiction . . . : that each episode illustrates some quality of fiction; that the major theme of Huck's development is his increasing preference for fiction over fact; and that the novel itself is deliberately devised to exemplify fiction's power to distort life. (209)

Benardete begins her argument from the discussion on language between Huck and Jim in Chapter 14. Jim lives in a world of nature where species determines identity, she concludes, but Huck lives in a world of language where it and the fictions it enables determine everything. The logic of the novel extends from Huck's growing awareness of the world of fiction, where "Huck, a half-literate urchin, is transformed into a knowledgeable reader who believes that men are defined by the language they speak" (213). This awareness begins at the novel's beginning with Huck's admission of his own fictiveness and grows through his adventures in the world of words. Even at the beginning, Huck accepts the power of words to create worlds. Though Huck rejects Tom's fiction for himself, he accepts them as Tom's truth. He writes, "I judged that all that stuff was only just one of Tom Sawyer's lies. I reckon he believed in the A-rabs and the elephants, but as for me I think different. It had all the marks of a Sunday school" (17). A statement's value might only match its measure of truth, but for Huck "the truth of a statement is not established by experience but by belief. His stories are better than Tom's because noone doubts them" (Benardete, 215).

In this interpretation, the novel recounts Huck's growth into a better, more literate storyteller; his literacy is perhaps the only thing about Huck which changes in the course of the novel. Huck's ability to read angers Pap more than anything else; he forbids Huck school in order to prevent the alienation of father and son and to retain the authority of illiteracy. But in Chapter 7, Benardete maintains, Huck "effectively dismisses Pap's rights in him by staging his own murder in a manner so bookish that Tom Sawyer will later admire it" (216). Huck's literacy gets a boost in the raid on the *Walter Scott*, which nets him "a lot of books" (93), which, he tells us, he read both to himself and aloud to Jim. This training helps him become an expert reader and creator of fictions.

Each following adventure depends increasingly on language. People's names determine their fate in the Shepherdson-Grangerford feud, which explodes into bloody massacre after the exchange of a written note. Benardete adds to the above interpretation of the Boggs-Sherburn incident that Sherburn's murder of Boggs before his time is up—a somewhat questionable assertion—undercuts the assumption that the gentry have a special respect for the word. She goes further: "Sherburn is unique in *Huckleberry Finn*, for his is the only voice explicitly condemning speech and the agreeable fictions that men live by. The importance of his statement may be underlined by its position at the exact center of the novel" (217). More, what excites the crowd into a lynch mob is not the murder itself, but the white-suited man's recreation of it. "Had Sherburn died, he would have been the victim of the storyteller's art, not of natural indignation rising spontaneously in the hearts of men" (218). Twain drives home this point in the difference between Huck's dispassionate, reportorial presentation of Boggs' ride and death and the excited engagement at the trick rider's clowning: only the show matters. We see in this that story gives events value. The Wilks incident likewise depends on story, language and writing. The King spins himself into a minister and is told a story by the waylaid young man. The King then adopts that story for himself and the Duke. The townspeople's attempts to end the fraud by examinations of writing, climaxing with a debate over marks on a dead man's chest, end in failure. Huck is incredulous that the King can continue the sham, but the King apparently knows something about the art of language: that it is suited more to creating falsehood than to revealing truth. Huck resists learning this lesson; but neither does he grasp its alternative: Huck fails "to see that art imitates life and that it is life which matters" (Benardete, 218).

Huck's fictive development reaches its climax in the evasion, when he participates in a fiction for the pure love of it. Huck accepts now that words can be made to mean whatever the storyteller wants them to mean: caseknives are pick-axes, lightning rods are stairs. Huck becomes Tom, and Tom Sid. Jim, at root of the novel a victim of the fictions of racism and slavery, pointedly objected to Huck's fictions in the trash episode of Chapter 15, but at that point

43

he thought he was free. Now in chains again, he acquiesces to the white master's fictions. Benardete points out that Jim's participation in the evasion "binds together the fiction of books and legal fiction" (222). To pull the moral from this we must first see that "the civil code does not get to the heart of the matter: . . . Jim is as free as a man can be, whatever his civil status, when he knows that all men are essentially alike" (222–23). Benardete wisely notes a source of the feeling of failure at the novel's end: "Jim's character becomes less noble when he is manumitted. His heroic potential in the novel is denied because he is not allowed to establish his freedom for himself" (223).

Because she focuses on *Huckleberry Finn*'s metafictive qualities, she attributes this event to the linking of civil and bookish fictions. I find some basic problems in Benardete's reading of the ending. She bases much of her argument on Jim's experience of being freed by Tom and Huck, but we have only speculation to help us know what Jim thinks, knows, and sees during the evasion. The well-known arguments that Jim becomes a "darkie" stereotype at the Phelps farm also inhibit any interpretation which endows him with the weight and range of more complete characters. Further, it seems clear that Jim's failure to contribute anything to his own freedom at the end of the novel carries weight not primarily because of this pairing of legal and narrative fictions, but because it echoes the failure of Huck's heroic potential and reflects the powerlessness of both blacks and poor whites, both in the work and in the world.

But Benardete's well-constructed metafictive reading of *Huckleberry Finn* also creates its own limits. Although it is a holistic insight into the organizing principles of the book's form, it leaves out much of the book's content. Benardete's argument does not account for Huck's passivity or his heroism, does not account for the prolonged presence of the Duke and King, does not account for the presence of the bulk of the book's questionably literate characters: in short doesn't account for the book's world, in which fiction is undoubtably a theme.

My writing this implies somehow that the two are separable but this implication is exactly wrong; particularly in *Huckleberry Finn* we cannot separate form and content. We must take stock of Benardete's formal considerations of the novel and look further for events which give them body. George Carrington's argument in *The Dramatic Unity of "Huckleberry Finn"* shares conceptual space with

Benardete's, but amplifies and specifies it. Benardete begins her construction from Huck's relationship to language, which leads her to discover, in the premises of constructed fictions, a formal organizing principle for the novel. Carrington uses and expands that same discovery, but he also generates from that principle a vision of the world rendered in the myriad mirrors of *Huckleberry Finn*.

Carrington begins his book, "The world that Mark Twain has imagined as the non-human basis of *Huckleberry Finn* is a world of disorder and chaos, but, being an imagined world, it is a structure of disorder and therefore orderly" (3). He finds the order in the novel by tracking down the instances of what he calls turbulence, a term he borrows from science to mean ordered disorder. To see this turbulence, the critic must conceive of the novel as process: "Description of the static elements is not enough to understand a novel whose basis is change" (6). The process in the novel, the sense of change, is always away from the excessive order of boredom or the excessive disorder of meaninglessness toward the erection of drama. Huck checks out the *Walter Scott* because "I can't rest, Jim, till we give her a rummaging" (81). Huck even makes a drama of picking up the King and Duke: instead of picking them up and paddling out quickly, losing the dogs just as effectively, Huck tells the con artists to "crowd through the brush and get up the crick a little way; then you take to the water and wade down to me and get in" (159). This pattern of resisting boredom and meaninglessness by the artifice of drama runs the novel. There are no overarching ethical rules determining the novel's action. In this world, drama makes its own rules. Situational rules govern the drama. This is why, Carrington argues,

> In Chapter 8 Huck sneers at 'low down cornpone' because he has just set his teeth into a loaf of 'baker's bread,' the food of the quality; but in chapter 17 he proclaims that 'there ain't nothing better' then 'cold cornpone' because it helps satisfy his ravenous appetite in the security of the Grangerford house after the steamboat hits the raft and throws Huck into a terrifying crisis. (16)

Only that which increases the intensity of the drama has virtue within this situational world.

Traditional criticism has postulated Nature as the ethical determinant in the novel, natural Huck in battle against unnatural

45

'sivilization'. Carrington argues that the high value placed on nature comes from the reader, not the novel. The simple division of nature = good and society = bad does not reflect the true organization of the novel. Carrington writes about Huck's anticipated journey to the wilderness Territory at the novel's end that

> Huck may remember those idyllic moments on the river—in fact, he just got through writing about them—but he cannot link memory to anticipation because that would require a coherent world, and he lives in a world of changing situations that he experiences as changing pressures and changing emotional responses to them. The only anticipation he has or can have is that something will turn up that he can turn into diversion. He does not set nature against civilization in general; he sets his own cycles of activities against the demands of the cycles of others. (38)

It is easy to overvalue nature in the novel because of the remarkable beauty of its portrayal and its degree of association with the hero, but Carrington believes it plays little role in a true comprehension of the world presented there. Carrington points out that Huck leaves the pastoral beauty of the river often enough of his own desire. Huck does not himself seem especially to value the experiences of Nature over the experiences of civilization; there seems little doubt he would choose the circus over the fog anytime he was offered the choice.

Carrington explains what other critics have read as the corrupt values of the Mississippi Valley as, instead, "the human need for drama, the central human activity of the novel." Caught between boredom and meaningless flux, every person in *Huckleberry Finn* builds small dramas which temporarily order "the alternate flatness and turbulence (both unbearable) of man's existence in nature" (49). This activity of giving arbitrary meaning to events which are essentially random as they occur to the individual is itself the purpose of life in this Twainian world. The completion of these dramas has little value. We learn this in the first chapter when Huck is "in a sweat to find out all about him, but by and by she let out that Moses had been dead a considerable long time; so then I didn't care no more about him; because I don't take no stock in dead people" (2). The outcome of the drama matters far less than the effect, on both the actors and the audience, of the drama's performance. Performance matters, not only because of the intense need people have for order in the vast uncertainty of the universe, but also because the quality of the performance determines the social status of the performer. What appears as corrupt civilization is in fact competition for prestige, just like the blowhard competition among the raftsmen in Chapter 16. Carrington notes that the undertaker at Peter Wilks' funeral gains respect not only because his efforts resolve the threat the rat-crazed dog posed to the ordering ritual of the service, but also because his public explanation of the disturbance increases the intensity of the ritual by widening the participation in the drama. His whisper earns him status because, as Huck says, "it was a great satisfaction to the people, because naturally they wanted to know. A little thing like that don't cost nothing, and it's just the little things that makes a man to be looked up to and liked" (233). The undertaker gets the gravy because he raises the level of the drama.

We never see this more clearly than at the novel's end, which has troubled critics for so long. Tom dominates the last fifth of the novel because his expertise as a dramatist vastly overshadows Huck's by now considerable skills. Tom berates Huck for his effective plan for Jim's release. "*Work?* Why certainly, it would work, like rats a-fighting. But it's too blame' simple; there ain't nothing *to* it. What's the good of a plan that ain't no more trouble than that? It's as mild as goose-milk. Why, Huck, it wouldn't make no more talk than breaking into a soap factory" (292). The value here is not effectiveness but effect, a foreshadowing of the passion of *Connecticut Yankee*'s master dramatist.

If we rebel against the book's ending we rebel for two reasons. First, because we do not like the novel's reality, the vision of the world the novel's author portrays for us. Twain's extended ending painfully forces us to realize that the drama we have been creating out of his fiction is as wholly artificial as the ones the characters within the fiction create. Each level of elaboration in the evasion produces a higher engagement between the reader and the text: What is Tom after? As the evasion seems more and more to produce nothing, to only worsen everyone's situation, we at last suspect we have been tricked into believing that this world has an identifiable good and that it might triumph. When we find out at last that Tom has been trying to "set a free nigger free," we know we have been had. Second, we rebel at the reduction of Huck. He is our hero: if there is any absolute moral value in the novel's world it must reside in him. But Huck does not reject the notion of drama, this reality we have grown to detest. Instead, he seems to embrace it. The only excuse we can make for him is that he is ignorant of the structure of his world. This, however, leaves us only a hero who cannot even see his own reality. "The real 'Providence' or ruling force of life is not at all what or where Huck thinks it is, but is rather the nature of the universe revealed in the nature and relationships of situations and of men, and Huck cannot read the signs" (106). Carrington has, I believe, put his finger on the nature of the house of mirrors, of the underlying organization of the ever shifting reality and images of it. The fiction Jane Johnson Benardete finds as the subject of *Adventures of Huckleberry Finn* is of a specific kind: George Carrington's drama.

But still, the drama of the novel itself seems to have slipped past Carrington's inclusive vision. He has detailed Huck's world with unarguable accuracy, but the novel is not just about Huck's world, but about the fundamental tension between Huck and his world, a world which in the end defeats a hero of such proportion that we have trouble believing he can be defeated. This tension is not just the tension between a novice and the enlightenment he or she hopes to achieve: Huck fails in his effort to remake his world; he never tries to master its wiles. Huck's unchangeability makes this plain. Although he is a shapeshifter, his essential goals and characteristics do not change in the course of the novel. In Chapter 1 Huck says he wants to go to hell, and he still holds that desire at the climax. Huck begins the book reviling civilization and ends it the same way. If he has simply become, as Carrington believes, a highly competent but morally void dramatist, he would accept his position in the Phelps' world and dramatize it as he prefers. Instead he lights out for the Territory for some temporary respite from the battle, a battle which many critics have pointed out will begin again before long, when the rest of civilization catches up with him. Neither Huck nor his world change at their core; they simply just spin out different versions of themselves. Reality generates new faces because of its situational nature; Huck generates his new personas as part of his heroic quest for freedom from this world. The battle is eternal. The tension between Huck and his world is fundamental and unchangeable. It erupts from their essential characters.

I started this investigation into the novel with a dissection of Huck as hero. What we discovered from that enterprise is that Huck is a traditional hero, a kind of superhuman force whose most distinguishing characteristic is not strength, or bravery, or intelligence, but rather a simple imperviousness to time: the hero grows up but he does not age. The traditional hero exists as an always-forever. He can only be said to have lived once upon a time, not in real time at all. Wherever his home, it does not exist on the same time continuum as our own; for the hero's audience, he lives in a world without time. Look again at the gaps between the three parts of the hero's tale. The absence of story between the events of his birth, his ascendance, and his death result not so much from an ignorance of a hero's childhood or kingly administration as from a ritual compression of the experience of the people he is meant to represent. The traditional hero is not real and was never meant to be. He does not exist in history. He has no biography. The events of his life happen all at once, in the presentation of the ritual or, in a literate culture, between the covers of a book. The hero is absolutely timeless.

If the traditional hero's birth, ascendance, and death mean themselves as symbols of the experience of his audience, then this timelessness only makes sense. The hero comes to us through our oral tradition, and an oral-based culture differs fundamentally from a literate one. Although a person, regardless of culture, lives his or her life in time, an oral-based culture as a whole does not. It has no history beyond memory; its identity is not its past but its present, which is structured by its traditions and rituals. In an individual life, birth, ascendance, and death come in time. In cultural life, though, they exist simultaneously, just as they exist simultaneously for Huck Finn and other traditional heroes. Huck is timeless in the way the ideal of culture he represents is timeless: they are both ahistorical.

Not so the world he occupies. Documents, bills, books, and papers—the material that transforms a relatively timeless society into one firmly time-based—proliferate in the novel. Almost every chapter not directly concerned with the fate of Huck and Jim on the river flows around a text of some kind. From the Bible in the first chapter, through Harney Shepherdson's note, Peter Wilks secret will, the Duke's runaway-slave bill, Huck's unsent letter and Tom Sawyer's authorities, to Huck's own bible, the text of the novel itself, writing dominates the adventures. Note too how many of these documents include time; some of them, like the note that sets off the feud's finale, are nothing but time. Even among the society's outcasts, like Pap, time and writing constitute the world. A quick review of Pap's "Call this a govment!" tirade finds both: the first paragraph concerns the law, the second the mostly time-based terms of freedom a free black must accept in a slave community. The King and Duke fetch the crowd to their Royal Nonesuch with a bill prohibiting women and children. The scam works on timing; the Duke says he "knew the first house would keep mum and let the rest of the town get roped in; and I knew they'd lay for us the third night" (198). Tom's crucial factors in the evasion are his books and time: "We can't resk as long digging him out as we ought to. By rights I reckon we ought to be a couple of years; but we can't. . . . We can snatch him out and rush him away the first time there's an alarm" (305). Everywhere in the novel the time and writing define the static qualities of the novel as surely as Carrington's rules of drama define its fluid ones.

I emphasize these elements because of the relationship they bear to history. Without descending too far into the philosophical maelstrom of R. G. Collingwood and Michel Foucault, I can safely assert that not only do time and writing make history, and not only do they enable it, they necessitate, almost define, it. Though one might quibble about the relative importance of the two elements—reasonable arguments have been made that writing itself creates the concept of historical time—few would argue that a community possessing them can avoid an historical concept of itself. This historical concept springs only in communities where concrete evidence of past social structures allows for, perhaps even forces, the notion of social change. Georg Lukacs writes, "History is precisely *the history of these institutions*, of the changes they undergo *as* institutions which bring men together in societies" (*History and Class Consciousness*, 48). History conceived with the most simple and broad notions is movement through time, but such movement can be detected only in variations from one moment to the next. In order for us to observe these changes, we must be able to see at the same time what things were and what they became. Without documents—pictures, ledgers, but mostly writing: laws, books and letters—there is no proof of the past. The twinned actions of time and writing make history. The world of *Huckleberry Finn* overflows with both. The novel presents still pictures of communities marked by a constant accumulation of writing and time. Sequences of these still pictures, following one after another, create the dramas George Carrington has described. These dramas, taken altogether, do not add up to history. That would be an idiotic assertion: the world of *Huckleberry Finn* is after all a fictional world, existing in many ways like the world of the traditional hero, outside of history. But we can at least say that the novel presents a reality which is conceived historically, a fictional world drawn not from day-to-day life, nor from the workings of the psyche, but from history.

Twain himself sounded suspiciously like Lukacs in his unpublished "Eddypus," which Roger Salomon calls "his attempt at a universal history" (*History*, 8), when he wrote that "the sole and only history-makers are circumstance and environment; . . . these are not within the control of man, but . . . men are in their control, and are helpless pawns who must move as they command" (quoted in Salomon, 21). This also sounds very much like the reality of drama already proposed, but with the name 'history' taking the place of the otherwise characterless terms of 'situation,' 'circumstance,' and 'environment.' We got into the question of the shape of *Huckleberry Finn's* reality through the house of mirrors. It seems clear now that the dizzying swirl of reality and its images which comprises the novel is designed out of a concept of history. This history is a complex web of interrelated and determined events from which an individual existence cannot be separated, just as the two Hucks, Twain, and the reader cannot be separated. In "Eddypus" Twain wrote of his universal historian that "He believed that while he wrote his personal histories, general history would flow from his pen of necessity" (quoted in Salomon, 9n). The particular reality of Twain's fiction recreates in metaphor the general reality of history.

In *Huckleberry Finn*, this harshly determinist history is opposed by concepts of freedom. From the first chapter's signal of Moses, the book informs us, if not of freedom's value, at least of its presence. Its value we learn through Huck's and Jim's continued efforts to find freedom. As any reader can surely recognize, Jim's freedom from slavery and Huck's freedom from 'sivilization' metonymically draws our attention to a more general sort of liberation. Twain hoped, according to Salomon, that history, although it is determined, might bring about circumstances which would approximate the experience of freedom for individuals bound up within history.

But as Salomon points out, for Twain, "At best, benevolent historical determinism was only a substitute for a moral and psychological freedom which he could dream about but not locate in human experience" (32). History might imitate freedom in theory, but in fact it cannot provide it.

That job falls to Huck, who as a traditional, ahistorical hero in quest of freedom combats a determined, documented, and calendared world that looks like history. "In *Huckleberry Finn* myth and history are forced into sharp juxtaposition; and it is from the disparity between these two modes of being that the larger meanings of the book emerge," Salomon states (166). In his view Huck survives the battle: "Only in the image of the flowing river and the boy who communes with it did Twain convincingly succeed in describing a mode of being apart from the tyranny of history" (166). Salomon's words are stirring, but untrue. Huck does not emerge from his war with history a winner. No one can. Huck fails in his quest: he does not free Jim and he does not free himself. By the novel's end he becomes more of a tool of his world than an instrument of change in it. Huck's escape from history mirrors Jim's: it is no escape at all, only an evasion. Jim evades slavery for a while. Huck evades history temporarily by lighting "out for the Territory ahead of the rest" (362). Jim does not have the right to determine his own freedom. There can be no true escape, just an end resulting from circumstances he can in no way control. Even Huck—an empowered hero, a representative of a whole people—is trapped. In the timeless world which birthed him, the traditional hero calls on his supernatural powers to defeat his enemies. But Huck has been taken out of that world and put into another, a reality construed from history. Time and timelessness battle for supremacy in a novel which hovers between discourse and writing, between Huck's talk and Twain's history. Huck cannot break free of that reality, because, once in it, there is no escape from history.

# 3

&#8766;&#8766;

# Huck and *Huck*: Jacksonian Ideals, Jacksonian Reality

Writing creates history, a recreateable past irrefutably different from the present. By recording static particulars—modes of dress, of work, of thought as much as possible—writing, or any form of documentary evidence, establishes our ability to distinguish one moment from a subsequent one. By stringing these written moments together we create for ourselves a sense of movement through time, a way to differentiate between who we were and who we are.

This theoretical construct of history allows us to see a fundamental source of conflict in *Huckleberry Finn*. A tension exists in the novel between Huck himself and the world he operates in, a tension deeper than the content-based struggle between a freedom-loving individual and a convention-ridden society. Huck is, we have seen in Chapter 1, a traditional hero. His heroism comes to us out of folklore, myth, and legend, from the preliterate past which remains, if not intact, then at least vital in even the most literate societies. Because his sort of heroism predates writing, it predates history: Huck's heroism comes to us from out of time. He is not wholly bound by the rules of the world of time. By shapeshifting—his assumption of new masks—Huck crosses the barriers of sex, of death, of color, of morality, of authority. His heroic powers border on supernatural.

Though he is from a timeless world, in his own novel Huck appears in a world not built for the exercise of supernatural powers. Though we do not see Huck bleed or hurt once he escapes Pap through death—that is, once he proves his unearthly heroism—his earthly identity is in the flesh-and-blood form of a pubescent boy in a world of absolute historicity. In Twain's novel, as Chapter 2 shows, the Mississippi Valley is constructed of paper and writing, of the recorded particulars of an historically conceived reality. As in history, the events of *Huckleberry Finn* come to us as unrelated events more or less coequal in time. That they follow the sequence of Huck's travels matters little to our understanding of the world under consideration; they are like the events of a picaresque, only observed by, not changed by, the picaro himself. The purpose is satire, not plot, a comic portrait of a time, not a rendition of a sequence of changes. Huck and the world portrayed are equally the novel's subjects. The story is in the conflict between the world and the hero, but the fundamental tension in the novel goes past a simple conflict of wills between Huck and his world. The tension is structural and lies in their very natures, between Huck's timelessness and his world's historicity.

The novel gives away its particular historical reality early. When Huck first escapes from the twin torments of the widow's 'sivilization' and his father's inversion of it, he goes to Jackson's Island, which he says he says is "good enough for me; I know that island pretty well, and nobody ever comes there. . . . Jackson's Island's the place" (41). Once the townsfolk give up the search for his body, Huck settles down to a three-day idyll—the traditional period between death and rebirth—but it seems an empty paradise to him:

> When it was dark I set by my camp fire smoking and feeling pretty well satisfied, but by and by it got sort of lonesome and so I went and set in the bank and listened to the currents washing along, and counted the stars and drift-logs and rafts that come down, and then went to bed; there ain't no better way to put in time when you are lonesome; you can't stay so, you soon get over it. (48)

At the end of his three days, Huck discovers he is not alone. In fact, the whole time he has been enjoying his antilife at the head of the island Jim has occupied the foot. The symbolic elements of this picture add up quickly: On an isolated American island called Jackson, an adolescent idyll of freedom shared paradoxically with slavery. Twain has inscribed Jacksonian America in miniature.

This reading gets encouragement from the title page. There

Twain sets the time of the novel at "Forty to fifty years ago." Some quick math gives us the range of possible dates. Twain began writing the novel in 1876 and published it in America in 1885. Forty to fifty years before stretches the scope to between 1826 and 1845. The latter date is the year Andrew Jackson died. The earlier is halfway between the Presidential election he should have won and the first he did: in 1824, the House of Representatives denied Andrew Jackson the Presidency, despite his plurality at the polls; but he won handily in 1828 and 1832. His top aide, Martin Van Buren, succeeded him, and the issues and ideals of Jacksonianism dominated the American scene until the question of slavery elbowed them from view in the years following Jackson's death. In his seminal work on the period, *The Age of Jackson*, Arthur M. Schlesinger, Jr. resists constructing a beginning or end for the age. Still, he begins his chronology in 1829 and extends "the days of Jackson . . . till about 1850" (488). A more date-minded historian, Glyndon G. Van Deusen, calls his book on the period *The Jacksonian Era, 1828–1848*. But as Twain leaves the specific year of the novel's action uncertain, these minor variations in contemporary interpretation of when the period begins or ends matter little. Whatever the summer Huck and Jim take their early freedom-ride, Jacksonianism—and what is meant by the term will be made clear in this chapter—ruled America.

Two bits of evidence restrict the time frame to the latter decade of Jacksonianism. First, any possibility of constructing a date before 1835, fifty years before the date of publication, lies outside the text, in biography. Without Walter Blair's reconstruction of the novel's composition, we must hang evidence for an earlier date on the raftsmen's passage in Chapter 16, which Twain intended to include in *Huckleberry Finn*, even after he published it as part of *Life on the Mississippi* with the note that it was part of a novel he had been working on for several years. Second, Huck claims to know that King William IV of England, who was succeeded by Queen Victoria in 1837, "was dead years ago, but I never let on" (221). This claim to knowledge, however, comes in the middle of the endless muddle he is making of life in England and so we have little reason to trust what Huck says he knows about the monarchy. Even admitting this evidence puts the action of *Huckleberry Finn* in the early 1840s, in the twilight of Jacksonianism.

This is especially appropriate; the failure of Jacksonianism and the failure of Huck as hero have some causes in common. As I have pointed out, the conflict between Huck's traditional heroism and his world's general historicity shows that the novel itself gives compelling reasons for the failure of its own hero. By further making the fictive world's historicity specific to Jacksonian America, we see a second level of conflict, that between Jacksonian ideals and Jacksonian reality, and a second realm of Huck's failure. *Huckleberry Finn*, in sharing the imaginative space it occupies with the imaginative space occupied by Jacksonian America, provides another structure in which its hero must fail.

The failure of Huck Finn as a hero has rightfully become axiomatic in Twain studies. Various explanations have been forwarded for the failure: that Huck's heroism is a sham; that Huck's character changes in the final fifth of the book; and that the reader, alerted by Twain's larger concerns, learns through the novel to reject Huck's heroism. I have tried in the previous two chapters to illustrate the difficulties in holding these positions. First, Huck's heroism is no sham, as the discussion in the first chapter shows. Second, with the important exception of his ability to write and dramatize, which more grows than changes, he undergoes no transformation from the beginning of the novel to the end. Huck's goals, character, and attitudes undergo no noticeable change between the first four-fifths of the book and the last one-fifth: his announced acceptance of going to hell in Chapter 31 only echoes the same announcement in Chapter 1; he is just as willing at the end of the novel as at the beginning to play Tom Sawyer's games, so long as there is some measurable good—Jim's release, for example, or seeing elephants—to be got out of it; and George Carrington's argument, that Huck continues to the novel's end practicing the ethic the novel enunciates, seems faultless. And third, we do not reject Huck in the face of Twain's larger concerns, such as determinism or the situational ethic; we simply resent Huck's capitulation to them. Our enthusiasm for Huck is a part of the novel's meaning, not a straw man set up to get us to read enough to see Twain's real point. Huck's failure is genuine because his heroism is genuine. The failure is more a necessary working out of the novel's elements than a rupture in plot when "the boys steal nigger Jim," as in Hemingway's view, or a disjuncture between readerly expectation and fictive delivery. We have faith in Huck because we have always had faith in heroes like him; that is why his

failure is so painful. If Twain has tricked us, it is only in that he
has, from the novel's start, given Huck the sort of heroism unable
to survive the world in which Twain forces him to live.

Huck has, in addition to this folkloric heroism, an historically
particular one. Part of our enthusiasm for Huck depends on this
specific configuration of his heroism, the kind of ideal Twain creates him to represent. One level of Huck's heroism, his ahistorical
supernaturalism, stands in opposition to the historically conceived
realism of the novel's world. But if that world represents an historical reality and Huck opposes it, Huck must represent an historical ideal; it is part of his heroism. Brewed out of the cauldron
of preliterate narrative, such a hero is programmed to represent
his culture's highest values. Though as a character Huck is a realistically executed thirteen-year-old boy, as a hero he symbolically
suggests the ideal. If, as a part of his role as traditional hero, we
think of him as an historically conceived ideal, an ambient representation of the high hopes of Jacksonianism, we can comprehend
the nature of the second level of tension between Huck and his
world.

This insight into the novel gains further justification through
a review of the historical literature on Jacksonianism, which strikingly resembles critical literature on *Huckleberry Finn*. After discussing the many areas of mutuality among historians of the era in
his introduction to *The Jacksonian Persuasion*, Marvin Meyers writes:

> Here agreement ends. The limits of the subject are in dispute.
> Is Jacksonian Democracy to be considered primarily an affair of
> party politics, or as a broad political, social and intellectual move-
> ment? What message did Jacksonian Democracy carry to society,
> whom did it reach, what did it signify in the setting of the times?
> These are yet unsettled questions, for all the wealth of industry
> and talent spent upon them. (5)

Edward Pessen echoes this sense of division in *Jacksonian America:
Society, Personality, and Politics*, writing:

> Whether it was an age of democracy or seeming democracy, the
> common man or the uncommon, idealistic reformers or artful
> dissemblers, the era remains one of seminal importance. If it was
> in fact what it long seemed, then of course its reputation would

be justified. If it was not an age of democracy or egalitarianism, the era if anything becomes more intriguing. For what is more interesting than the existence of a vast gulf between appearance and reality. (3–4)

Twain scholars recognize in Pessen's construction of the problems of comprehending Jacksonian America a confluence of our author's obsessions: history, appearance, reality. It should be no surprise then that in *Huckleberry Finn* we find these concerns worked to startling detail. But critics of the novel have pursued the issues without seeing the overlay between fiction and history. The general boom in scholarship after World War II notwithstanding, the coincidence of academic interest in *Huckleberry Finn* and in Jacksonianism over the past forty years demonstrates this overlay. Early work on Jacksonian America concentrated on the results of the political idealism which fueled the age: the expansion of the suffrage, the defeat of centralized money power, the emphasis of state's rights over federal rights, and of individual rights over property rights. Early Twain criticism concerned Huck and his role as representative of freedom, dignity, and morality—the "triumph of a sound heart over a deformed conscience." By 1970 both fields of scholarship sought to prove that the surrounding reality did not support the ideal conception. Jackson's actual political actions rewarded wealth, encouraged currency speculation, expanded federal involvement in contemporary life, and in the end collapsed over the issue of slavery. So too among Twain scholars concern shifted from the idealism of the novel's hero to the gritty reality of his starkly deterministic, degrading and amoral world. These parallels seem persuasive.

## Huck and Jacksonian Cultural Ideals

A small leap nominates Huck as a Jacksonian ideal, by which I mean that the same ideological structure which made a symbol of Jackson makes a symbol of Huck. John William Ward's *Andrew Jackson—Symbol for an Age* articulates part of that ideology successfully by showing how the American people of the first half of the last century created a hero out of a man. Ward writes in his coda on symbolism, "The symbolic Andrew Jackson is the creation of his time. Through the age's leading figure were projected the age's leading ideas. Of Andrew Jackson the people made a mirror for themselves" (208). And he concludes his essay, "To describe the early nineteenth century as the age of Jackson misstates the matter. The age was not his. He was the age's" (213). I offer a further qualification: Jackson belonged to what we now conceive the ideals of the age to have been. This does not revise Ward's thesis, only recognizes that all history, in its attempt to construct something true about the past, builds on the foundation of the present, which did not then exist and therefore could not contribute to that truth. If we can believe that America of the time could see Jackson as an embodiment of certain ideals and can in that belief ourselves see Jackson as that embodiment, we can also see Huck in the same way. Ward argues that three more or less inseparable ideas—Nature, Providence and Will—"are the structural underpinnings of the ideology of the society of early nineteenth-century America, for which Andrew Jackson is *one* symbol" (10). I will use Ward's ideas to point out how Huck Finn is another.

Jacksonian America's conception of Nature was, according to Ward, an uneasy compromise between the savagery of uncivilization, as identified with the Indians, and the moral decay of too much civilization, embodied in the Europeans. "The ideal of the admixture of nature and civilization was a static one. It could be achieved only in the pioneer stage when the wildness of nature had been subdued but the enervating influence of civilization had not yet been felt" (45). Jackson's defeat of the British at New Orleans was seen symbolically as the defeat of European decay. A cartoon representation of the "Spirit of the Times" provides an insight into the American perception of Europe's dissipation and corruption. In it, Europe is represented by castles, a vertical flagpole, armies and caricatures of leaders as domesticated animals. Across the ocean, America is represented by a cornfield surrounded by a split-rail fence, a flag draped horizontally, wildfowl and snakes, and an eagle as a caricature of leadership. This American ideal differed from a Rousseauean embrace of noble savages and their habitat. Ward explains, "Americans were willing to accept the idea that nature, symbolized by the forest, was the source of vitality, but their attitude was ambivalent. They celebrated nature, but not wild nature" (33). Wild nature belonged to the Indians.

> As they advanced into the interior of the continent, pushing the
> Indians before them, Americans tended to see themselves as the
> advancing frontier of civilization. . . . But always at their backs
> was Europe, the culmination of the process of civilization, which
> was inextricably involved in the American mind with tyranny
> and decadence. (40)

Andrew Jackson's Indian policy solved this problem for Americans.
"The answer was incredibly simple. America would save the Indians *for* civilization by rescuing them *from* civilization" (41). Jackson,
like many early heroes, was prized as an American Cincinnatus,
called from the plough into service for his country. This careful
mix—civilized enough to write, raw enough to retain innate moral
values, one who turns wilderness into productive land—was the
human embodiment of America's ideal of Nature.

Though in recent years critics have withdrawn support for the
vision of Huck Finn as a child of Nature, the impression remains
with readers of the novel. The initial chapters of the book encourage this interpretation, even if they do not wholly endorse it. Huck,
caught between the poles of the widow's stultifying 'sivilizing' and
Pap's brutal uncivilizing, the second defined against the first, escapes both by plunging into the relative wilderness of the Mississippi river, then the boundary between the tamed states and the
untamed territories. Huck writes of the moment just before releas-
ing the canoe into the current, hovering on the precipice of freedom, "Everything was dead quiet, and it looked late, and *smelt* late.
You know what I mean—I don't know the words to put it in" (42).
This passage points to two aspects of Huck's relationship to Nature:
his rare ability to detect the minutiae of nature, like the odor of
night, and the resistance such natural phenomena have to language. Once Huck achieves his independence he overcomes the
resistance. Out on the Mississippi Huck becomes the mouthpiece
for Nature: "The sky looks ever so deep when you lay down on
your back in the moonshine; I never knowed it before. And how
far a body can hear on the water such nights!" While his knowledge
of Nature never seems more than adequate—when Mrs. Loftus
questions him about the rising patterns of animals, for example, or
in his river-mastery during the fog—Huck's ability to speak for Nature binds Huck and Nature in our imagination. Even during the
terror of the fog, his sense of personal relationship to Nature im-
presses us more than his knowledge: "I was floating along, of

course, four or five miles an hour; but you don't even think of that. No, you *feel* like you are laying dead still on the water; and if a little glimpse of a snag slips by, you don't think to yourself how fast *you're* going, but you catch your breath and think, my! how that snag's tearing along" (100–101). This power of speaking for Nature becomes more apparent when periodically throughout the novel Huck takes his moments of peace to enjoy it. His description of the sunrise at the beginning of Chapter 19 is the classic passage of the type. These passages appear infrequently, as contemporary critics point out in their arguments against conceiving of Huck as Nature's child, but when they do occur they establish an alliance between Huck and Nature, better understood as a partnership than as a familial relationship.

This sense of alliance gains substance in passages which reverse Huck's speaking for Nature; that is, when Nature appears to speak for Huck. We see this in the liberating lightning storm which ends the Wilks episode and in the church-going hogs in Chapter 18, who well represent Huck's view of religion. *Huckleberry Finn's* best example of Nature's voice comes in the description of Bricksville in Chapter 21. After Huck has vilified the citizenry for three pages, he switches to a brief description of the town itself, where on the river front houses prepare to cave into the water. "Such a town as that," Huck writes, "has to be always moving back, and back, and back, because the river's always gnawing at it" (183). I argued in the last chapter that Twain here uses the river as his symbolic agent against the town. As an agent of Nature, it also seems to share Huck's moral evaluation of Bricksville. We must conlude therefore that, despite modern revisions of the concept of Huck as Nature's child, evidence in support of some sort of relationship remains convincing.

Ward's delineation of the second concept, Providence, begins with the popular belief that God intervened on Jackson's and America's behalf in the astounding War of 1812 victory over the British at New Orleans. Though in the flurry of panegyrics after the battle Jackson was made an equal to the deity, in time he settled for a role as, in his own words, "the humble instrument of a superintending Providence." This Providence particularly superintended America. Ward writes:

> Perhaps the most durable among the many ideas that have fallen under the generic term, nationalism, is the belief that God will

see to it that America will succeed. . . . Americans of the nineteenth century, preoccupied with immediate tasks, argued that a
self-conscious social philosophy against which all change must be
measured was unnecessary because man, in America, would in-
tuitively trod the path to justice. (111)

This moral intuition is a fundamental characteristic of America's
ideal relationship to divine will. God's word mostly came to Americans through the Bible and the lessons of Nature, and careful rea-
soning about right and wrong meant less than instinctive ethics.
Even the superb reasoner Thomas Jefferson expressed the belief
that in moral cases a ploughman will decide as well as or better than
a professor, and Andrew Jackson, Western farmer elevated to
America's moral and political leader, embodied proof of that belief
for his time. In the strictly political arena Manifest Destiny strikingly shows American belief in the divinity of its leadership, a belief
grounded in the conviction that we have a natural, god-given morality. The deity behind this morality is not precisely the ruler of
Nature; Jacksonian America saw only the creation of Nature, and
not its direction, as proof of God's power. Instead,, God has a plan
larger than Nature, and America and Andrew Jackson were significant parts of it.

Huck shares with Jackson this direct relationship to the divinity; that Ward and Huck use the same word for it makes this
relationship easy to prove. Huck refers to two experiences of divine
intervention within a few pages of each other at the story's moral
climax. Finding himself in a moral corner about Jim in Chapter 31,
Huck writes:

> And at last, when it hit me all of a sudden that here was the plain
> hand of Providence slapping me in the face and letting me know
> my wickedness was being watched all the time from up there in
> heaven, whilst I was stealing a poor old woman's nigger that
> hadn't ever done me no harm, and now was showing me there's
> One that's always on the lookout, and agoing to allow no such
> miserable doings to go only just so fur and no further, I most
> dropped in my tracks I was so scared. (268–69)

Many critics have pointed out the verbal ambiguity of this sentence:
Who hadn't done Huck any harm? Which miserable doings? Allow
how, or what? Others have shown a structural irony in that this

slapping God seems not only to allow these goings on but to encourage them; in that Huck in fact rejects this God's interference;
and in that Huck's subsequent cleansing of sin in fact leaves the sin
and cleans out the morality. But before we can confront these ironies and ambiguities we have to grant Huck's perception that God
does interfere directly in his life. The irony and ambiguity actually
depend on the temporary sincerity of Huck's perception that God
watched him and tried to stop his immorality. Huck later backs
down from this perception, but his belief in a false case of providential interference prepares the reader for a true intervention on
his behalf in the subsequent chapter. Wandering up to the Phelps
house wishing for death, Huck "went right along, not fixing up any
particular plan, but just trusting to Providence to put the right
words in my mouth when the time come; for I'd noticed that Providence always did put the right words in my mouth, if I left it alone"
(277). Aside from this being a succinct expression of Ward's concept of innate moral divinity, it is reliable prophecy. Providence
lives up to its name, providing Huck through the Phelps with an
identity and words to fill it. "But if they was joyful, it warn't nothing
to what I was; for it was like being born again, I was so glad to find
out who I was" (282). Huck's "chin was so tired it couldn't hardly
go," so many words did Providence put in his mouth. The false
Providence of Chapter 31 leads us to trust the Providence of Chapter 32. God appears to have chosen Huck.

Will, Ward's last concept, removes the responsibility for differences in people's accomplishments from the larger forces of Nature
or Providence and places them with the individual. "From the time
of his victory in 1815 to his death in 1845, Jackson was constantly
before the American imagination as the embodiment of the success
that awaits the man of iron will, the man who can overcome insu-
perable opposition simply by determination" (158). While this faith
in the self-made man does in the extreme negate the importance
of Providence and Nature, its practical danger lies in demagoguery.
Against this, Ward asserts, the American ideal of Will had moder-
ating attributes.

> A highly fluid society, such as the United States in the early years
> of the nineteenth century, faces the problem of insuring social
> conformity and establishing social direction without the aid
> of traditional institutions which implement such purposes. . . .
> What actually seems to happen is that the individual incorpo-

rates society's demands into his own consciousness and thereby
is led to strive even harder because the demands of the society
seem to be the demands of one's own self. (172–73)

America created out of Andrew Jackson a man of indomitable will
who dearly loved his wife, adopted a score of children, and had
nearly impeccable scruples. This modified concept of Will—
indomitable desire soft at heart—protected society from a Napoleon, the age's emblem of a harder sort of will. America watched
Napoleon with great interest and reserved admiration; Jackson's
own library contained five biographies of the French leader. If the
internalized rules of society and native kindness were not sufficient
to protect society from an iron will, America could appeal to a
higher authority. "The universal stress on the fact that the man of
iron will had in the end bowed to God"—Jackson turned to religion
before his death—"proved that in the last analysis God ruled the
universe, that the man of iron will offered no threat to society because he too had his master" (204).

I cannot prove Huck Finn a boy of iron will without stretching
the novel. Part of the novel's grievously frustrating ending is Huck's
inability to make Tom Sawyer accept anything he says, to the point
that Tom even changes the meanings of Huck's words while they
are still in his mouth. Tom's willful "psychopathic personality,
for whom all that counts are energy and charisma" (Carrington,
*Unity*, 173) easily dominates Huck. But Ward's concept of Will
is not merely a matter of energy and charisma; it includes self-
determination and moral responsibility. These two elements have
long been the central focus of appreciation of Huck Finn. Traditional interpretations of the novel, starting with those by T. S. Eliot
and Lionel Trilling and continuing to the present day, stress Huck's
moral development, his eventual acceptance that, in the problem
of human cruelty, "The solution, simply, is human love" (Rubenstein, "Moral Structure," 59). More recent criticism, in shooting
down the notion of Huck's moral enlightenment, erects yet another
defense of Huck as an embodiment of Will by stressing Huck's increased skills as a maker of situations, a player of roles, a fabricator
of his own life in the form of a book called *Adventures of Huckleberry
Finn*. Further, Huck's inability to completely embrace Will is partially mitigated at the novel's end by his partnership with Tom,
whose ability to make things happen by just saying so is proved to

have no power outside the realm of fiction. Will has endless effect in the personal world each of us creates with lies, but in the reality of the novel, we are shown, Will has limits. For Huck to possess Tom's absolute will would abrogate to the novel's final thrust and Huck's final lesson: That the world of history cannot be manipulated, even by Huck's heroic powers. If supernatural force cannot change history, how can Will? In this novel, Will is less subject to Providence than to whatever force creates history.

## Huck and Jacksonian Socio-Political Ideals

Huck, then, shares with the popular conception of Andrew Jackson the ideological space which made Jackson a hero. The confluence of Nature, Providence, and Will—the last of these concepts modified out of Ward to suit *Huckleberry Finn's* larger purpose—establishes a matrix of cultural beliefs which an effective Jacksonian hero will symbolize. These cultural ideals shared the Jacksonian imagination with certain socio-political ideals, ideals we might identify as even more certainly Jacksonian than Ward's cultural ones. Alexis de Tocqueville's *Democracy in America* remains the best source for abstractions about the ideals behind Jacksonian society. Tocqueville

> was less interested in describing the American actuality than in explaining the inevitable tendencies of an abstract or generalized democracy. . . . His interest was not in fact but in ideas. . . . His characteristic method was to have an extended discussion with a prominent personage, then to indulge his great powers of deduction and imagination to create a logical theoretical structure based on the idea he had extracted from the words of his informant. (Pessen, 44)

In short, Tocqueville is the premier contemporary observer and systematizer of Jacksonian beliefs. His passion for political and social structure restricts his value as a journalist, but earns him vast worth as delineator of socio-political ideals.

We can see easily how Huck Finn embodies the three core ideals Tocqueville saw. The first of these—the notion of independence, of freedom, of individuality—shares ideology with the last of Ward's concepts. Those three terms, used with a bewildering interchangability in some histories of the period, all concern the same value: the right of an individual to make and follow his [pronoun employed with knowledge] own rules within territory solely his own. Tocqueville writes, "There's a general distaste for accepting any man's word as a proof for anything. . . . Each man is narrowly shut up in himself and from that basis makes the pretension to judge the world" (430). I have already noted in my discussion of Neil Sapper's "'I been there before': Huck Finn as Tocquevillian Individual" the degree to which Huck fills Tocqueville's prophecy that individualism—perhaps the best of term for this concept— born of democracy "isolates [men] from their contemporaries. Each man is forever thrown back on himself alone, and there is danger that he may be shut up in the solitude of his own heart" (508).

The second socio-political ideal of Jacksonianism is democracy. In Tocqueville's view the dangers of individualism are offset by a kind of democracy of free association. The frequent exercise of voting rights means that political "direction really comes from the people, and though the form of government is representative, it is clear that the opinion, prejudices, interests and even passions of the people can find no lasting obstacles preventing them from being manifest in the daily conduct of society" (173).

The maintenance of this ideal depends on the third, equality. Tocqueville believed that the equality of condition that reigned among European colonists in New England encouraged them to do away with most aristocratic distinctions. Even Southern aristocrats conceded the virtue of rule of law, a fundamental political tenet in the ideology of equality, and laws restricting inheritance forwarded the cause of economic equality. In Tocqueville's view a belief in equality is a precondition of the universal suffrage which gave American democracy its unique and idealistic quality. "The more I studied America society," Tocqueville claims, "the more clearly I saw equality of conditions as the creative element from which each particular fact derived" (9).

Readers of *Huckleberry Finn* need very little argument to see in Huck the particular embodiment of the abstractions of equality, democracy, and individualism. Huck regards the King and the Duke with the same indulgence he grants Silas Phelps, though the con-artists' shrewd evil matches measure for measure the farmer-preacher's simple-minded goodness. Huck treats both sorts of people with equal dishonesty, lingers illogically in their company, and still presents them to the reader with a brutal directness. For all Huck's acknowledgement of the differences in social status he leaves no doubt that moral value and community rank have nothing in common. Sherburn is "a heap the best dressed man" in Bricksville and a murderer; though Pap and Col. Grangerford differ in style, they share in the most bald-faced hypocrisy. Huck's inconsistency over bread—sneering at cornpone because he has the bread of "the quality," then claiming nothing is better than cornpone cooked right—owes as much to his levelling eye as to his world's situational ethic (Carrington, 15). Huck's equalizing extends up to, but does not embrace, Jim. Even so, in the novel he is far and away the white person most accepting of black people's humanity.

Huck's democratic impulse shows itself in the few situations he finds himself in a group. When the Duke and the King first show on the raft, Huck determines to allow the group to settle its differences to its own satisfaction, in ignorance of the facts. No one present holds the power of arbitration; this power belongs to the group as a whole. When the Duke and the King negotiate a solution to their difference over social rank, a final handshake "took away all the uncomfortableness, and we felt mighty good over it, because it would have been a miserable business to have any unfriendliness on the raft; for what you want, above all things, on a raft, is for everybody to be satisfied, and feel right and kind toward the others" (165). This version of democracy reappears in the Wilks episode, where the doctor accepts the communal judgment of his dissent and backs off; he makes no unpopular crusade against the duly elected frauds. Later, in the same sequence, when the second pair of possible shysters show, truth is left to people's judgment: one set of brothers will be the Wilks' family heirs because the people say so. Huck's democracy is like Tocqueville's idealized version: a tyranny of the majority tempered by a decentralized administration always conscious of minority opinion. The final ploy of the raftsmen's-passage ghost-story shows just this sort of democracy at work: "'Say, boys,' said Bill, 'less divide it up. Thar's thirteen of us. I can swaller a thirteenth of the yarn, if you can worry down the rest'" (120). This equal responsibility for the working out of matters pertaining to the group is precisely the form of democracy Huck represents.

The argument for Huck's individualism has already been well made and needs no repetition. I wish only to add a sinew of connection between Sapper's argument for Huck as Tocquevillian individual and Carrington's perception of Huck's continued movement away from ennui into action. Tocqueville notes that the social fracturing caused by democratic individualism is mitigated by the drive to voluntary association, the slow discovery of the social interdependence of morally independent men (509–20). Huck's voluntary movement from the isolation of the raft to the integration of the shore grows in part from this necessary modification of individualism, as well as from the emotional need for drama.

I have made this argument about Huck not to pull back from my earlier assertion of Huck's traditional heroism but rather to show that the generic hero can also have historically particularizing qualities. Huck's complexity—if he weren't complex, could he fascinate us so?—is precisely this mixture of a character older than time with characteristics specific to a certain time. Embodying Ward's Nature, Providence, and Will on one side and Tocqueville's individualism, democracy, and equality on the other, Huck becomes a symbol for the ideals of Jacksonian America. These elements, and minor others not here articulated, are what we believe Americans in the second quarter of the nineteenth century hoped their country was. These concepts, applied to Huck, cast him as the Jacksonian ideal in the particular historical drama of the novel, a role concurrent to his in the narrative drama as a traditional hero in tension with an historically conceived reality.

## The World of *Huck* and Jacksonian America

That the ideals of Jacksonian America and its reality share almost only a space on the calendar should surprise no one, except blind idealists. Evidence of Jacksonian reality abounds. America in that period attracted an endless stream of foreign visitors, almost all less perspicacious and theory-minded than Alexis de Tocqueville, but many just as willing to commit their observations to paper. Further, the expansion of the country, population, and democratic rule created a need for more effective communication, and newspapers of the day provided it. Tocqueville himself observed that "There is hardly a hamlet in America without its newspaper" (185). This virtual flood of primary documents has sustained a generation of historians and—accepting the caveat that history is written mostly from a time rather than of a time—contributed to a full picture of American life under Jackson and his successors.

Edward Pessen has collated observations of Jacksonian America and determined that they "fall into four not always distinct categories: emotional traits or attributes of personality; mental or intellectual traits; manners, habits or customs; and values— themselves, of course, manifested in behavior" (10). Pessen's work structures my attempt to find correlations between the historical reality of Jacksonian America —the America described by its visitors and inhabitants and later interpretations of that place—and the America Mark Twain gives us in *Huckleberry Finn*.

1. *Personal traits.* According to Pessen, visitors found Americans cordial, generous, and curious, but also rude, humorless, dull, cold, cruel, violent, selfish, insecure, thin-skinned, boastful, and complaining. Pessen gives each of these traits a paragraph of substantiation from his primary sources; I can hardly be as thorough from Twain's novel without steeping my reader in boredom. A review of the novel will provide many examples of each. I have included below at least one incident in the novel each characteristic brings to mind:

cordial: the King's informant about the Wilks (205–208)

generous: "America was the land of assorted benevolent associations, the leaders of which clearly were not themselves suffering from the abuses they sought to correct" (Pessen, 11) = the slave hunters' two gold pieces for the small-pox victim (127)

curious: "'They cannot bear anything like a secret,' was the conclusion of [English Captain Frederick] Marryat, one of whose confidants had advised him that the Ursiline Convent had been stormed more because of curiosity about the life behind its sealed gates than out of bigotry" (Pessen, 12) = the mourners' need to know what caused the disturbance at the Wilks funeral (223) rude: British entertainer Fanny Kemble saw in her hosts "a singularly felicitous union of impudence and vulgarity, to be met with nowhere but America" (in Pessen, 12) = as the good people of Concord realized, the novel is a document of rudeness, so much so that only acts of politeness stand out; the most outstanding rudeness comes when Huck asks a fellow river-traveller if the shore lights ahead are Cairo (129)

humorless: According to Pessen, Tocqueville believed of Americans that, "as social upstarts of a democratic community, they took themselves too seriously" (13) = we see this in the King's and Duke's offense rather than laughter at each others' obviously humbug nobility (161–65) dull, cold, cruel: the Bricksville loafers (181–83)

violent: Pessen notes that "In Kentucky one man came near to killing another for opening a coach window ... Stabbing, shooting, gouging out of eyes, biting off of nose or ears are not uncommon" (14–15) = the shooting of Boggs fits this pattern (184–87)

selfish: One visitor remarked, writes Pessen, "that there was something in his training that led the American to the ignoble feeling that the purpose of life was nothing more than the satisfaction of 'his own good pleasure'" (15) = Tom keeps Jim's freedom secret to open up an opportunity for his own amusement (284)

insecure, thin-skinned, boastful, and complaining: the raftsmen's entire interaction (107–20).

2. *Intellectual traits.* "In matters of mind," Pessen writes, "The American was above all practical. . . . Americans were clever but not profound. . . . They were not gifted conversationalists. . . . Americans loved scandal and were quick to believe the worst" (18–19). We see all these traits beautifully in Tom Sawyer's dominance at the novel's end. Though Huck would argue against the practicality of Tom's plan, we must agree, after we have found out that Jim is already free, it is absolutely practical. The goal, after all, is not to free Jim, but to entertain two pubescent boys. Tom keeps his mind on the passing weeks, not because he wants to evade before Jim can be sold—his say-so will stop that—but for the same reason he hides

Aunt Polly's letters: because he "knowed they'd make trouble" (359), the only possible trouble being an end to his pleasure.

The style Tom throws into the evasion grows out of cleverness, not profundity. Jim's burdens are stolen piecemeal from romance novels, the only authority Tom seems to recognize. Tom assembles bits of other people's inventions cleverly, but with no real comprehension and no insight. The same books Tom steals from also fuel the boys' often inane conversation:

> "Why look at one of them prisoners in the bottom dungeon of the Castle Deef, in the harbor of Marseilles, that dug himself out that way. How long was *he* at it, you reckon?"
>
> "I don't know."
>
> "Well, guess."
>
> "I don't know. A month and a half?"
>
> "*Thirty-seven year*—and he come out in China. *That's* the kind. I wish the bottom of *this* fortress was solid rock."
>
> "*Jim* don't know nobody in China."
>
> "What's *that* got to do with it? Neither did that other fellow. But you're always a-wandering off on a side issue. Why can't you stick to the main point?" (304)

For idiotic talk it compares with the Bricksville loafers' endless squawking about tobacco.

Lastly, the conversation among the Phelps' neighbors once the boys have successfully evaded has equal shares of inanity and something else: the babbling church-folk do as much petty scandal-mongering as commiserating. "The nigger was crazy," one woman says (345). "Ther's ben a *dozen* a-helpin' that nigger, 'n' I lay I'd skin every last nigger on this place, but *I'd* find out who done it, s'I; 'n' moreover, s'I—" "A *dozen*, says you!—*forty* couldn't a done everything that's been done" (346). While there is a degree of sympathy for the Phelps family, there is also implied fault: that the Phelps have so little power over their own slaves that the blacks can run a complete African cult out of the prisoner's shack. Aunt Sally punctuates her comments with "People to *help* him . . . they slides in right under our noses . . . *sperits* couldn't a done better" (347), anything to create the impression it was not the family's own slaves responsible.

Pessen further finds that "The American was a conformist, in the opinion of the foreigner and native, to the sympathetic as to the jaundiced. In an essay in *The American Democrat*, Cooper wrote that "'they say,' is the monarch of the country.' . . . Related to the American's deference to the opinions of others, was his need to associate himself with them in every manner of activity" (20–21). These associations and their dominance over individual integrity of opinion play a master's role in the novel's Mississippi Valley life. From the indecisiveness of the killers aboard the *Walter Scott* to the same indecisiveness among the investigators of the Wilks frauds, group-think rules. Individuals rarely make decisions and stick by them; according to Sherburn's indictment of America, North and South, making a courageous decision takes a man, and this country has very few of them. "If only *half* a man—like Buck Harkness, there—shouts 'Lynch him, lynch him!' you're afraid to back down— afraid you'll be found out to be what you are—*cowards*" (190). Some historians suggest this accedence to local norm resulted from the tremendous mobility of Americans, who, wanting acceptance in their new place, would seek to join whatever activity or idea presented itself. The King's and the Duke's first foray together is an extreme version of this. The Duke steals the use of a printshop for a day and makes money with a lie about being new to town that people somehow seem to believe easily. The King, against all logic in this town hundreds of miles from the nearest ocean, works the crowd with a converted-pirate con. But the people for some reason buy in to such a degree that the King remarks that "heathens don't amount to shucks, alongside of pirates, to work a camp-meeting with" (174). Huck himself finds the need to become someone new wherever he goes, showing in high relief the sort of transformation of the individual required in a massively mobile society. Huck's very movement itself recreates the movement epidemic in Jacksonian America.

3. *Customs.* Twain's picture of Jacksonian life extends to the smallest manners and behavioral foibles. Frances Trollope's *Domestic Manners of the America* became such a well-known index of *faux pas* that "subsequent visitors observed that the cry, 'a trollope! a trollope!' went up from America audiences when one of their number happened to be caught in that public slouching that had so offended their critical visitor. Americans slouched in theaters, they slouched in church, they were even discovered slouching when attending sessions of the supreme court" (Pessen, 23). Americans chewed and spit tobacco, drank to excess and gambled widely and

wildly. The simply-prepared plenty of American tables did nothing to slow down consumption: "speed and silence were the rule" at table (26). With the exception of the baker's bread floated down-river to find the fictively dead Huck, the food in the novel seems more plentiful than excellent. On the raft Huck and Jim eat "corn-dodgers and buttermilk, and pork and cabbage, and greens" (154). Huck always wants to "go right to eating, but you had to wait for the widow to tuck down her head and grumble a little over the victuals, though there warn't really anything the matter with them" (2). Gambling metaphor infects Huck's language and gambling appears not only in the plain and fatal form Pap practiced, but in all forms of speculation, legal and otherwise. The Duke and the King speculate in everything they do: Shakespeare does not pay, but the Royal Nonesuch does; making up the Wilks' 'deffersit' only looks like a sure thing. Even Silas Phelps, the noble one-horse-plantation farmer-preacher—the man who is the backbone of Jacksonian political idealism—speculates in human flesh with his purchase of Jim. A load of alcohol gets consumed in *Huckleberry Finn*, from the light morning bracer at the Grangerford's to Pap's foul excess; the only judgment against drinking comes when someone other than the drinker himself is threatened by the alcohol, as with Pap's DTs. The citizens of Bricksville are only the extreme variety of slouching tobacco-spitters in the novel, but they can serve as the model for the rest: "There was empty dry goods boxes under the awnings, and loafers roosting on them all day long, whittling them with their Barlow knives; and chawing tobacco, and gaping and yawning and stretching" (181). Even if we did not know from the title page and the subsequent symbolism where and when Twain had set the novel, we could likely figure it out from the habits of its characters.

4. *Values.* Pessen discovers in the primary documents a portrait of American values—lived values, he stresses, not idealized ones, though some do cross over. Egalitarianism, distinct from the concept of equality discussed above, meant, according to Pessen, "that one man—particularly an American—was as good as any other, certainly that he should be treated like any other. White Americans simply would not be known as 'servants.' Those who worked in other people's homes would not be summoned by bells" (27). This often accounted for a rudeness about possessions, with people making a show of keeping the best for themselves. "The transcendent American value according to most contemporaries

was materialism" (29). Money often seemed to be the only material of any reliable value. Wealth was the only successful measure of distinction in this egalitarian society and Americans spared nothing in its acquisition. "If Americans were opportunistic, if amoral behavior was countenanced and shrewdness applauded, it was clearly because the worship of gain was such, that in Juvenal's old phrase, it smelled sweet no matter its source or by whatever means secured" (31). Oportunism and materialism were the values most regularly observed, but foreigners also noticed the lack of educational and artistic values, and "American hypocrisy towards Negroes and Indians was most severely censured" (28). Foreign visitors almost universally recorded their observations not only of the cruel violation of American promises to the Indians and the institutionalized brutality practiced on enslaved blacks, but also the regular and random violence against people of color North and South. Every Jacksonian visitor seemed unlucky enough to witness racist communal stonings, lynchings, or rapes.

These values and lacks show up plainly in *Huckleberry Finn*. In order to find the novel's egalitarianism we need to further distinguish egalitarianism from equality. Equality as a value only appears in the character and ideals of heroic Huck, not in the world of the novel. Equality means the undifferentiated worth accorded each human being simply for being human. Thus we see characters who begin sounding like the voice of authority, such as Col. Grangerford, in the end inculpating themselves by some inhuman horror, in his case by the senseless slaughter of the feud, while thorough scoundrels, such as the King and Duke, achieve a sort of moral pardon by becoming victims of extreme cruelty. The judgments that level these diverse people, however, come from Huck. He creates the equality between Col. Grangerford and the con artists by writing of the feud, "I ain't going to tell *all* that happened—it would make me sick again if I was to do that. I wished I hadn't ever come ashore that night, to see such things" (153), when the alternative to coming ashore was death by the river; and then writing of the King and Duke tarred, feathered, and ridden on a rail, "Well, it made me sick to see it; and I was sorry for them poor pitiful rascals, it seemed I couldn't ever feel any hardness against them any more in the world" (290). Equality in the novel is a transcendent quality, an other-worldly assertion of the balance of human worth issued by the only character able to move between worlds, heroic Huck.

Egalitarianism, on the other hand, is the real-world revolt against differences in status. The duped crowd at Bricksville shows this value. Rather than admit themselves 'sold' by the Duke and King, they buy their leader's argument: "We don't want to be the laughingstock of this whole town, I reckon, and never hear the last of this thing as long as we live. *No*. What we want, is to go out of here quiet, and talk this show up, and sell the *rest* of the town! Then we'll all be in the same boat" (197). This egalitarianism, a value which owes next to nothing to the metaphysical proposition of human equality, dominates this Mississippi Valley world. The concept of equality in the real world gets trampled early. In Pap's abortive redemption in Chapter 5 he uses the language of equality, claiming he was once an animal and is now a man, worthy of human dignity. But Pap's redemption is a hoax: he ends as he begins. Equality is clearly not a workable concept with Pap, but egalitarianism is: he expresses exactly that position in his tirade against the government (33–34).

Materialism affects every portion of the book, as the number of times Huck himself simply lists his possessions demonstrates. Respect for material values outstrips respect for egalitarian values, just as in Jacksonian America. We see this when Huck goes to the ferry-boat captain to alert him to the danger aboard the *Walter Scott*. In his egalitarian description of himself as the gamut of river-boat society, from owner to watchman, he says, "I ain't as rich as Jim Hornback, and I can't be so blame' generous and good to Tom, Dick and Harry"—a phrase from the Jacksonian era—"as what he is, and slam around money the way he does, but I've told him many a time 'tIwouldn't trade places with him; for, says I, a sailor's life's the life for me, and I'm derned if *I*'d live two mile out of town, where there ain't nothing ever goin' on, not for all his spondulicks and as much more on top of it" (88–89). This noble sentiment fades in the space of a page. Huck spins a story about danger aboard the wreck and the captain responds, "By Jackson, I'd *like* to [help], and blame it I don't know but I will; but who in dingnation's agoin' to *pay* for it?" When he finds out Jim Hornback's niece is among the threatened, his resistance to help transforms itself to enthusiasm: he realizes who will foot the bill. Except when Huck and Jim are alone together, and often even then, money or possessions figure in every sequence in the novel, from the threatened sale of Jim, the murderers' haul on the wreck, the Grangerfords' decor, Huck's free passage into the circus, and all the King and Duke do, down to the final sucking of a dime from Huck. Money no longer seems to count for much at the Phelps' plantation, where Aunt Sally simply gives up hope of keeping track of her rapidly vanishing goods, but this only seems the case. Here, all the surface materialism has been removed to reveal what has been the fundamental question of possession throughout the novel, that of slavery, the human ownership of human beings.

The novel presents a society with next to no interest in education, art, or any element of elite culture. If the novel is to be believed, not a single artifact of high culture, with the exception of John Bunyan's *Pilgrim's Progress*, exists in the entire Mississippi Valley. The two extended considerations of material with artistic or educational rather than market value appear close together and treat their subjects with remarkable similarity. Huck has equal enthusiasm for the Grangerfords' possessions as for the Duke's Hamlet, but that enthusiasm is in each case tempered by an ironical distance between Twain and his narrator. Twain encourages us to laugh at Huck's ignorance. The disrepair of the Grangerfords' art objects and the poor attendance at the performance of Shakespeare mean one of two things: either the people of the Valley see with Twain and us the absurdity of calling these particular productions art, or they grant no value to the goods except material value. This choice becomes clear by the presence of *Pilgrim's Progress*. To the Grangerfords, the book is just one of the objects of 'culture' their house holds; they can no more differentiate between it and the rest than Joanna Wilks can between a Bible and a dictionary. Huck, however, seeing the statements in Bunyan's book as "interesting, but tough" (137), has a sense of value outside the simply material. This puts him halfway between Twain and the created world of the novel.

Huck also occupies this central position in regard to the book's racism. Sound arguments, especially in Woodard's and MacCann's "Blackface Minstrelsy," have been made about the racist quality of *Huckleberry Finn*, arguments to which I have only the following to add: The novel itself presents different degrees of racism. We think of the Twain presented as author of this book as thoroughly antiracist because, of all the partially separable voices in the novel, Twain's is the least racist, the most like contemporary readers. We can see this through Huck's reflection on Jim's tears that "He was thinking about his wife and children, away up yonder, and he was low and homesick; because he hadn't ever been away from home before in his life; and I do believe he cared just as much for his people just as much as white folks does for theirn. It don't seem natural, but I reckon it's so" (201). The last sentence looks two ways: first, it sets Huck off at an ironical distance from Twain, letting us know that the author knows that familial love knows no race; and second, it sets Huck off at a distance from his world by letting him understand as natural a thing his world believes is not. To successfully demonstrate Twain's racism, critics must step out of the novel into his life, because in the novel itself he is the least racist, a giant step better than Huck, who is himself a giant step better than the rest of his world.

In personality, mentality, habits, and values, the world of *Huckleberry Finn* closely mirrors the Jacksonian America recorded by contemporary visitors. Twain's historical conception of reality is realized through a brilliant conception: an overwhelming attention to the detail of the age. The difficulty of negative arguments notwithstanding, I feel secure in maintaining that nothing in the novel, except Huck's heroic character and the scenes with Huck and Jim on the river, disturbs the sense that the world presented is an integral whole which looks very like our concept of Jacksonian America.

Now we have a fuller picture of *Adventures of Huckleberry Finn*: Huck is a traditional hero placed in a realistic world. Huck's heroism is of a folkloric and so ahistorical nature, unrestricted by the historical world of time, writing, causality, or law. The world Huck operates in, on the other hand, is not only restricted by all these things, but is, in fact, defined by them. It is a world conceived historically, a realism of historicity. This is the source of the most basic conflict in the novel, that between Huck as a traditional hero from outside the realm of history and a world with history in its very nature. This abstract conflict has an analog in the historical time of the novel's events. In this analog, Huck's world's particular historicity is the age of Jackson, America of the second quarter of the nineteenth century. The world is presented with a comprehensive realism, a vision seconded up and down the line by contemporary documents of the period collated by modern historians. The ideals of Americans of the period, their abstract hopes and underlying, unremembered dreams, can be seen to coalesce in the character of our traditional hero Huck. Just as history in the abstract defeats Huck's timeless heroics, so the particular historicity of *Adventures of Huckleberry Finn*'s Jacksonianism reality shows the failure of Jacksonian idealism, of which Huck Finn is our emblem.

# Part II

❧❀❧

*A Connecticut Yankee
in King Arthur's Court*

# 4

⋅⋖⋟⋅

# Inside Hank Morgan

Although critics have written much on the character of Hank Morgan in Twain's *A Connecticut Yankee in King Arthur's Court*, surprisingly little appears on his heroism. The debates concern themselves primarily with understanding Hank's complexities and contradictions. The role this character plays in the novel comes second, and often as not the critical methods used in the attempt to fit the Yankee into his book more suit psychological realism than whatever it is we have in *Connecticut Yankee*.

Those critics who do see Hank Morgan formally put forth more convincing interpretations of the novel as a whole. Casting Hank as daimonic entrepreneur, as American individualist, or as Manifest Destiny made flesh shapes our reading more effectively than do investigations into Hank Morgan's character; interpretations which view Hank Morgan as a type allow a much easier access to the historical issues the book begs readers to contemplate. But simplifying Hank's complexities and contradictions by historical metaphor turns him into a paper-thin hero and, in the end, does the same to the book which is almost exclusively his document. An interpretation of Hank, capitalizing on both the psychological and the historical streams of criticism, would seem to offer the richest lode. My earlier discussion of *Huckleberry Finn* shows the fundamental formal and ideological consistency of that novel by interpreting the conflict between Huck and his world in terms of literary types and historical symbols. *Connecticut Yankee*, another tale of confrontation between a gigantic hero and an even larger world, invites the same investigation. If we can unify the two driving interpretations of Hank Morgan—the psychological and the historical—we will have brought to bear a method which might well answer the central difficulties of the novel.

As with *Huckleberry Finn*, I begin this investigation with the book's nominal maker. Two issues come up repeatedly in the literature assessing Hank's character: first, his personal integrity, which introduces questions not only about his unrestrained ego and altruism, but also about his honesty and authority as narrator; and second, his humor, which includes not only praise of it but also resistance to it, particularly in its more violent manifestations. Almost all critics assessing Hank's character note either Hank's ambiguity or their own ambivalence toward him. Gerald Allen manifests this rampant critical ambivalence his "Mark Twain's Yankee" with one statement: "Hank Morgan is by no means an unequivocally ironic figure" (446). Chadwick Hansen writes "The Yankee's mind is, in fact, full of contradictions, and on dozens of subjects" (70). In "Hank Morgan: Artist Run Amuck," John S. Dinan describes this divided character most completely:

> Though he remains oblivious of the fact, Hank is a dangerous and consummate hypocrite. He is inhumane in the name of humanity, undemocratic in the name of democracy, and brutal in the name of kindness. He pours forth democratic ideals and platitudes about basic human dignity and worth even as he deliberately trains young boys to be unfeeling, capitalist mass murderers. He breathes his dreams into machines without realizing that the two are made of different stuff. (73)

These ambivalent responses to Hank Morgan deserve special attention because, unlike Henry James' characters, whose ambiguities are themselves the subject of the fictions, Hank Morgan is himself rarely ambivalent. His ambiguity depends on a readerly account-keeping. We respond ambivalently because the novel itself contains few instructions on how to view Hank's ambiguity.

This ambiguity presents itself in an inconsistent characterization. Hank's integrity might seem too broad a topic to handle briefly, but my purpose in this discussion is not to illuminate the disparate aspects of Hank's character but to demonstrate the near impossibility of producing intelligible interpretation of the novel from just Hank's character. A first glance at Hank produces the interpretation of many earlier critics of the novel: that he is a man with a noble purpose and a few flaws whose heroic efforts fail. "In 1889," Everett Carter writes in "The Meaning of *A Connecticut Yankee*," "most readers, the illustrator Dan Beard among them, thought they were reading a book about a Yankee's praiseworthy attempt to make a better world" (419). This reading lives on the premise that Hank truly believes in democracy, truly despises despotism, truly embraces materialism. Hundreds of passages in the book support this premise, and dozens more document that the actions he takes have as their purpose the redesign of Arthurian England according to the American plan. Hank is honest with us, and, although egotistical in the extreme, Hank needs this egotism in the face of his eventual failure: "The ultimate expression of the egotism" manifests itself in "the conviction that he is too good for the world in which he finds himself. It is pearls before swine, Hank Morgan and the 'human muck'" (Fetterly, 672). In this interpretation, Hank is scrupulous from the smallest detail to the largest, marrying Sandy to prevent compromising her, exterminating 25,000 knights so that a people may be free.

Contemporary critics, on the other hand, take what Everett Carter calls the soft line on the Yankee. Hank Morgan's virtues are at best ambiguous, and an ambiguity of virtue here argues against a refined personal integrity. As Chadwick Hansen observes:

> Critics have consistently but carelessly called the Yankee a humanitarian. It should be apparent, however, that humanitarianism, like much else the Yankee thinks he believes in, is very much on the surface of his personality—that at bottom the temperament which enjoys the spectacle of acres of people groveling on the ground is anything but humanitarian. (64)

In this construct, all the Yankee's values are suspect. His intention from the beginning is despotic rule of the country and he will permit nothing, including scruples, to bar him from accomplishing his goal. Hank's ego becomes his enemy and "as his strength in Camelot grows, his sense of altruism is overpowered by his sense of self-importance" (Turnbull, 21). This exaggerated vision of his own value skews his perception of the world. The reliability of his narration—already questionable considering its fantastic premise—becomes flimsier and flimsier with each explosive effect. The problem of reliability in Hank's narration will become more important when we look into the Yankee's world in the next chapter. Here I only need note that the evidence for the soft view of Hank Morgan balances that for the hard view of him. We simply cannot decide which of these two men he really is, and he simply cannot be both.

The same problem appears when we turn to the novel's humor, "which depends for the most part on a rendering of the ridiculous, ludicrous aspects of chivalry and feudalism," Reid Maynard writes, and "is the story's forte, or the main element which holds our attention" (4). Hank Morgan's humor comes light and dark and not many shades in between. Critics most absorbed by the light humor turn to Twain himself for confirmation of *A Connecticut Yankee's* mild intentions. James D. Williams states in his "Revision and Intention" article that, "Even with the novel nearly half finished, Mark Twain insisted that 'fun' was its primary purpose and planned to accompany it with a free copy of Malory" (289). Everett Carter, echoing this position, maintains that

> Until the final pages, when Twain's rage against aristocratic privilege got out of hand, Twain was working confidently in the comic world of frontier humor where overstatement about death and destruction was a standard mode of evoking laughter. Many of the seemingly inhuman reactions of Hank take this form, a form linked to the author's own perhaps tasteless but nevertheless comic hyperbole. (422).

Several critics argue that Hank Morgan has the character of Tom Sawyer grown up and, though Tom and Hank might be insensitive or just tasteless in their humor, they are not cruel.

Unless you happen to be Jim, say, or the musicians at Morgan Le Fay's castle, or Sir Dinadin, or the knights dynamited into a long rain of sheet metal and horseflesh. Even the ambiguous comedy, such as the conversion of the hermit into a power source, turns dark at the end, when Hank goes from praising St. Stylite's mechanical motion to reducing his entire identity to the level of a weary machine, which Hank later unloads on several knights in a flimflam deal. Readers will recognize in the St. Stylite episode the pattern observed by Bergson and other major theoreticians of humor, the mechanization of human action. The light comedy of this mechanization, however, becomes brutal when the humanity of

the comic object disappears entirely into the machine. The repeated brutality of some of Hank Morgan's humor moves Judith
Fetterley to remark that "Ultimately, of course, Hank's aggression
is uncontrollable and his attempts to divert it through jokes and
philosophy fail" (676). An investigation of Hank's humor leads us
to the same place an investigation of his integrity does: on one
hand his humor keeps us reading, and on the other the humor is
too violent to succeed even as the blackest humor. There's an
equivalent weight between these two streams, and the book itself
offers no way to decide between them which promises the truest
interpretation of Hank Morgan's character.

These divided interpretations result from an attempt to saddle
the character of Hank Morgan with critical tools appropriate to
understanding personality, looking in it for some sort of integrated
whole which realistically represents a human being. Our current
critical prejudice is to see the Yankee as a man with a shimmering
surface of humor and virtue which barely hides his brutality and
egomania. The flaw in this formulation comes in thinking of the
Yankee as a man. A host of critics have plunged into Hank Morgan's personality armed with Freudian and Jungian constructs and
emerged with interesting but, it seems to me, artificial interpretations of his character. We have in Hank Morgan a parallel to what
we discovered in *Huckleberry Finn*: in the earlier novel, the inseparability of voices warned us off of standard deconstructive methods;
in *A Connecticut Yankee* the impossibility of creating a cohesive character warns us off approaching Hank Morgan with psychological
weapons drawn. Even the best of these efforts, Judith Fetterley's
"Yankee Showman and Reformer" and Susan K. Harris' *Mark
Twain's Escape From Time*, while generating interesting questions
about the relationship between politics and personality, fail to produce any insights into the novel itself. Some critics have noticed this
difficulty. David E. E. Sloane observes in *Mark Twain as Literary Comedian* that "By refusing to confine Hank to consistency of character, Mark Twain freed his point of view to entertain a wide
spectrum of social and intellectual issues. Such breadth and freedom enable Mark Twain to suspend belief as well as disbelief in a
confined 'fiction'" (157). Sloane might well be right, but he leaps
ahead too quickly: Agreeing Hank has no consistency of character,
must we then leave him no character at all and reduce him to a
simple point of view? In "a confined 'fiction'"—and I am assuming

the phrase to mean an integrated fictional world—we credit characters with personality, and the less personality they have the less good they are as characters. But in an unconfined fiction—and I only mean by this the negative of my earlier assumption—perhaps personality cannot adequately measure character. Very few critics or readers consider Hank Morgan an inferior character, even given the impossibility of defining his personality; the very attempt to understand his personality implies he is a superior character. But Hank, a superior character refusing personality, occupies some other sort of fiction. It would be a hopeless task to abandon Hank now and scurry after a definition of what sort of fiction he occupies. Hank, as teller of his own tale, provides readers the only access to the fiction; as critics, our portal to the book is the same. We go through Hank or we get nothing at all.

This should not daunt us. The book provides a host of easy clues as to how to think of Hank Morgan without forcing him into critical molds he can never fit. The most obvious is the title itself: *A Connecticut Yankee in King Arthur's Court*. The first word gives us the broadest message. Hank himself says in his exultation at his title, The Boss, "It was a pretty high title. There were very few THE'S, and I was one of them. If you spoke of the duke, or the earl, or the bishop, how could anybody tell which one you meant?" (69) Dukes, earls, and bishops live with the burden of the indefinite article, and so, despite his vanity, does Hank Morgan. He is *A* Connecticut Yankee, one of a group, and the most that can be said for him as an individual is that he represents that group. This implies what we have already found: that the particularization of personality in Hank Morgan matters little in the context of the story. What Hank Morgan accomplishes in Arthurian England, the title seems to say, any Connecticut Yankee would have accomplished.

This leads to the second message of the title. Hank Morgan is a Connecticut Yankee. Hank provides us with some information about this group when we first meet him. "I was born and reared in Hartford, in the State of Connecticut—anyway, just over the river, in the country. So I am a Yankee of the Yankees—and practical; yes, and nearly barren of sentiment, I supposed—or poetry, in other words" (4). Even before we get past the title to this statement, though, we bring to the book a stereotypical image of a Connecticut Yankee. Various sources contribute to this stereotype. Personal experience adds a small share, but experience tends to weaken rather than strengthen stereotypes. Most of this image comes from a now nearly defunct cache of folktales which featured the Connecticut Yankee. These tales and jokes all show the same thing, that the Yankee's apparent stupidity masks a brilliant shrewdness; whoever tries taking advantage of the Yankee pays in the end. We must remember that there is no personality in any sense behind this folk character. Rather, all similar stories become attached to a figure called Connecticut Yankee. The phrase 'Connecticut Yankee' becomes a magnet for a kind of story. Walter Blair, in his wonderful introduction to *Native American Humor,* gives a detailed account of the appearance of the Connecticut Yankee in nineteenth-century writing. This type appears rarely outside of detective fiction in contemporary writing, but some jokes featuring a Vermont farmer seem to make use of certain of his attributes. For example:

> A New Yorker driving in Vermont comes to a fork in the road. A sign with arrows pointing both ways says Montpelier. The New Yorker gets out of his car and approaches the farmer working there his field. "Does it matter which road I take to Montpelier?" he asks.
> And the Vermonter says, "Not to me it don't."

This possible survivor of the Connecticut Yankee stories retains some traces of the old character. When we encounter Mark Twain's Connecticut Yankee, we carry images like these with us.

We should not be surprised, then, if Hank Morgan has no true personality. He is primarily a type, not a person at all. But because he occupies an enormous written story, something much larger than any of the folktales which spawned him, he becomes a type-like character. Not one-dimensional, as a joke-character must be, but not exactly human either. Hank Morgan cannot be said to represent a human being. Instead, he represents a type in a tale, much as does the traditional Connecticut Yankee, holding a fictional space into which fall certain stories we already associate with the type.

Armed with this understanding of Hank Morgan we can begin to reassess his character. It would be a mistake to believe that, because Hank is a character of more type than personality, he has been reduced in any way. Types do not have to observe the limits of realism, as personalized characters do. They are free to behave on a larger, more heroic, scale. A realistic modern American, from Connecticut, Kentucky, or Kalamazoo, would be more apt to gape first and set about becoming rich later, if unfortunate enough to be transported to King Arthur's realm. Reconstructing the society might occur somewhere down the line. But since the Connecticut Yankee is not a person so much as a type, his self-interest equals the interest of his type, the group he represents, and the interests he pursues in the novel do not reward him so much as they reward his type. But what is his type? We can see by the novel's success over the past century that a broad constituency identifies with him. His type stretches beyond the simple Connecticut Yankee bettering a citified outsider into a realm of grander action. Hank Morgan does not just outsmart some business rival—in fact, his small-scale traditional-Yankee toying with Dowley backfires—he nearly masters an age. Hank acts on an heroic scale, and his self-interests represent the interests not only of those parts of us which admire a Connecticut Yankee, but also those parts which admire a hero. This is why we identify with Hank Morgan so strongly, and so broadly.

Grasping any sense of identity in fiction is like fishing bare-handed; the few things you can grab are hard to hold onto. While the evidence for identity in human life has almost no end, evidence in fiction is limited, suggestive rather than conclusive. Our conventional tools, the application of a contemporary understanding of psychology to the scanty evidence of fiction, prove minimally productive in grasping Hank Morgan's identity. We must therefore reconceptualize our approach to the text, look for other tools which work better with this particular novel. One possibility for unscrambling Hank's identity is to distinguish between Hank's narrative self and his fictive self. The fictive self is the imagined person, the self the critics I have spoken of thus far have considered. The narrative self is the role a character plays in the story. What we have seen so far is that the fictive self, as constructed in *A Connecticut Yankee in King Arthur's Court*, refuses integration. He is a mass of contradiction, an exploded self. We recognize there exists some sort of self at the core of the explosion, but for the most part the interests of this self can be easily reduced to ego-aggrandizement. Everything

Hank Morgan says he does pushes himself forward in his own eyes; ego seems all that is left the fictive self. Hank's more convincing and complex narrative self has interests less easily identified. I hope the coming pages will clarify these interests and, with them, the nature of Hank Morgan's identity.

I do not mean, by demonstrating the resistance of Hank Morgan's personality to definition, to show up critics who have turned their attention to this problem. Hank is vexing, there is no doubt about it. "We line up behind him," John S. Dinan says, "because there seems no respectable alternative. Furthermore, since he is the one telling the story, we get to like him, and tend to make excuses for him. He is all we have" (72). But, on the other hand, Hank insists on showing us his sores and scars. We smile at his despotic determination to rule the asylum, where Hank figures he must be if still in the nineteenth century, or to "boss the whole country inside of three months" (17) if he was in the sixth. We smile again five pages later when Hank says the knights are like boys who

> meet by chance, and say simultaneously, "I can lick you," and go at it on the spot; but I had always imagined, until now, that that sort of thing belonged to children only, and was a sign and mark of childhood, but here were these big boobies sticking to it and taking pride in it clear up into full age and beyond. (22)

We smile here, though, because Hank, in describing the knights as children, describes himself the same way. He has just met the country the way he says two boys meet—and he claims he can lick it.

The unconscious inclusion of himself in the critique he makes of the knights gathered at the Round Table becomes even clearer when we try to resolve what he means by "beyond full age": it could refer as easily to Hank, "thirteen hundred years" (17) and ages beyond anyone else in the room, as it could to men past their prime. Chapter by chapter, Hank shows his violence, pettiness, and stony lack of sentiment, and at some point—hopefully before he kills 25,000 people—we have to cease identifying his interests with our own. We have to get out of line and refuse to follow him any longer, no matter where his story leads. Hank Morgan's incremental repulsiveness, more than the actual genocide of medieval knighthood, creates the problem of reader identification and leads to the quandary contemporary readers find in Hank: that "he seems like the Hitler to whom one 'soft' commentary has come close to comparing him" (Carter, 421). But the problems of Hank's fascistic politics, while present in the criticism, come second to the problems of Hank's identity and reader identification. These quandaries occupy much more critical thought and prompt the bulk of psychological inquiry into Hank Morgan. The limited success of psychological inquiry into the Yankee does not give us the right to dismiss it, however. The very fact that critics and readers turn to psychology in their attempts to come to terms with Hank instead ought to tell us just how important the drive toward understanding Hank psychologically is.

Which is where this equation becomes most interesting. Readers must identify with Hank, at least for a while; if we do not, we get no story. We must also at some point refuse to follow Hank, to therefore end our identification. This conflict has moved critics to look for Hank Morgan's identity, that thing with which we identify. Looking for Hank's identity in his personality, where we normally find identity, leaves critics empty-handed, because Hank's personality refuses cohesion. There is no identity there. We must therefore look for Hank Morgan's identity elsewhere, if we hope to find that with which we first identify and follow and then refuse to follow. We must still use psychology; what other tools do we have for understanding identity? We must follow the title's suggestion and look at Hank as a type and as a hero. Types do have psychology; Jungians might argue that types begin and end psychology. Heroic types have a particularly well developed psychology and have attracted scholars of all stripes. In literary study, one man, and one book in particular, has perhaps best investigated the psychology of the heroic type. The man is Joseph Campbell. The book is *The Hero with a Thousand Faces*.

*The Hero with a Thousand Faces* needs little introduction, but my use of it here benefits by explanation. The path which has led me to Campbell in this essay shows the limits I apply to my use of his wonderful book. Just as I greatly admire Lord Raglan's *The Hero*, while at the same time recognizing its critical shortcomings, I admire *The Hero with a Thousand Faces*. The book is brilliant, learned, far-ranging, and thought-provoking. It also constructs its arguments more by association than by rigor, relies on debatable premises, and invokes an awkward reverence toward its own materials. Only because a major war and a change of worlds stand between the publication of Raglan's book and Campbell's have we not seen the kind of rampage against Campbell that we have seen against Raglan. I have faith that the reaction will come: the books have so many of the same flaws—and the same greatnesses. In my use of *The Hero*, I ignored most of Raglan's hypotheses about ritual origins. Though much of what he wrote was generated by these hypotheses, very little was dependent on them. So it is with Campbell. A reader need not embrace the Jungian premise of the monomyth to make good use of Campbell's idea that the traditional hero's journey to the underworld represents the common human's journey to the self. Do not assume that because I use Campbell extensively I endorse all he says. I use Campbell for the same reason I use Raglan: their books offer frameworks which when applied to *Huckleberry Finn* and *A Connecticut Yankee* ease recurrent confusions about these novels.

Joseph Campbell's project in *The Hero with a Thousand Faces* is massive. Stated briefly, he argues that our myths, legends, and other stories portray the struggle of the psyche to discover its own identity. These narratives "are spontaneous productions of the psyche, and each bears within it, undamaged, the germ power of its source" (4). While the solutions to the psyche's struggles vary from culture to culture, the problems and the goals do not; we therefore find a remarkable similarity of myth across cultures. Boiled down to its essence, this myth runs: "A hero ventures forth from the world of common day into a region of supernatural wonder: fabulous forces are there encountered and a decisive victory is won: the hero comes back from this mysterious adventure with the power to bestow boons on his fellow man" (30). Not all journeys into this underworld meet with success. Many heroes fail to achieve a decisive victory; others, having been victorious, elect to remain in the underworld. To Campbell, this "region of supernatural wonder" is the psyche, and the battles engaged there are battles for a mastery of self. The victor gains what Campbell calls, following a host of myths from assorted cultures, "The World Navel." This is the center, the point of contact between the natural and the supernatural. The hero so situated is the master of both worlds. More to Campbell's point, he is a healthy or complete human, worthy of admiration and emulation.

Without accepting the fullest range of Campbell's argument, we can assent to the use of his structure of the hero's journey and recognize, at least within our own culture, its analogous relationship to the psyche. While Campbell implies that his interpretation of narrative explains the meaning people find in myth, legend, and story, we only need to acknowledge that it is one possible explanation, more applicable to some stories than to others, more present in some cultures, some genres, and some heroes than in others. None of this renders *The Hero with a Thousand Faces* invalid. Many people today have the same circumscribing response to Freud. Limiting the fields in which Freud or Campbell are right does not make them less right, perhaps only less divinely inspired.

The strength of applying Campbell to *A Connecticut Yankee* becomes clear in his first chapter. He writes:

> The hero, therefore, is the man or woman who has been able to battle past his personal and local historical limitations to the generally valid, normally human forms. Such a one's visions, ideas, and inspirations come pristine from the primary springs of human life and thought. Hence they are eloquent, not of the present, disintegrating society and psyche, but of the unquenched source through which society is reborn. The hero has died as a modern man; but as an eternal man—perfected, unspecific, universal man—he has been reborn. (19–20).

We can easily see the application of this description to Hank Morgan, who in a battle with Hercules leaves his time. His light humor—the joke image that started Twain writing the novel, for example: the impossible discomfort of armor—emphasizes his transcendent humanity. What motivates Hank's efforts at social reconstruction, or at least what adds fire to them, are his direct experiences with personal tragedy: the flayed slave, Morgan Le Fay's prisoners, the small-pox family, the young girl hanged for petty theft. Although critics have sometimes complained that these episodes are sentimentalized, Twain assembled most of them from fact, from lived life, and thus Hank's visions and ideas grow out of history, the primary spring. Hank's mixture of Americanisms and archaisms which becomes his speech by the middle of the book emphasizes the timelessness of his expressed hopes of reforming society. Hank does not survive the novel as a modern man, as his speech in the frame demonstrates. His timelessness is apparent to the Mark Twain character, the frame's narrator, who writes that

Hank's smile was "not a modern smile, but one that must have gone out of use many, many centuries ago" (2). That Hank Morgan is one face of Joseph Campbell's hero seems clear. More detailed examples of the correspondence between the hero of *A Connecticut Yankee in King Arthur's Court* and *The Hero with a Thousand Faces* will show us just what face Hank Morgan wears.

Like Lord Raglan, Campbell provides a structure for heroic adventure; like Raglan's, the adventure comes in three parts. But, because Raglan's and Campbell's goals are not the same, neither are the actual details of their patterns. Instead of a numbered list of actions the true hero will fulfill, Campbell presents a series of possibilities, some mutually exclusive. Rather than demonstrate how Hank Morgan fulfills or fails to fulfill each of the permutations Campbell describes, I will show briefly how we can understand Hank's heroism in Campbell's terms. I provide Campbell's variations from his table of contents.

*DEPARTURE*
- The Call to Adventure
- Refusal of the Call
- Supernatural Aid
- The Crossing of the First Threshold
- The Belly of the Whale
*INITIATION*
- The Road of Trials
- The Meeting with the Goddess
- Woman as Temptress
- Atonement with the Father
- Apotheosis
- The Ultimate Boon
*RETURN*
- Refusal of the Return
- The Magic Flight
- Rescue From Without
- The Crossing of the Return Threshold
- Master of the Two Worlds
- Freedom to Live

I will attempt to keep short the illustration of how Hank suits this map of the hero's travail. We gain less by seeing how he suits this model of the hero than by understanding how this sort of heroism works with the rest of the novel.

## Departure

The Call to Adventure, Campbell writes, can begin in many ways. "A blunder—apparently the merest chance—reveals an unsuspected world, and the individual is drawn into relationship with forces that are not rightly understood. As Freud has shown, blunders are . . . ripples on the surface of life, produced by unsuspected springs. And these may be very deep—as deep as the soul itself" (51). Very often, though not absolutely, the call comes in the voice of some creature lowly regarded or of mysterious origin, or might emanate from an idyllic place, possibly the common world's navel. The call may not actually strike the hero's ears as a call when it first comes; he or she may return to everyday occupations for a time, but the hearer of the tale will know that the hero has been marked by the call. It "signifies that destiny has summoned the hero and transferred his spiritual center of gravity from within the pale of his society to a zone unknown" (Campbell, 58).

Hank Morgan's departure, like his return, come to us vastly foreshortened. We encountered the same balance of thirds in *Huckleberry Finn*, you will remember, with the middle section, the romance, grown large compared with the birth and death of the hero. While Campbell and Raglan have unequatable models of the hero, each has a sort of balance. The beginnings and ends inform us of the supernatural qualities of the hero, while the middle mostly relates his story. Twain, because of his times unable to tell a believable story involving the supernatural, compresses those aspects. What might be construed as supernatural if played out, becomes in this compressed state simply metaphorical. The Yankee's departure, until he crosses the threshold into the underworld of King Arthur's territory, consumes under three hundred words.

But even these few words suit Campbell's pattern. Hank's calling, the Colt arms factory, is also his call. There he learned his "real trade; learned all there was too it; learned to make everything: guns, revolvers, cannon, boilers, engines, all sorts of labor-saving machinery. Why, I could make anything a body wanted—anything in the world" (4). Hank becomes a god-like creator and the supervisor of the godlets around him. By willing himself into this position he also wills himself into his blunder. Hank confesses to being full of fight and having "plenty of that sort of amusement" until he is sent out of his world by "a misunderstanding conducted with crowbars" (5). Hank has no opportunity to refuse his call. Campbell explains that heroes often cross the threshold with supernatural aid, often in the form of a protective figure who provides the hero with necessary potions and amulets. Hank's magic is technology; it remains his amulet throughout the novel. He is not endowed with this power by a supernatural force. Rather he already possesses the power in his natural world, which is, compared with the underworld, a supernatural world. This is an important and curious reversal of the traditional hero narrative. The hero goes from a more powerful to a less powerful world; this inversion becomes more meaningful as we look at the worlds involved. Within this context we can say supernatural aid hurls Hank across the barrier between worlds: Hercules' crowbar pushes Hank over the edge. Beyond this edge, Campbell writes, "is darkness, the unknown, and danger; just as beyond the parental watch is danger to the infant and beyond the protection of his society danger to the member of the tribe" (77–78). So Hank explains the effects of the blow: "Then the world went out in darkness, and I didn't feel anything more, and didn't know anything at all—at least for a while" (5).

Danger presents itself immediately; Campbell points out that "folk mythologies populate with deceitful and dangerous presences every desert place outside the normal traffic of the village" (78). These creatures beyond civilization always have special powers and mysterious ways; the hero passes through the first defender easily, but soon after is trapped in The Belly of the Whale. Hank survives the threat by Sir Kay with comic ease and is conducted to Camelot. The entrance there has a mouthlike quality: "the head of the cavalcade swept forward under the frowning arches; and we following, soon found ourselves in a great paved, with towers and turrets stretching up into the blue air on all the four sides" (12). Campbell compares the entry of the hero into the whale's belly to the entry into a temple; buildings can be whales too. He writes:

> The idea that the passage of the magic threshold is a transit into a sphere of rebirth is symbolized in the worldwide womb image of the belly of the whale. The hero, instead of conquering or conciliating the power of the threshold, is swallowed into the unknown, and would appear to have died. (90)

This image closely parallels the events of Chapters 2 through 6. In *A Connecticut Yankee*, the hero both conciliates the threshold guardian and finds himself in the dungeon womb, stripped naked and sentenced to death. Campbell says this approach of death has the markings of self-annihilation; Hank seems to charge headlong into his own death by the threat of the eclipse, and it is only through the various accidents of feather-headedness on the part of Clarence that Hank's death and the eclipse coincide. Instead of finding himself consumed in fire—the full impact of this not happening can only be understood in terms outlined by David Ketterer in his "Epoch-Eclipse and Apocalypse: Special 'Effects' in *A Connecticut Yankee*"—the Yankee places himself at the center of a world grown as dark as his womb-cell. Before the eclipse lifts, Hank becomes clothed once again, but now he is clothed like a prince of the underworld. The world, with Hank aboard, emerges from the darkness as an infant does the womb. Hank's passage into the underworld is complete.

## Initiation

"Once having traversed the threshold," Campbell writes, "the hero moves into a dream landscape of curiously fluid, ambiguous forms, where he must survive a succession of trials. This is a favorite phase of the myth adventure. It has produced a world literature of miraculous tests and ordeals" (97). In Campbell's view, these adventures fall into categories of relationship, often following a certain sequence. First comes the complex relationship with women, symbolized by goddesses, temptresses, and animas of all sorts. Then comes what Campbell, following others, calls "Atonement with the Father," in which the relationship of hostility, admiration, and oneness with the male finds resolution. The initiation sequence often ends with the hero's apotheosis, his final empowerment with the knowledge of this new, strange world, the world of the self. Having come to terms with the mother, the father, and the self, the hero can return to his own world.

*A Connecticut Yankee* follows this pattern with an almost curious devotion. After the four chapters establishing Hank as the focal person in King Arthur's world—"I was no shadow of a king; I was the substance, the king himself was the shadow" (63)—he finds himself compelled to hit the road in search of adventure. These adventures can be broken down into four sequences: Hank's travels with Sandy, including the stop at the castle of Morgan Le Fay (chapters 11 through 21); Hank's accomplishments at the Valley of Holiness (chapters 21 through 26); Hank on the road with the king (chapters 26 through 38); and his consolidation of power and its ultimate disintegration (chapters 39 through 43). I will make brief arguments, more along the lines of suggestion than conclusion, that Hank's experiences with Sandy and Morgan Le Fay offer an abstract of heroic resolution with the female, that Hank's experience with King Arthur offer an abstract of heroic resolution with the male, and that the final sequence produces a form of apotheosis for Hank. Hank's near success in each endeavor provides insight into what many critics have seen as his heroic failure.

## COMING TO TERMS WITH THE FEMALE

Campbell describes two different sets of experiences through which the hero comes to terms with the female in the underworld of the self. One "is commonly represented as a mystical marriage of the triumphant hero-soul with the Queen Goddess of the World" (109); this marriage "represents the hero's total mastery of life; for the woman is life, the hero its knower and master" (120). But this pure Goddess can only be married after the hero has gotten past the corruption of her flesh and his own.

In the sequence concerning Hank's travels with Sandy he at first regards Sandy's phrasemaking as a vast emptiness. Hank asks Sandy to explain to him the identity of the knights they captured in Chapter 14, called "Defend Thee, Lord," but realizes his "mistake, at once. I had set her works agoing; it was my own fault; she would be thirty days getting down to those facts. And she generally began without a preface, and finished without a result" (127). But after his experience with Morgan Le Fay, his view of Sandy changes. Not only do his interactions with her take on the aspect of conversation—with only exceptional and playful reference to her mouth as machine—but he accepts behavior in her which he would ridicule if he found it elsewhere. When Sandy throws herself on the pigs mistaken for royalty, Hank says he "was ashamed of her, ashamed of the whole human race" (186), a net which must include himself. But he goes on to excuse Sandy:

97

> Here she was, as sane a person as the kingdom could produce;
> and yet, from my point of view she was acting like a crazy
> woman. . . . I had to put myself in Sandy's place to realize she
> was not a lunatic. Yes, and put her in mine, to demonstrate how
> easy it is to seem a lunatic to a person who has not been taught
> as you have been taught. . . . Everybody around her believed in
> enchantments; nobody had any doubts; to doubt that a castle
> could be turned into a sty, and its occupants into hogs, would
> have been the same as my doubting, among Connecticut people,
> the actuality of the telephone, and its wonders,—and in both
> cases would be absolute proof of a diseased mind, an unsettled
> reason. (191)

What is remarkable here is Hank's acceptance not only of Sandy,
but also of the legitimacy of Sandy's perceptions. Hank has been
transformed. Between the time he set out on his quest with Sandy
and the time he achieved its end, he crossed some invisible
boundary. Campbell writes that as the hero "progresses in the slow
initiation which is life, the form of the goddess undergoes for him
a series of transfigurations: she can never be greater than himself,
though she can always promise more than he is yet capable of comprehending" (116). This describes Hank's relationship to Sandy
admirably.

The key transfiguration of Hank's relationship with Sandy
takes place at the castle of Morgan Le Fay. The king's sister is in
many ways the most remarkable character in the book, next to the
Yankee. Twain gives her perhaps the longest description of any
character, and he describes the very image of the temptress: wicked
within, compelling without. "I was most curious to see her; as curious as I could have been to see Satan. To my surprise, she was
beautiful; black thoughts had failed to make her expression repulsive, age had failed to wrinkle her satin skin or mar its bloomy
freshness" (142–43). Critics who have said that Merlin's final stroke
against Hank is the book's only true magic neglect Morgan Le Fay's
eternal youth. But her eternal youth appears less a result of magic
than of narrative. It is only one of many aspects of her character
which parallel Hank's; remember, Hank remains young 1300
years. Aside from the obvious linking of their names—note that
Twain changed the Yankee's name from an early-draft Robert
Smith—Hank and Morgan share behaviors and attitudes. A hand-
some young page bumps her knee by accident and "She slipped a

dirk into him in as matter-of-course a way as another person would have harpooned a rat!" (144)—or as Hank himself would kill the entire knighthood. The logic by which Hank convinces himself to accept her murder of the page—the logic that leads to his "training is everything" speech (162)—he uses to excuse himself later: She believes that "the law that permitted her to kill a subject when she chose was a perfectly right and righteous one" (162); Hank believes he is justified in exterminating the knights if the act ends the institutional crime of knighthood. It is killing rationalized by politics in either case. Morgan Le Fay's murderous habits find another parallel in Hank Morgan's. He prohibits her from killing the grandmother of the slain page, but arbitrarily encourages her in more arbitrary violence. The queen wants to kill the composer for his bad music, so Hank listens to the song again. "Then I saw that she was right, and gave her permission to hang the whole band" (152). Both Morgans are imperious, intelligent and magical, and why not? If this underworld is the self, Morgan Le Fay is the female persona, the anima, of Hank Morgan. Look how the episode between them ends. Morgan Le Fay is in no way defeated; Hank simply releases the prisoners from her dungeons. She is herself ignorant of what she keeps in her own castle, a clear symbol for common psychological confusion, a plain representation of the hero's state before he begins his journey.

The most detailed and poignant episode from the dungeons is the story of the old lovers, held for a decade ignorant of the other's being. Hank brings the male and female together in the dungeon of Morgan Le Fay,

> But it was a disappointment. They sat together on the ground and looked dimly wondering into each other's faces a while, with a sort of weak animal curiosity; then forgot each other's presence, and dropped their eyes, and you saw they were away again, and wandering in some far land of dreams and shadows that we know nothing about. (166)

Hank's ignorance of the lovers' far land is in the end something which defeats him. As we will see later, his attempt to bring together the male and female in the dungeon of his own psyche fails, much as does this attempt to bring them together in the dungeon of his female self. Following Campbell's heroic pattern, Morgan Le

Fay is Woman as Temptress—who is more tempting than our own anima or animus? Hank succeeds in sidestepping her and returns to the road with Sandy.

Hank's marriage to Sandy becomes at this point inevitable. Having succeeded in his quest of herding the pigs into a stranger's castle, Hank makes ready to get back on the road, to which Sandy replies, "I also am ready; I will go with you" (194). She reacts to Hank's doubt with an explanation of the rules of the underworld: A maiden remains with a knight until he has been defeated and she has been won over by another; she considers it betrayal even to think that might happen. "'Elected for the long term,' I sighed to myself. 'I may as well make the best of it.' So then I spoke up and said: 'All right. Let's make a start'" (194). A full colon ending a paragraph on the following page strengthens this sense of a new beginning; in English, this punctuation is found most typically in the Bible, where it is used to set off God's words. Sandy initiates Hank into an understanding of the rules of his new world, particularly that the ties to the goddess cannot be shirked. His eventual marriage with her demonstrates his final appreciation of these ties. He marries her, he says, only because his New England morality made him feel that she would be compromised by any other arrangement. But once he marries Sandy his perspective changes. "Now I didn't know I was drawing a prize, yet that was what I did draw. Within the twelvemonth I became her worshiper; and ours was the dearest and perfectest comradeship that ever was" (407). Hank acknowledges Sandy as a goddess, and Campbell's pattern of coming to terms with the female is nearly complete.

I say only nearly, because readers do sense an ambiguity about this bond. Nearly twenty pages slip by between Hank's deliverance from slavery and death (380) and any further mention of Sandy (400). The fact of the marriage itself seems a narrative afterthought, coming as it does in the first paragraph of the chapter titled "The Interdict." This ambiguity is one crystalline sign of Hank Morgan's failure as a hero. Campbell writes, "The goddess guardian of the inexhaustible well . . . requires that the hero should be endowed with what the troubadours and minesingers termed the 'gentle heart.' Not by the animal desire of an Actaeon, not by the fastidious revulsion of such as Fergus, can she be comprehended and rightly served, but only by gentleness" (118). Though we admire the gentleness that leads Hank to cast aside the business of government in favor of scrupulous attention to his child's health, we also know he has not fully accepted Sandy's wisdom. His gentleness is sentimentality only. Though these characteristics often appear the same, we have learned throughout the novel that sentimentality, such as that produced by the nearly endless array of beleaguered women and children Hank runs across, is not the same as gentleness. Frequently Hank's sentimentality only provokes him into a vituperant outburst, hardly a sign of a gentle heart. "Furthermore," as Chadwick Hansen notes, "—and this is the most conclusive evidence of the Yankee's sentimentality—his feelings are not really a matter of sympathy for others, but an emotional bath for himself" (71). Hank produces this self-conscious soul-wringing in place of a true sympathy; he seems to feel only to write about those feelings later, an egotistical representation of his moral superiority. Hank's ego, his preoccupation with self, marks the difference between gentleness and sentimentality. The ego cannot join with another. Thus, Hank Morgan's ego also marks the difference between a truly successful union with Sandy the goddess and one which only verges on success.

### ATONEMENT WITH THE FATHER

The next of the hero's tasks is an atonement with the father. Campbell, in one of his most interesting passages, explains:

> Atonement (at-one-ment) consists in no more than the abandonment of that self-generated double monster—the dragon thought to be God (superego) and the dragon thought to be Sin (repressed id). But this requires an abandonment of the attachment to ego itself, and that is what is difficult. One must have a faith that the father is merciful, and then a reliance on that mercy. (130)

This battle with the male force has certain similarity to the battle with the female, in that the final victory comes through an abandonment of self to the power of the force. But the battle with the father has a further complexity in that the successful hero eventually must supplant the father. The vanquished father reveals himself as the initiating priest, the mystagogue, who will "entrust the symbols of office only to a son who has been effectively purged of all inappropriate infantile cathexes" (136). In the end this means that the hero comes to terms with the essential paradox of creation: one dies that another may live. "The hero transcends life with its peculiar blind spot and for a moment rises to a glimpse of the source. He beholds the face of the father, understands—and the two are atoned" (147).

In *A Connecticut Yankee in King Arthur's Court,* Arthur is the obvious father. He is responsible for Hank's initial delivery from the womb, countermanding Merlin's instruction to "Apply the torch!" (48) Like a contract killer, Hank receives half his complete payment, the king's power, up front, with Arthur holding the other half until Hank completes the deed. Arthur is the only man in the kingdom who appears to be Hank Morgan's equal. Yet, in a book echoing with one challenge after another, Hank never challenges Arthur. They clearly battle in a different realm than Hank and Merlin or Hank and the knights. Hank wants nothing more than to defeat, displace, and humiliate Merlin and the knights, but he is content to allow King Arthur to rule until death. Although an argument can be made that Hank will not displace Arthur because he believes this will alienate the people, in fact he never maintains this. Hank objects to kings, not to King Arthur.

Between Hank's delivery from the stake and the king's arrival in the Valley of Holiness, Hank documents no direct interaction between them. In recording his first four years of co-rule with Arthur he does not refer to the king at all, except to say that "the king thought I ought now to set forth in quest of adventures, so that I might gain renown and be more worthy to meet Sir Sagramour" (80). He also makes what might be a reference to Arthur in his discussion of the danger of earthly despotism (81–82), but the most interesting aspect of this discussion is Hank's implication that he himself shares more qualities with the divinity than with his companions in humanity. Since we cannot really decide whether or not Hank Morgan is divine in the context of the novel, we must conclude two things: if he is not divine, yet is intent on becoming a despot, he must defeat Arthur but in the end establish the same flawed government; or, if he is divine, his divinity confirms that his story is myth, the interaction of the gods with humans, and subject to the rules of myth, in this case an inevitable battle with the father, Arthur. In either case the result is the same—war with Arthur, however submerged. The Yankee's improvements on King Arthur's realm and the details of his government, though, occupy a small portion of the narrative. Hank Morgan seems to realize he has other difficulties to overcome: first he must resolve his relationship with the female through his travels with Sandy and his meeting with the king's sister, his own anima, Morgan Le Fay; only then is he ready to resolve his relationship with Arthur the father.

That Hank and Arthur oppose one another comes clear in their first direct interaction after the eclipse. In Chapter 25, "A Competitive Examination" for posts in Hank's new standing army, we find an interesting form of opposition. Arthur believes in the natural merit of setting a condition of four generations of noble birth for an officer's post; he is "staggered" by the revelation that the Boss' candidate is the son of a weaver. He tells Hank, when the Yankee objects to the law's exclusion of his candidate, "*You* can permit it an you are minded so to do, for you have the delegated authority, but that the king should do it were a most strange madness and not comprehensible to any" (248). Arthur both executes the law of his realm and instructs Hank in it, much as Sandy, not seeing how staying with Hank might compromise her, stays with him and explains why: it is the rule in her world. In both cases, Hank feels himself forced to "yield"; he is "down in the bottomless pit of humiliation" (248). He responds to Arthur as a child must respond to a parent, finding a way to get his own goals met within the confines of parental authority.

The lines of opposition between Hank and Arthur have been established by Chapter 25; they are set on the road to solution in the first paragraph of Chapter 26. On the road Arthur and Hank undergo a parallel decay in status. In the Valley of Holiness both are among the few THEs in the kingdom. We can see their decline clearly in the company they keep. Their initial encounters on the road are with nobles, then with freemen, and at last with slaves. They end as convicts and only by a true *ex machina* rescue do they avoid becoming corpses. Each step down they take comes at the hands of the kind to which they nominally and temporarily belong. In other words, their candidacy for any status in the kingdom, except that which is truly their own, is rejected by those people who have that status, the only people seemingly empowered to confer it. The King and Boss eject themselves from their own rank. The nobles, despite Hank's successful exploding of a clatch of them, boot them down to freemen. The freemen hound them into slavery. The slaves turn them into convicts. This series of exclusions isolates Hank and Arthur and focuses reader attention less on the decay of their social status and more on the resolution of their own opposition. Stories recounting a character's social deprivation typically show either the nobility (as in *Huckleberry Finn*) or the savagery (as in *The Lord of the Flies*) of the human heart unrestrained by civilization. But this tale of decayed social status shows neither. Instead, the relationship between the king and the Boss, between the father and his emerging son, remains central to the narrative. As the novel strips away society, that primal conflict remains.

Their journey has a prologue in Arthur's touch for the king's-evil. In Hank's telling, little of the narrative concerns the affliction or its cure; instead he dedicates more than a page to the improved economics of distributing a nickel rather than gold to those touched. "I judged that a sharp, bright new nickel, with a first-rate likeness of the king on one side of it and Guenever on the other, and a blooming pious motto, would take the tuck out of scrofula as handy as a nobler coin and please the scrofulous fancy more; and I was right" (254). But Hank has only devalued the ritual, cut into the distribution of wealth to the people, and mocked Arthur in an icon. Granting that the laying on of hands seems mumbo-jumbo to him, Hank sees only the people's belief as the cause of their recovery. He misses entirely that symbolically the ritual redistribution of wealth and reformation of Arthur from oppressor to savior in fact relieves not only the king's-evil, but also the evil of kings. By replacing gold coins with nickels, he works counter to his stated intention to raise up the people.

Arthur and Hank begin their journey in earnest with Hank cutting Arthur's hair, an act against the father of symbolic import. "He was no longer the comeliest man in his kingdom, but one of the unhandsomest and most commonplace and unattractive" (264). But no matter what reduction of the king Hank works toward, he does not achieve equality that way. He says, "it would not be good politics for me to be playing equality with him when there was no necessity for it" (265). But still, Hank continues his efforts to degrade the king. Nobles approach the king and Hank flies to his side with supernatural speed—"desperation gives you wings"—with the hope of convincing the king to act a peasant. Arthur is incapable and his punishment for being what he is, regardless of appearance, falls on Hank Morgan. Hank's comment, as Arthur cannot master his mastery and unthinkingly obtains a knife, is telling: "I persuaded him to throw the dirk away; and it was easy as persuading a child to give up some bright fresh new way of killing itself" (267). The death wish implied here, the ultimate reduction of self, appears misapplied. Hank means that the king is the child chasing death, when it is he himself who wishes the king's end. But Hank's blindness is his egotism: he sees himself as godlike and believes he has entered a natural world from a supernatural one, rather than the other way around. We read in Hank's entire attempt to get the king to reduce himself something other than what Hank himself states, something far more complex. Campbell writes of the fight against the father image:

> The ogre aspect of the father is a reflex of the victim's own ego—derived from the sensational nursery scene that has been left behind, but projected before; and the fixating idolatry of the pedagogical nonthing is itself the fault that keeps one steeped in a sense of sin, sealing the potentially adult spirit from a better balanced, more realistic view of the father, and therewith of the world. (129–30)

The hero, according to Campbell, imagines the father-image to be an evil force intending death for the child. The heroic process is not so much a defeat of the father-ogre as a stripping away of the false image the hero attempts to put on him.

This precise opposition continues throughout Hank's journey with Arthur. The second encounter with nobility goes no better than the first. After being nearly ridden down, "The king was in a flaming fury, and launched out his challenge and epithets with a most royal vigor" (270). Arthur's kingliness imperils both Hank and himself. At the dinner Hank buys for Marco, Dowley, et al., Arthur's kingly ignorance of agriculture (338) launches them into danger again. The peasants recognize them as hoaxes, but are wrong about their true identities; only Hank can see that Arthur's kingliness plunges them into danger again. By the third crisis, the uprising against the slave-trader and the subsequent gallows scene, Arthur has been stripped of his royal trappings, but not for Hank and not for the reader. When we are told about the slave uprising we know, given what has been told us about the slaves previously, that Arthur led the revolt, but we have no real evidence. As the peasant retelling the event responds to Hank's question as to how they would determine which of the slaves performed the violence, "*Which* ones? Indeed they considered not particulars like to that. They condemned them in a body" (368). At the gallows the people respond to Arthur's proclamation of himself king with jeers and laughter. They cannot see the kingliness which endangered Hank, but Hank can, remarking about Arthur's dignity under this contempt, "He certainly was great, in his way" (377). Hank achieves the recognition that the sham of royalty—the king's ogre-nature in this case—covers a true greatness. As the world strips Arthur's royalty from him, it reveals a sort of kingliness Hank cannot help but respect.

This final perception is also the culmination of the other thread in the opposition between Hank and Arthur, the connection which eventually allows Hank to come to terms with the king, to atone with the father. Even at the beginning of their travels, Hank grudges the king some respect: "It was a wise head. A peasant's cap was no safe disguise for it, you could know it for a king's, under a diving bell, if you could hear it work its intellect" (269). But to identify an intellect as a king's does not, in Hank Morgan's vocabulary, prove its greatness. In the very next chapter, Hank says that Arthur "wasn't a very heavy weight, intellectually. His head was an hourglass; it could stow an idea, but it had to do it a grain at a time, not the whole idea at once" (276). Critics have been unfair to Hank and Twain in seeing these paired statements as contradictory. Instead, they reveal a conflict, the same conflict revealed in Hank's remarks as he ends his chapter "Drilling the King": "Words realize nothing, vivify nothing to you, unless you have suffered in your own person the thing which the words try to describe" (278–79). For both narrating Hank and authoring Twain, this seems a negation of the very fact of the book, whose purpose is to realize and vivify an experience with the impossible. But, in both cases, what appears as contradiction is in fact conflict, and the final result is a synergy of the opposed forces.

According to Campbell, the transformation of the hero occurs

> When the child outgrows the popular idyl of the mother breast
> and turns to face the world of specialized adult action, [and so]
> passes, spiritually, into the sphere of the father—who becomes,

for his son, the sign of the future task. . . . The traditional idea of initiation combines an introduction of the candidate into the techniques, duties, and prerogatives of his vocation with a radical readjustment of his emotional relationship to the parental images. (136)

Keeping in mind the recognition ending Hank's experience on the road with Arthur, that royalty and kingliness have little to do with one another, we can see our way through Hank's apparent contradictions. Hank ends his paragraph decrying the hollowness of word and "the very law of those transparent swindles, transmissible nobility and kingship" (279). But Arthur shows the difference between kingship and kingliness in the very next chapter, "The Small-Pox Hut." I quote the passage at length because it is one of the most beautiful and stirring Twain has written, more breathtaking in almost every way than Huck's commitment to save Jim in Chapter 31 of *Adventures of Huckleberry Finn*.

There was a slight noise from the direction of the dim corner where the ladder was. It was the king, descending. I could see that he was bearing something in one arm, and assisting himself with the other. He came forward into the light; upon his breast lay a slender girl of fifteen. She was but half conscious; she was dying of small-pox. Here was heroism at its last and loftiest possibility, its utmost summit; this was challenging death in the open field unarmed, with all the odds against the challenger, no reward set upon the contest, and no admiring world in silks and cloth of gold to gaze and applaud; and yet the king's bearing was as serenely brave as it had always been in those cheaper contests where knight meets knight in equal fight and clothed in protecting steel. He was great, now; sublimely great. The rude statues of his ancestors in his palace should have an addition—I would see to that; and it would not be a mailed king killing a giant or a dragon, like the rest, it would be a king in commoner's garb bearing death in his arms that a peasant mother might look her last upon her child and be comforted. (285–86)

I cannot here give this passage the commentary it deserves; I must restrict my observations to a few of the many points salient to this discussion. First, we see the king emerging from darkness and descending, like a hero going through darkness into the underworld.

He faces an invisible and tremendously dangerous enemy, like the psyche; he carries death in his arms. Unlike the traditional heroes, killing giants and dragons in a quest for glory, Arthur kills nothing, defeats nothing, receives nothing; he is simply a conduit for love, yet another invisible force. Hank admires him, and rightly. Arthur achieves with serene bravery the very task the Yankee finds himself in the midst of: not the succoring of a dying mother, but the heroic quest. This is the king's kingliness—the absolute spiritualizing of Hank's task.

Though Hank can perceive this greatness, he cannot equal it. His efforts come out poorly in the next episode, the extended involvement with Marco. Hank sparkles with insight here, perceiving Marco's tie to the injured family and the pain his need to assist in their execution causes him, but his efforts to relieve this pain produce a shambles. In contrast to Arthur's efforts in the small-pox hut, Hank's show requires an audience and reward. "I never care to do a thing in a quiet way; it's got to be theatrical, or I don't take any interest in it" (309). He wants "to surprise the guests and show off a little" (313). He maneuvers Dowley into creating a text within the text, one in which he is himself the hero; but Hank's goal is only to trump him. Hank's original noble purpose, to do some good for the beleaguered and sorrowful Marcos, has been forgotten in the swell of his own ego. And when "the first statesman of the age, the capablest man, the best informed man in the entire world, the loftiest uncrowned head that had moved through the clouds of any political firmament for centuries [is] . . . apparently defeated in argument by an ignorant country blacksmith" (328), this massive ego reacts, and for no good but to salve itself. When he defeats Dowley and company at last, he holds death in his hands, as Arthur did, but the death he holds does not risk his own life but the lives of others, and that changes the matter entirely. While Arthur's royal ignorance pushes the duo into the chasm of slavery, Hank's flawed imitation of the king's greatness drew them to the precipice. Arthur's act was a sign of Hank's future task, as Campbell says, but signs, like words, are pale imitations of the thing itself; and what passes for a heavy-weight intellect—the kind that could plan and execute as fine an effect "as I ever produced, with so little time to work it up in" (333)—cannot compare itself to the brilliant spirituality that illuminated Arthur's actions.

So, while Hank has been introduced to the techniques and

prerogatives of heroism, he has not mastered them, and cannot until he comes to his atonement with Arthur. That is the function of the final stage of their journey together in slavery. The man who accepts them into slavery "bore all the marks of a gentleman" (343); but a gentleman's marks and a gentleman's soul share no more common space than do kingship and kingliness. The sixth-century slaveholder is himself as degraded as his nineteenth-century counterpart. The slave system remains the same, one era to the next. The slaves do too: they are "worn and wasted wrecks of humanity" (344); Hank never describes any slave, except the king and himself, any differently. But while Hank is willing to take himself down a notch or two to avoid punishment, the king shows no thought of doing the same. Prospective buyers regard him as "a two-dollar-and-a-half chump with a thirty dollar style. Pity but style was marketable" (351). But style is no more marketable than spirit; each have value only to the person possessed of them. The slave-driver's attempts to break Arthur's style and spirit fail, "So he gave up, at last, and left the king in possession of his style unimpaired. The fact is, the king was a good deal more than a king, he was a man; and when a man is a man, you can't knock it out of him" (352).

But while this passionate acceptance of King Arthur has the appearance of atonement, we see in the continuation of the slave-journey that Hank has not achieved his transcendence. Campbell notes that the final struggle between the hero and the father begins where the hero not only recognizes the father's perfect knowledge, but also sees where the possibility of his own perfect knowledge has been impaired. "The problem of the hero is to pierce himself (and therewith his world) precisely through that point; to shatter and annihilate the key knot of his limited existence" (147). Of course, Hank Morgan does not do that. Hank's point in his narrative is the lessons the king learns. He is willing to take desperate chances for freedom only after the king agrees he would abolish slavery. But Hank here falls victim to the same flaws that had toppled him with Marco and Dowley: "I set about a plan, and was straightway charmed with it. . . . One could invent quicker ways, and fully as sure ones; but none that would be as picturesque as this, none that could be made so dramatic" (353). Tom Sawyer has escaped from *Huckleberry Finn* and landed as an adult in King Arthur's realm, having learned nothing in between. Hank has been able to observe and appreciate the king's perfect knowledge, but, again, he cannot emulate it. To sincerely emulate another one must negate oneself, and Hank Morgan has too much ego for that. Hank retains his affection for abstractions, particularly for the products of his own mind, such as ego. Hank reasons himself from the "pitiful incidents" he witnesses as a slave to the dangerous outrage which leads to the explosion at the novel's end. The king, on the other hand, resents the material incidents of his life, his concrete experience. Hank expects the king to brood abstractly "about the prodigious nature of his fall," but "the thing that graveled him most, to start with, was not this, but the price he had fetched" (350). Hank's ego does not allow him to see past the products of his mind—the ideas he has about his own experience—to the experience itself. Hank Morgan thinks too much of himself to negate himself. Because of this, he cannot fully atone with Arthur. Just as Hank managed to follow the well-worn trail of the hero's attempts to come to terms with the female only to fall just barely short, so he also falls just barely short in his "at-one-ment" with Arthur. His ego, his affection for his own abstractions from reality, deter him from the understanding which is the fundamental greatness of the hero.

APOTHEOSIS

The third stage of the hero's initiation is his apotheosis. Having come to terms with the female and male aspects of the godhead, the underworld, and the self, the hero links the two and lives the remainder of his life with beneficence and insight. Campbell breaks this finale into two parts: where the hero achieves a transcendence of the values of the old world; and where he becomes identified with "The Ultimate Boon," which Campbell metaphorizes as food for the self. I am not sure that I see these ends as so very different; nor do I see that the hero's mastery of his adopted world takes place only after his return to his original one. I cannot tell if my doubts about how to understand this phase of the hero's journey come from Campbell's inarticulateness about it or my lack of personal experience with this particular mystical transcendence. The clearest statement I can find about the linking of the male and female aspect in the hero comes in his comparison between the modern teachings of psychoanalysis and the traditional teachings of mythology. The goal of the traditional hero is not to cure the individual back again to the general delusion, but to detach him from delusion altogether; and this is not by readjusting the desire (*eros*) and hostility (*thanatos*)—for that would only originate a new context of delusion—but by *extinguishing* the impulses to the very root. . . . With the final 'extirpation of delusion, desire, and hostility' (Nirvana) the mind knows it is not what it thought: Thought goes. The mind rests in its true state. (164–65)

Heroes who achieve this transcendence, Campbell writes, are the immortals. Often in the tales of heroes, we find the final goal achieved easily. Raglan views the fact of the struggleless final victory as evidence of the purely ritual origins of the battle. Campbell's view, that "the ease with which the adventure is here accomplished signifies that the hero is a superior man, a born king" (173), supports Raglan. While Raglan looks for the cultural and historical progression which have led to current hero tales, Campbell looks to the psychological reasons for them. It is perhaps in this difference that we can distinguish between the end of Raglan's hero program and the end of Campbell's. Raglan's hero achieves a physical satisfaction—marriage, kingship—which he fails to retain, and then he disappears in what looks more like a mystical transformation than a death. According to Campbell, though, while the hero certainly does achieve marriage and kingship, represented in each case by a god figure and representing in each case an ascension to a godhead, "what the hero seeks through his intercourse with them [the gods] is therefore not finally themselves, but their grace, i.e., the power of their sustaining substance" (181). Where this final quest lands the hero, Campbell cannot well explain. He equates personal limitations with thresholds individuals must cross and with dragons heroes must slay. But then, "finally, the mind breaks the bounding sphere of the cosmos to a realization transcending all experiences of form—all symbolizations, all divinities: a realization of the ineluctable void" (190). It reduces Campbell's prose, but not his substance, to compress his view of the hero's end as follows: After accepting the male and female aspects of the self, the hero becomes both male and female and accepts death.

The application of this to *A Connecticut Yankee in King Arthur's Court* encounters trouble as much from Hank's failure to achieve his goal of a republic as from Campbell's shadowiness. But certain transcendent parallels become clear in even a cursory review of the novel's final chapters. The sequence begins with the tournament, the culmination of the challenge issued by Sir Sagramour before Hank achieved his heroic stature; it was what pulled us into the story from the start. Hank achieves his goals with comic ease. Even the challenge issued against the five hundred knights, "squally" at first, produces a battle of just over a hundred words. It is a scene reminiscent of Sherburn's turning back of the Bricksville mob in *Huckleberry Finn,* but without words and without the chilling effect of the temporary reduction of Huck to an ironic point of view. In this novel, the scene depicts the hero's struggleless victory; Hank Morgan becomes the Sherburn no one dares counter. "When I broke the back of knight-errantry that time, I no longer felt obliged to work in secret. So, the very next day I exposed my hidden schools, my mines, and my vast system of clandestine factories and work-shops to an astonished world" (396).

While not the exact apotheosis Campbell describes, it is a seeming apotheosis. Throughout the novel, the nineteenth century has appeared to be the land of the gods. By finally producing the nineteenth century for the sixth, Hank seems to achieve an apotheosis. But the difference between Campbell's model and *A Connecticut Yankee* illuminates for us what we must consider Hank Morgan's failure as a hero. Falling short of true atonement with Arthur, falling short of a true bond in his marriage to Sandy, Hank cannot possibly achieve a complete integration of the male and female aspects of himself. And, failing this integration, Hank must fail to gain the grace which is the true reward of the hero. This suits the pattern of the boon bestowed on heroes and near heroes:

> The boon is simply a symbol of life energy stepped down to the requirements of a certain specific case. The irony, of course, lies in the fact that, whereas the hero who has won the favor of the gods may beg for the boon of perfect illumination, what he generally seeks are longer years to live, weapons with which to slay his neighbor, or the health of his child. (Campbell, 189)

Hank Morgan wishes each of these things, but perhaps most of all wants power. He expects to outlive Arthur, whose practical power he seems to have usurped after his victory over the knights, and allow royalty to pass away with the king. In its place he claims to want a republic, but readers have reasons to think otherwise. "I may as well confess, though I do feel ashamed when I think of it: I was beginning to have a base hankering to be its first President myself. Yes, there was more or less human nature in me; I found that out" (399). Throughout the novel, Hank's politics seem a mixture of outrage and ego, his social actions as much despotic as enlightened. Returning from France to find the Interdict in place, Hank issues his proclamation establishing the republic. He does this from "the executive authority vested in me" (423) and makes himself The Boss of it. But this gesture of ego has no effect. The Yankee's power has become at this point only the power to destroy, not to build. The true power belongs to the Church.

Though I will examine this transformation in more detail in the next chapter, some points need to be made about the Church in this context. Though Hank has given us some good abstract reasons to dislike established churches in general, our extremely limited practical experience with the one in this novel can be described in primarily benign terms. After his first mention of the Church, calling it "a trifle stronger" than Arthur and the Boss put together (63), it plays no role at all in the narrative. All the readers and writers in the world are priests. Hank grudgingly records the good works of some. The monks at the Valley of Holiness, in the novel's most prolonged exposure of the Church, appear unsurprised by Hank's scientific approach and are altogether the most intelligent denizens of Arthur's England. The Church and its representatives seem nothing but grateful for all of the Yankee's improvements. We have only Hank's word that he restrained himself from working publicly because the Church would resent his accomplishments. When the Church shuts Hank down in the end, the action arrives in the text *deus ex machina*, unbelievable except that in this world the Church both represents God and possesses the true power. It seems clear, then, that at least in some ways the Church bestows on Hank "The Ultimate Boon"—power. But Hank has already shown himself to be a failed hero and so the Church must take back the boon and Hank must end his heroic progression ironically. Power in Hank's hands affects his world as Midas' ability to turn all he touched to gold affected his. Midas in the end transforms his prized daughter into a golden statue; Hank turns his scientific republic into dust and death.

How much of this failure we can attribute to Hank's incompletely resolved crises regarding the male and female powers in his life cannot be known, but a small theme in the novel suggests Hank has not touched a central conflict of sex and gender. When Hank first meets Clarence, he says, "He was pretty enough to frame"; before that he says Clarence's tights "made him look like a forked carrot" (15). The possible double reading of the phrase 'forked carrot' suggests homosexuality, a suggestion deepened by continued references to Clarence and other young boys as beautiful objects. When Merlin begins to speak at the Round Table, "The boy nestled himself upon my shoulder and pretended to go to sleep" (25). After a seven-year association, Hank says of Clarence that he "was my head executive, my right hand. He was a darling; he was equal to anything" (83). Clarence throughout the first hundred pages gushes and pours and drips, his character constructed liquidly, so differently from the hard lines normally reserved for male characters in the novel. Even his name, Amyas le Poulet, suggesting a translation 'my chicken love,' contributes to the sense that Hank has a romantic affection for young boys. When Hank returns from his adventures this sense is renewed. Clarence saves Hank from hanging with a wink (380) and is by his side to the end. Also by his side are the 52 boys fully trained under the Yankee's program, about whom Hank writes, "Ah, they were a darling fifty-two! And pretty as girls, too" (430). Dan Beard's portrait of one (425) exactly represents the sexual ambiguity of these nameless boys submerged deeply in Hank Morgan's affection. This homosexual theme in Hank's character seems unchanged by his attempts to come to terms with the male and female aspects of his self, untouched by his marriage to the goddess or his atonement with the king. Whether or not this keeps him from achieving the true union of these aspects of self in the bisexual apotheosis we cannot say. What we can say is that Hank's expulsion from this underworld comes from Merlin, who not only makes the Yankee sleep thirteen centuries in the most plainly magical event in the novel, but also performs this act in the guise of a woman. He dies a woman, laughing; "I suppose," Clarence writes, "the face will retain that petrified laugh until the corpse turns to dust" (443). Merlin laughs because he has achieved in the end what Hank Morgan could not, what Hank Morgan perhaps did not know he should have wanted to achieve: To bring the male and female together, to have true magic, and to speak as Merlin speaks at the end: as a god.

## Return

In the final phase of the journey, the hero returns to his original world. This return voyage has many permutations, according to Campbell: sometimes the hero chooses not to return, sometimes he cannot; sometimes the gods of the underworld send him back with a task, sometimes they fight his return; sometimes the natural world rescues the hero, sometimes the hero discovers he never left the natural world. None of these permutations seems to fit Hank Morgan, who does not seem less of a hero because of the nature of his return. Hank Morgan has, by the time of his return to the nineteenth century, failed as a hero; to give him a hero's send-off would misappropriate the myth. Hank's journey home is more passive than his journey to the underworld. He was a man full of fight and got himself sent over because of one, but for his return he merely sleeps, his power gone from him, his destiny out of his control, his very being in the hands now of a force he believes simply cannot exist. Hank's final passivity gives us the last proof we need that he has failed as a hero. Traditional heroes control their destinies, or are made great by them; Hank Morgan is made a fetus by his, sleeping away the centuries in a cave awaiting a new birth.

But we cannot consign the Yankee to the role of an ordinary mortal swept up by heroic events. His failure to achieve initiation is slight, as often the result of hubris as anything else. The presence of this fatal flaw suggests that, despite the humor of *A Connecticut Yankee in King Arthur's Court*, Hank is a tragic hero. Even more interesting, closer to the text, is the fact that for some reason the Yankee has been saved. Think of the magic involved in the final image by Clarence:

> We were glad to have this woman [Merlin in disguise], for we were short handed. We were in a trap, you see—a trap of our own making. If we stayed where we were, our dead would kill us; if we moved out of our defences, we should no longer be invincible. We had conquered; in turn we were conquered. The Boss recognized this; we all recognized it. If we could go to one of those new camps and patch up some kind of terms with the enemy—yes, but the Boss could not go, and neither could I, for I was among the first that were made sick by the poisonous air bred by those dead thousands. (443)

The defeat of the victors is not a simple switch of fortune. They are in fact defeated *by* their victory, killed by dead people. This would simply be a lively irony if not for the purposeful blindness Twain has written into Clarence, into the ending: If the boys are trapped in a mountainous circle of corpses, how did the old woman—only later found to be Merlin—enter? Wouldn't Hank have questioned her? and if he was not able, wouldn't Clarence have done the same? But no. Merlin's presence does not serve any purpose of realism, but only provides an escape, so Hank could eventually meet Mark Twain and hand him his manuscript. Merlin comes to rescue Hank from certain death. Whatever the meaning behind Merlin's petrified laughter, his final victory is the preservation of Hank Morgan's life.

The near-hero thus travels back to his own world. According to Campbell, the return from the underworld brings to the hero a consciousness of the links between the two worlds. "The two worlds, the divine and the human, can be pictured only as distinct from each other—different as life and death, as night and day. . . . Nevertheless—and here is the great key to the understanding of myth and symbol—the two kingdoms are actually one" (217). The returning hero has trouble accepting the reality, not of his journey, but of the real world. Often the time spent in the underworld feels to the hero like a year, while the real world has passed a century; sometimes the hero returns old to his own youth. The hero also has problems maintaining the "cosmic standpoint in the face of an immediate earthly pain or joy" (223). The hero must survive all these traumas and meet his final requirement: "to knit together his two worlds" (228).

Hank Morgan achieves something like this. We have very limited exposure to Hank Morgan after his long sleep, but in those passages he seems painfully aware of the ties between his two worlds. In this novel's first paragraph, Mark Twain's character admires Morgan's "candid simplicity" (1), a characteristic few would grant Morgan before his return across the threshold. He seems "to drift away imperceptibly out of this world and time, and into some remote era and old forgotten country" (1). But inside this unification of worlds, best signified by his unification of idiomatic speech—"'Wit ye well, *I saw it done.*' Then, after a pause, added: 'I did it myself.'" (2)—we find a spiritual exhaustion. When Hank first broaches the subject of having lived thirteen centuries before,

"He was so little interested . . . that he did not notice whether I made him any answer or not" (2). Only at the end of the novel do we find that the pain of his bifurcated life seems not to have enlightened him, only to have darkened and befuddled him. His return finds him "a stranger and forlorn in that stranger England, with an abyss of thirteen centuries yawning between me and you [Sandy]! between me and my home and my friends! between me and all that is dear to me, all that could make life worth the living!" (447) According to Campbell, the rewards of the returning hero are the mastery of both worlds and the freedom to live. The hero "no longer resists the self-annihilation that is the prerequisite to rebirth . . . and so becomes ripe . . . for the great at-one-ment. . . . The Law lives in him with his unreserved consent" (237). The peace and freedom of these final rewards escape Hank Morgan, and we find once again what we have already known through reading his story: that the Connecticut Yankee strives to be a hero but cannot in fact be one. His addiction to ego—the name we give to the abstract construction of the self we tell ourselves we are— opposes at the root the psychological quest his actions represent. Hank's addiction to effect, the concrete representation of the ego, remains with him until his death. Though he seems to have been reborn twice already in the novel, neither rebirth has redeemed him from his old life, and so he must now die. We cannot escape the tragic proportion of Hank Morgan's heroism.

Though not as much has been made of failure in *A Connecticut Yankee* as has been made of failure in *Huckleberry Finn*, the critical assumption of this novel's failure is as widespread as for the earlier one. Gerald Allen's comment in concluding his essay, "Mark Twain's Yankee," is a typical one: "Successes put forth answers, while failures define the questions more precisely. *A Connecticut Yankee* hovers in a most engaging way above the gap between question and answer, and, as a failure, it suggests so much about other works of the time" (446). Kenneth Anderson notes that the ending fails readers by leaving obscure Twain's opinion of Hank Morgan. And Robert Regan writes in *Unpromising Heroes* that there is no excuse for "the shambles into which the book's structure and its intellectual and emotional tenor fall" (184).

It seems to me, though, that calling a novel, in print and widely read for a century, a failure mistakes the meaning of the word. Just as with *Huckleberry Finn*, the failure is not the novel's, but the hero's. Just as contemporary critics of the former novel have not had to go far to point out its internal consistency, so we must begin to re-evaluate *A Connecticut Yankee*, not in terms of its failure, but in terms of the success of its hero's failure. What has made this process so difficult in both cases is that the novels seem simply extensions of their central figures. Huck, we have seen, is cast in the mold of a traditional hero, but in a world which makes success at that trade impossible. Hank, too, promises to achieve a certain sort of heroic level and fails. Can this failure be a fundamental part of the book's formulation? Can we interpret the book without confusing the hero's clear failure with the purported failure of the novel, by instead seeing Hank as the major feature in the book's design, a design which itself necessitates the failure of its central feature?

We have seen that Hank fails in his heroic endeavors because of his ego. His constant eye on effect, on how he looks, prevents him from the release of self necessary to truly marry the goddess, atone with the father, or become the wise god. We need to distinguish between one's ideas and feelings about the self and the self itself, between the ego and the id. In a kind of Freudian shorthand, Hank fails to achieve his promised heroism because he confuses the ego with the id. He is only what he tells himself and others he is. Since the heroic journey described by Joseph Campbell is a journey into the self and the Yankee's self is simply a mock-up of a self, not a real one, Hank achieves the semblance of success on this journey without the substance. The only self he ever encounters, and that we ever encounter with him, is the image of the self we call ego. However accurate this image—since we have no vision at all of a self within Hank's ego we might as well assume it is accurate—it cannot be authentic. The con man is a literary type, but in him we can see the difference between the surface man and the inner man; that is his appeal. We envy the con man his knowledge of the difference between who he is and how he is perceived. The Yankee, though, is only perceived. Even he only sees himself as though from the outside, through the ego. There is no man behind the ego to distinguish this image from. This is the ultimate cause of Hank Morgan's failure.

In his recent *Lost in the Cosmos*, Walker Percy argues for a semiotic understanding of the self. This fascinating construction from the brilliant Southern writer permits me to offer an new interpretation of Hank Morgan's failure and, as a result, a new understanding of *A Connecticut Yankee in King Arthur's Court*. Percy, following well-established traditions of semiotic thought, distinguishes between the dyadic relationship between all nonhuman beings and things and each other and the triadic relationship between humans and all other beings and things. Only human beings exist not only in an environment but also in a world created by the symbolic relationships we establish. Thus the explosion of the space shuttle Challenger in 1986, while having impact on the environments of very few Americans, becomes an event of pivotal importance in the worlds of almost all Americans. The importance of the Challenger explosion occurs in the world of symbols, which is the world most of us occupy most of the time. It is not the Challenger itself which affects us, but what we have made the Challenger symbolize. The Challenger only has the meaning we consensually give it.

In this view, what distinguishes human beings is what distinguished Adam in the Garden of Eden: we have the power to name. By naming, we grant objects and beings a symbolic as well as a natural importance. We live very little in the environment of nature and almost exclusively in the world of symbols. In Percy's view this system works well enough, except for one tragic problem: "Semiotically, the self is literally unspeakable to itself. One cannot speak or hear a word which signifies oneself, as one can speak or hear a word signifying anything else" (106–07). We exist for ourselves as the unnamed and unnamable namer at the center, not of the environment of nature, but of the world of symbols. According to Percy, we attempt to combat this experience of self as an unnameable nothing through totemism (identifying the self with something else), pantheism (identifying the self as god and the world as a product of imagination), theism (we name everything in our world, but god names us), scientism (logical proofs of the self by transcendence of symbols), and aestheticism (emotive proofs of the self by transcendence through symbols). In the end, though, we are trapped in our world of language. We return to our nothing selves where, as the ultimate source of names, "all signifiers fit" and we are "at once the secret hero and asshole of the Cosmos" (107).

In this understanding of the semiotic self, all the names we throw at ourselves—names which become, when taken all together, the ego—become symbols of self, adequate to the self's function in the symbolic world, but in fact simply a hollow shell around the true self, which remains nothing, unnamed, unsymbolizable. The more names we throw at ourselves the more "immanent," using Percy's word, we become. "The self sees itself as an immanent being in the world, existing in a mode of being often conceived on the model of organism-in-an-environment as a consequence of the powerful credentials of science and technology" (113). This immanent self sets up dyadic relationships between its conceived self or ego and conceived objects and beings or symbols. As should be obvious, by taking the thing's symbol for the thing itself, we maintain the semblance of a dyadic relationship, but at the cost of truth about the self and the world, about the thing and its environment. We can see by this how words and language both save and plague the immanent self.

Heroes in literature often fight a battle against this immanence. Hamlet fights against the appearance of things, against his own ability to be immanent, to "be bounded in a nutshell and count myself a king of infinite space" (II, ii). But Hank Morgan embraces his immanence. He fully accepts the symbol of himself as his true self. All of his relationships to things are simple. We can see this most clearly in the one portion of the book I did not discuss earlier, the episode at the Valley of Holiness. To everyone else in his world, the cessation of water from the well is an event of gigantic proportion. When the report of the calamity comes, nameless pilgrims ask, "Has someone been washing again?" and Sir Ozana replies, "Nay, it is suspected, but none believe it. It is thought to be some other sin, but none wit what" (201). This event, coming on the hooves of Sandy's pigs, suggests that the sixth century embraces the mystery of symbols. No one can ascertain the direct relationship between the dry fountain and behavior, but they know it to be there. Hank finds no such confusion. Having no belief in the symbolic content of events, he plunges into the well, finds the hole and plugs it up. Merlin's efforts to pierce the veil of symbolism to the core of the enchantment fails; Hank's technology succeeds. And yet it is the magic of words, especially the speaking of a magic name, which Merlin credits with the rejuvenation of the fountain. Hank says at the end of the tournament, his penultimate battle with Merlin, "Somehow, every time the magic of fol-de-rol tried conclusions with the magic of science, the magic of fol-de-rol got left" (393). This appears to be true until the end of the novel, when the suspicion of failure which has grown in the reader has been at last confirmed, when Hank's ego and ideology combine to produce the slaughter of 25,000 innocents, when even the most die-hard Hank supporters waver in identifying with him. Then we find that Merlin's magic has a legitimacy we did not before suspect, and the hole which is Hank Morgan's true self looms like a terrifying chasm.

Hank's terrible trouble with language starts after he crosses the threshold into the new world. If we knew the signs then, we could have read the outlines of his coming failure. The first words he hears after Hercules' blast are "Fair sir, will ye just?" He can only respond, "Will I which?" (5). Once at Camelot, he decides whether his first interlocutor is an inmate of the asylum or a keeper by the language he speaks. Hank refuses to be named by the king. Instead he wants to be named by the people. Being named by one person implies a private language, but being named by many creates the fiction of consensual agreement that the name for a thing is the thing itself. This is a true language for Hank, one devoid of symbols; being called The Boss means he is the boss. But the phrase 'true language' is oxymoronic, and so Hank's belief in one only exacerbates his difficulties with real language. Reviewing Hank's first conversation with Sandy, we see that his frustration and anger result from his inability to reduce her talk to technology, concrete information about a concrete world. She cannot say how far or in what direction unseen objects lie—who can, except by a belief in true language? But Hank will not be deterred. He attempts to technologize communication as quickly as possible: telephone, telegraph, newspaper, writing. He wants all language made concrete. Hank's response to the first newspaper is telling: "It was plain I had undergone considerable change without noticing it. I found myself unpleasantly affected by pert little irreverencies which would have seemed but proper and airy graces of speech as an earlier period of my life" (258). He wants language desymbolized. He wants to believe things are simply what one says they are. We see this all the way to the novel's conclusion, where the declaration of the republic is to Hank the same as the establishment of one. His first real defeat is in fact a defeat of language, when the people of England switch their allegiance from the word 'republic' to the fact of feudal authority. They, with Merlin as the emblem of this relationship, still believe in a transcendent relationship between words for a thing and the thing itself. They still believe in the symbolic power of names and words. They remain conscious of the impossibility of true language. And so, we are shown, does Twain, perhaps despite his own desire to believe as Hank believes.

Hank has no self, only a representation of self, an ego. He tries to establish, primarily through science and technology, a dyadic relationship between this ego and the world. But the symbolic nature of the world traps him; he can only establish this dyadic relationship symbol to symbol, name to name. There can be no direct relationship of self to object in a world mediated by words. This direct relationship is the heroic goal, according to Joseph Campbell. The journey into the self, if completed successfully, results in a transcendence of symbol. "Symbols are only the *vehicles* of communication; they must not be mistaken for the final term, the *tenor*, of their reference" (236). Thus, Hank Morgan follows the pattern of the hero, looking for the direct link between self and object. But, burdened with only words for the self and symbols for the object, his goal is impossible to reach. His failure, in some ways, is that he must write, name his experience, mediate everything with words. It should come as a very small surprise that Hank Morgan fails to finish his own memoirs, which, being all words, is truly his last effect.

# 5

◆◆◆

# A Yankee's World

After understanding Hank Morgan, the thorniest critical problem in *A Connecticut Yankee in King Arthur's Court* is pinpointing its subject. Critics agree only in the most general terms with William Dean Howells' post-publication assessment that the novel is as much about the nineteenth century as it is about the dark ages. Susan K. Harris' *Mark Twain's Escape from Time* includes an extended note at the beginning her chapter on *A Connecticut Yankee* (44–46) which offers as complete a review of the variations on this theme as I could produce here. Harris notes that critics all agree Twain attacks some institution in the novel, but that they disagree as to whether he is after the long-ago or the contemporary world. As I noted at the beginning of the last chapter, Harris' own criticism concerns "Hank's reflection of Mark Twain's psychological stances" (46n), but her synopsis of the critical field of battle helps us move forward into what I hope will provide a new interpretive synthesis of the novel's political and social reality.

One question rises first out of this confusion. In what way does *A Connecticut Yankee* concern itself with the nineteenth century? Not quite ten pages of this long novel take place outside King Arthur's realm. The few direct references to the later century—the discussion of slave-holder morality, for example, or the reference to the murderous church tithe in modern Wales—hardly constitute a true presence in the novel; they amount to little more than necessary contrasts to assist our understanding of Arthurian England. Actual evidence of the nineteenth century is limited to the products of the Yankee's mind or work-shops and are, like Hank himself, out of place. They only show the dark ages in higher relief.

But still, the impression lingers that, when we read *A Connecti-*

*cut Yankee,* we read about the nineteenth century. We may understand a large part of this phenomenon by an extension of the last
chapter's discussion. If the world into which Hank Morgan voyages is the world of the self, and given that whatever self Hank
has, being a type and not a person, is a nineteenth century self,
then—though populated with characters out of myth and sketched
along medieval lines—the world will be at root a nineteenth century one. The frame story suggests that Hank's construction might
be dream or delirium; several critics note Twain's growing suspicion that dreams had the same veracity as the different reality experienced while awake. From this it becomes clear that Hank's
dream-self experiences a more acute awareness of its own historicity than does his historical self. This will be a continuing interpretive reference point in this chapter.

The discussion in the last chapter also suggests that King
Arthur's world as portrayed in the book is more allegorical than
historical. We can say for certain it does not have the sort of historicity we discovered in *Adventures of Huckleberry Finn,* where the
time referred to in the novel is accurately represented in both the
hero and his world. Hank does represent his own time, as critics
have long recognized. But what does King Arthur's world represent? This question more accurately defines the problem Susan
Harris and a score of other critics have noted, that as historical
reality, King Arthur's England is a sham. In James D. Williams view,
"Mark Twain's attempts at historical accuracy in *A Connecticut Yankee* were sporadic and strictly limited by the demands of farce, outrage, or the theme of progress" ("Use of History," 102). Howard
Baetzhold's *Mark Twain and John Bull* focuses most of its reading of
the novel on source study; he concludes that, rather than drawing
from one century or even one period, Twain's sources "represent
most of the ages of Western history from Roman times until his
own" (131). Most critics have assumed that the novel simply assigns
all of history's injustices to an age enough removed to have been
able to contain them. By sweeping all the dirt into a sixth century
pile, Twain can trash it more simply by the direct application of the
broom of his progressivist assumptions.

This may be true, but it ignores a fundamental objection: that
the world Twain portrays is not meant historically, but rather allegorically, at least in significant measure. This argument seems to

me irrefutable. Our hero and narrator, more of a caricature than a person, gets sent not so much across centuries as across fictional boundaries, from possible fiction into impossible fiction. After all, have readers ever believed in the historicity of King Arthur, Merlin, and the Round Table knights? The stories come to us from the oral tradition of a lost time; few experts will say for certain whether or not the stories themselves predate the age they are now said to be about. Contemporary readers cavil at seeing Twain's rendition of King Arthur's time in anything close to historical terms. Clarence's fictionality seems no more pronounced than Arthur's; Arthur seems no more historical than Clarence. The emblematic qualities of the characters who populate this world spring to our critical eyes once we have begun to interpret Hank's voyage in psychological terms, but we have trouble understanding them if we insist on viewing the novel itself in historical terms. The discussion in my last chapter can extend to cover the further questions which arise when we consider the nature of the world Hank Morgan finds himself in. As pure history, *A Connecticut Yankee in King Arthur's Court* is pure bunk. The novel renders its imaginary world so as to suggest, not depict, its true nature; it represents by ideational association, not by particularized description. Whether we want to attribute this shadowiness to Hank's peculiar vision or to the nature of the world itself, we must admit we picture King Arthur's realm abstractly and not concretely.

But still, the historical interpretation will not go away. King Arthur's realm is shared land, partially symbolic in terms of the psychological allegory outlined in the previous chapter, and partially representing some aspect of history. Some of the reasons for this need little repetition: Hank tells us he went into the past; if we grant Arthur any sort of fictional reality, and we must to read the novel, that reality must be in part historical; and the novel does discuss many historical matters taken from discoverable historical sources.

Beyond these obvious ones, a few observations about this historical representation can be made without contradiction. First, a sort of meliorism overrides the novel. Hank Morgan believes his technological wonders combined with democracy and education must create a utopia. Readers do not share Hank's belief, because the novel itself undermines it with Hank's violence and egotism.

But readers do accept that the world Hank desires greatly improves on the world he occupies and that most of the changes he makes will lead to that better world.

Second, and this because of the first, Arthur's world represents something before the world Hank came from. This seems simplistic, but is not; some critics, notably Louis Budd in *Mark Twain: Social Philosopher* and Howard Baetzhold in *Mark Twain and John Bull*, have found contemporary sources for Twain's outrage in British journals and newspapers. I make the point that Arthur's England is not merely different from Hank's native world, but that it actually predates it, that on an historical time line Arthur's world comes before the Yankee's. The discovery of Twain's use of contemporary sources for the creation of Arthur's world forces us to rethink the meaning of the word 'before' in the above premise. If the world improves in material happiness and moral integrity, as meliorist notions hold, then a civilization which passionately clutches onto its material and moral history must of necessity lag behind a civilization which does not, even if their contemporary cultures have reached identical development. This clarifies what has been seen as Twain's ambiguity about England in the novel: he chastizes England to let go of what holds it back, its past. King Arthur's realm is so much more backward than even the most radical version of England in the 1880s that calling one an accurate representation of the other misses the point. Twain's sixth century might look familiar to critics of British civilization, but only in the way a portrait of an ancestor looks like a descendant. No matter how close the resemblance, one is not a portrait of the other. So we must conclude that the world the Yankee finds himself thrown into must represent something older and worse than England in the 1880s.

Third, the novel represents its object in some other way than realistically. Twain has already demonstrated both his historical knowledge and his ability to render historical reality in fiction, but chooses not to do that in this novel. Though "The ungentle laws and customs touched upon in this tale are historical," Twain tells us in the preface, "It is not pretended that these laws and customs existed in England in the sixth century." So what the novel represents as King Arthur's realm we are not to understand as an historical King Arthur's realm, but as something else, part historical, part allegorical. But what does that really mean?

Critics have attempted to answer this question with source studies, but given the fact that Twain is not looking to represent his subject realistically, such studies must fail to produce results. Unfortunately, critics have found their apparatus for moving past source studies very limited. James D. Williams shows this in "The Use of History in Mark Twain's *A Connecticut Yankee*" by preceding eight pages of source study with the comment that "the following examination of Mark Twain's use of history does not aim at a detailed description of sources" (102). Perhaps Williams is right; he does not present the sources in detail. Instead, he presents in detail the form the sources take in the novel. Sliced either way, it is a source study, helpful in recreating Twain's thoughts in composing, but only marginally useful in helping us determine the nature of the novel's historical reality.

Hank Morgan himself provides an extremely valuable clue in interpreting what King Arthur's realm represents. We know, for example, what the world Hank Morgan hatches represents: American Industrialism. This point seems too obvious to require proof. Hank builds telephones, telegraphs, railroads, factories, newspapers, advertising—most of these things valueless, except as curiosities, in a country without a reading public, freedom, reason, or money to travel, or friends or business at a distance. He does all this with a speed even more astonishing than that at which America itself managed the same development in the decades following the Civil War, and he does it alone. But Hank Morgan, we remember, is not a person. He is a type, an emblem of a group, and so we cannot think of his accomplishments as solo flights. All the work he does represents the work of his group. Critics have long quoted Hank's claim to a barrenness of sentiment—I myself did so earlier—but the words surrounding that claim mean more in this context: "I am an American. . . . My father was a blacksmith, my uncle was a horse-doctor, and I was both, along at first. Then I went over to the great Colt arms-factory and learned my real trade" (4). By the time we meet Hank Morgan, he is an expert at making armaments and machinery, as was America in the late 1880s. But before, what was he? A blacksmith and horse-doctor. Does this represent a different sort of America? Can Hank Morgan produce the changes in King Arthur's England because he had already experienced those changes in himself? Is King Arthur's realm much different from America before our own massive industrialization?

We can get answers to this question by taking a short-cut through the criticism. The two interpretive streams we have been slogging through so far show that *A Connecticut Yankee*'s world is both allegorical and historical. We can blend these approaches and perhaps understand the world's construction as historical allegory or allegorical historicity. The first of these two schemes has been productively explored in the criticism. Henry Nash Smith's *Mark Twain's Fable of Progress* argues in essence that the world of the novel is historical allegory. As Smith writes, "The burlesque tale expresses a philosophy of history and a theory of the capitalist system created by the industrial revolution—and the story breaks under the pressure of the thought and emotion that the writer poured into it" (7).

Discussions since the 1964 publication of this reading have accepted Smith's point, and I have no issue to take with the first part of his assessment, except that it leads to his second. When we see the novel as an allegory on the philosophy of history, the story does break down, but this breakdown is tautological. Critics attach the sense of failure in the novel to its inability to maintain the consistent philosophical point of view they claim the book attempts to hold. But the failure in *Connecticut Yankee* is, as I have already shown, Hank's unrealized heroic promise, not a flaw in the novel, but a failure as essential to the novel as Hank's rivalry with Merlin. We must look for a way to interpret the novel which accepts the particular failure in it. Assuming that the novel's world represents an historical allegory has produced some interesting criticism, but has not produced a reading which accepts the Yankee's failure as hero as fundamental. I believe looking instead for the novel's allegorical historicity might.

What does this phrase mean? Only that the historical quality of King Arthur's realm is presented allegorically rather than realistically. The key implication of this understanding of the workings of the novel reaches further: we see the nineteenth century in King Arthur's Court because what we already know to be nineteenth century America finds allegorical equivalence in the world of the novel. This further focuses Twain's project away from a discussion of the more abstract principle of meliorism—a subject on which critics have found the novel divided—and toward a consideration of the more concrete problems America faced as we grew into an industrial power. Toward this end, I will try to show in the following few pages a sort of identity by association between the world as described in our contemporary histories of America in the 1870s and 1880s and the world in *A Connecticut Yankee in King Arthur's Court*. We cannot construe these associations to be proof, only evidence of allegorical constructions. As with most allegories—as with language itself—weight and meaning accumulates through repetition rather than through any natural likeness. This allegorical historicity does not require a neat fit between the worlds; we will not find the particular historicity we found in *Huckleberry Finn*. In fact, for every bit of King Arthur's world which looks like industrial America under development, we can find another bit which looks very strange to us, like something entirely alien. But it is this very division, which the critical tool of allegorical historicity makes visible to us, which permits us to see the world of *A Connecticut Yankee* accurately. I believe it is in the very sense, in which we see both something familiar and something unutterably strange in King Arthur's realm, that a true meaning of the world of the novel becomes clear.

Historians of industrial America have a text which is as fundamental for them as Tocqueville's *Democracy in America* is for historians of Jacksonian America. *The American Commonwealth*, by James Bryce, first published in 1888, "had at once a profound effect on Great Britain and undoubtedly paved the way toward that improvement of Anglo-American relations" (vii) obtaining when Louis M. Hacker wrote this in his introduction to Putnam's 1959 edition. Bryce's fascinating and minute analysis earned him an international reputation. We must leave unanswered whether or not Twain knew of this book while still at work on *A Connecticut Yankee*; it seems unlikely, given that Twain's comments on a 1907 speaking engagement in which he shared the podium with then-Ambassador Bryce include no reference to his important book. The nation which comes through *The American Commonwealth*, however, has a familiar feel to readers of Twain's novel. Much that Bryce writes applies equally to America in a time of almost unimaginable change and to any world undergoing Hank Morgan's program. "Religious teaching," Bryce writes of the average American, "though it has become less definite and less dogmatic, is still to him the source whence he believes himself to have drawn his ideas of duty and conduct" (495); Clarence says the same thing about his people on Hank's return to an interdicted England. Bryce explains that American education is still under development with the observation:

> If we define a university as a place where teaching of a high order, teaching which puts a man abreast of the fullest and most exact knowledge of the the time, is given in a range of subjects covering all the great departments of intellectual life, not more than twelve and possibly only eight or nine of the American institutions would fall within the definition. (464)

Though Bryce found few examples of institutional inequality, he did note that "The total absence of rank and the universal acceptance of equality do not however prevent the existence of grades and distinction in society which, though they find no tangible expression, are sometimes as sharply drawn as in Europe" (521).

While few of these observations surprise us, they do produce a picture of America—studied over the course of two decades—similar to Hank Morgan's growing Arthurian industrialism. John A. Garraty wrote in *The New Commonwealth*, a conservative but reliable history of the period:

> My thesis is that between 1877 and 1890 the character of American civilization underwent a basic transformation, a change so pervasive as to justify the word 'new' in my title. This change took the form of a greatly expanded reliance by individuals upon group activities. Industrialization with its accompanying effects—speedy transportation and communication, specialization, urbanization—compelled men to depend far more than in earlier times on organizations in managing their affairs, to deal with the problems collectively rather than as individuals. (xiii)

This is precisely the world Hank Morgan attempts to construct. When Hank and the King fall to the lowest point in society, they are saved only by the speed of the Yankee's new communication and transportation technology. Knights move from the generalized activity of knight-errantry, lambasted in the early going of the novel, into specialties in business, railroading and sport. Hank constantly sends people he meets in the country into population centers; the novel itself moves from the country to the city. Hank organizes so much group activity many critics see him as a fascist.

Garraty's discussions both of the mid-1880s strikes over scrip payment (154–55), against workers being paid in company-issued, overvalued currency, and of the controversial government policy of encouraging land and currency speculation sound remarkably like Hank's argument with Dowley in Chapter 33. Garraty also describes one of the period's most determined and productive groups of political activists, civil service reformers, as "genuinely idealistic if somewhat naive in their belief that the antique virtues of the early days of the Republic could be restored merely by establishing a merit system among federal workers" (256); the Yankee's idealism over his civil service reform (249–50) also seems a bit naive: "All the boys would join, I was sure of that; so all existing grants would be relinquished; that the newly born would always join was equally certain" (250). The Grange movement agitated for public money for agricultural colleges and experimental farms through this period and won their point. "By 1891, the stations were employing more than 450 persons, most of them skilled professionals, and distributing over 300 bulletins and reports to some 350,000 readers" (65). Hank Morgan's push for science and literacy, paired with Arthur's painful ignorance of agriculture, suggests this same pattern.

*A Connecticut Yankee in King Arthur's Court* poses the Roman Catholic Church as the ultimate power, the enemy against which Hank claims all his work is directed. But the church itself is invisible in the novel; we see a couple of priests—one as a reporter and another as a true help to the oppressed—and the gang in the Valley of Holiness, and they seem altogether benign in this truly cruel world. About the worst that Hank can say about actual representatives of the Church is that they do not wash. Since they clearly want to, this criticism lacks punch. Hank objects more to the lack of choice among the people than to Catholic beliefs themselves. Rather than thinking of the Church as a fount of evil power, it seems wiser to think of it allegorically as orthodoxy, the vast invisible power which, without being in and of itself good or evil, circumscribes the extent of a people's imagination. Orthodoxy presented vicious problems for people living in the midst of American Industrialism. Page Smith writes of the post-Civil War spiritual trauma in *The Rise of Industrial America* that

> Stated in its simplest terms, the problem was how to reconstruct the ruins of the old theistic world; how to build a new scientific world that would meet the deepest needs of the human heart, or, conversely, how to defend the old theistic scheme against the new heresies. The life-and-death nature of that struggle domi-

> nated the mental world of America. . . . Everybody and every
> institution defined or, in some cases, redefined himself, herself,
> itself in relation to that issue. (559)

Smith concludes his chapter on religion with the observation that, while many American intellectuals "embraced some form of spiritualism . . . , the old orthodoxy crumbled and out of its lumber a new consciousness was constructed" (586). Smith's view notwithstanding, the success of this spiritual replacement remains a matter for debate among historians. *A Connecticut Yankee* creates this same ambiguity: Hank's ideal of a go-as-you-please church (398) is his fight against orthodoxy, and the failure of this ideal reflects the era's inability to operate without an orthodoxy of some kind.

Critics have long seen the slavery in *A Connecticut Yankee* as an allegorical version of American slavery. The apparent use of Charles Ball's *Fifty Years in Chains* as a source for the novel confirms this for many readers. One interpretation holds that Hank Morgan's struggle is in fact against the Old South. A phalanx of fine critics—Henry Nash Smith, Louis Rubin, Lewis Leary, and many others—have successfully established this interpretive point. While I happily admit its validity, I do wish to suggest an alternative which more completely accounts for common readerly experience with the novel.

The argued equivalence between King Arthur's realm and the Old South—a point of view itself a vision of allegorical historicity—turns the book into a unique historical novel, in which the conflicts of the past find representation in conflicts of the further past. This seems to me quite strange; by the time Twain began writing *A Connecticut Yankee*, the Civil War had been over twenty years. We can see what happens to a work of literature with this historical time-shifting if we consider Arthur Miller's *The Crucible*. Written in the 1950s, first viewers easily accepted the intended allegory between the Salem witchhunts and McCarthyism. Today, though, the play seems nothing but dated. It works neither as historical drama nor as social criticism. To write a novel dated by its very conception seems foolish, and *A Connecticut Yankee* is neither foolish nor dated. The critical method used here is correct, but the particular history refered to allegorically seems not to be. In looking for an allegorical historicity, the dates of the primary document's sources matter little; we are looking for the feel of a time, not its reality.

In the novel, the slaves are always portrayed as a part of a larger social structure. Freemen sneer at them and the distant upper classes respond callously to a scene of one being whipped (199–200). It is only towards the end of the novel that a slave actually speaks, and then only to identify Hank for the purpose of having Hank's company on the gallows. No slave is personalized; none is given a name. They represent a small percentage of the population—just how large we cannot say from the information in the novel—but their faceless mass represents an important presence in King Arthur's world. Because we learn so little about them, what they represent in the allegory can only be understood through the relative positions of the other classes.

Hank writes that freemen were called that only "by a sarcasm of law and phrase. . . . Seven-tenths of the free population of the country were of just their class and degree: small 'independent' farmers, artisans, etc.; which is to say, they were the nation, the actual Nation" (109). But over the next two pages Hank catalogues their deprivations and shows they are hardly independent at all. They look more than a bit like the workers in Gilded-Age America. In that period, America witnessed vast accumulation of capital and industry in a very few hands. What had been before the Civil War a nation of small freeholders became in the 1870s and 1880s a nation of workers. Bonanza farms, often derived from federal grants for railroads, replaced independent farmers, whose small acreage made the use of newly developed machinery uneconomical. Everyday items, once made in small shops by artisans, now came from enormous factories. These rapid changes led to "the increasingly bitter war between capital and labor" (Smith, 134). While "real wages went up sharply—by between 10 and 20 per cent in the seventies and by at least 25 per cent more in the eighties" (Garraty, 128)—worker independence and satisfaction went down; whether this resulted from alienation or a relative decrease in the workers' standard of living depends on which interpretation of history one favors. In any case, strikes developed, matched by violence from employers. "The corporation was more than a match for labor, and when backed by public opinion and governmental action proved invincible. Considered by many to be contrary to the American ideal of individualism, unions and strikes were publicly condemned and blamed for violence and labor unrest" (Hoogenboom, 66). But of course it was not the unions but the concentration of capital and industry which robbed people of individualism. Workers were forced into signing "yellow dog" contracts, promising not to join unions; they often lived in company housing, shopped in company stores, were paid in company currency; they worked an average of ten hours a day, six days a week; complainers were dismissed; and workers had no wage guarantees. While the freemen of King Arthur's realm suffer more physical deprivation than did nineteenth century workers, their relative positions in society are analogous. We could say that the trials of the class have gotten less severe through history, but as a class the American worker and the Arthurian freeman are one.

And the slaves? The slaves of the American South had been replaced by 1880 with immigrants in the North and freed blacks elsewhere. In the South, black tenant farmers and sharecroppers performed the roles that the new mechanized combines did in the bonanza farms of the West. In the city, immigrants crowded in sweatshops, working endless hours for pay not equal to subsistence. These immigrants, Lafcadio Hearn wrote, "labor in tanneries, slaughter-houses and soap factories, receiving small salaries upon which an American worker could not support his family, and doing work which Americans instinctively shrink from" (in Hoogenboom, 98). Reports of immigrant laborers being sold upon arrival in this country appeared frequently in newspapers, and city, state, and federal government investigations of the sweatshop system uncovered repulsive conditions. Further, the sections of cities in which immigrants lived often had no sewers but their unpaved streets, no plumbing of any kind, and street after street of airless, lightless, firetrap tenements. Violence and prejudice against immigrants ran high, particularly among native-born workers, who worried that foreigners would steal their jobs. Also, the fear of Catholicism provoked vandalism and beatings. Again, though the conditions had improved—many of the immigrants had in fact left Arthurian slaves' chains and forced marches to come here—the social positions of slaves and immigrants in each world is the same.

I must repeat: I have not tried to show that Twain represented nineteenth century America realistically in King Arthur's realm. I only point out that we see the nineteenth century in *A Connecticut Yankee* because it is there, allegorically at least. We see it in part in the technological dreams Hank Morgan has and in part in the world he seeks to change. The social conscience of the novel comes not only in the contemporary political ideas that Foner, Baetzhold, and others show that Twain included, but also in the world depicted. The representation, unlike the realism of *Huckleberry Finn*, is allegorical, but the novel's historicity, the presentation of industrial America, comes through clearly.

But King Arthur's realm also appears as something quite different from Gilded-Age America, which did not contain such fairytale accoutrements as magic, aristocratic rights, hermits, and holy fountains. Hank expresses his astonishment of the world of difference in response to Sandy's belief in magic: "My land, the power of training! of influence! of education! It can bring a body up to believe anything" (190–91). Behind this passage is the assumption that Arthurian society is so different from Hank's nineteenth-century America that the sanest inhabitants of one will appear insane in the other. The novel, which has presented its world so that readers see in it an allegory for industrial America, simultaneously maintains that that world is something so entirely unlike industrial America that the definitions of sanity in each do not so much as overlap. The other half of Arthur's England represents an alien community.

In Arthur's world, an arbitrary and childlike aristocracy holds the visible power, yet even this unrestricted civil force bows to the virtually invisible presence of the Church on one hand and the mystification of magic, personified by Merlin, on the other. The people, even the best educated, unswervingly believe spoken words over the evidence of their own eyes, regard human life as interchangeable with money, and appear to have no concept of time or space, at least as Hank and we understand time and space. What does this aspect of King Arthur's world represent? Henry Nash Smith answers, "This medieval setting is obviously not meant to represent any actual place or time. It is a backdrop designed to allow a nineteenth-century American Industrial genius to show what he can do with an undeveloped country" (*Fable*, 36). Smith seems on the right track; many critics have followed him there. But we cannot fairly consider the world a backdrop, nor think of Hank Morgan as a genius, which would imply Hank is an individual, a position the argument of the preceding chapter makes difficult to maintain. If we generalize Hank Morgan into a force of American Industrialism and accord Arthur's Kingdom its central presence in the novel, we begin to see the drama of *A Connecticut Yankee* in a

135

new light. Hank Morgan goes to a distant and backward country and develops it. It is American Industrialism overseas; put succinctly, American Imperialism.

No scholar of Mark Twain doubts his fervent anti-imperialism, but very few have recognized Hank Morgan's exploits in King Arthur's Court as a fictional representation of American Imperialism. Nancy S. Oliver does make this connection in "New Manifest Destiny in *A Connecticut Yankee in King Arthur's Court*." She writes, "The Manifest Destiny of the 1840s developed through a metamorphisis [*sic*] of Social Darwinism to become the new Manifest Destiny and the basis for imperialism in the late nineteenth century" (28). She argues that the Yankee's belief in his superiority swept away any doubt he might have entertained that he should impose his world on the sixth century. She concludes, "Perhaps in a somewhat metaphysical sense, Twain anticipated our nation's involvement in early twentieth-century imperialism and suggested a possible danger to a race which accepts the tenuous position of superiority" (31).

Oliver is overcautious in placing American Imperialism in the twentieth century. We certainly began our military intervention in South and Central America and in the Pacific in the early 1890s. Ernest May points out in his *Imperial Democracy* that the mid-1880s "saw numerous Americans talking again of 'manifest destiny'" (8), and Garraty writes, "Recently, a number of historians have found in the foreign policies of the Presidents of the 1870s and 1880s a foreshadowing of the imperialism of the late 1890s. They suggest that American foreign policy during these years was heavily influenced by economic pressures, especially by rapid industrialization" (282n). Lloyd C. Gardner, introducing his *A Different Frontier*, a collection of readings on our economic expansionism of the Gilded Age, traces our later military imperialism to the pressing need for markets for the surplus of American Industrial expansion.

Several critics, including Henry Nash Smith, notice that Hank Morgan is an entrepreneur. As Lorne Fienberg remarks:

> The Yankee is not specifically an inventor, as James Cox has suggested, nor does he, except in his own imagination, assume the dimensions of businessman or 'capitalist hero.' Rather, Hank's are the characteristic talents and functions of the *entrepreneur*, or innovator, and his program is susceptible to all the crises of en-

trepreneurship as that role was evolving in the late nineteenth
century in the United States. (157)

Fienberg's argument brings us full circle, back to the perspective
that King Arthur's world looks suggestively like the world we assume Hank Morgan came from. King Arthur's realm is both nineteenth century America and the site of an experiment in American
manifest destiny, a victim of economic expansionism which ends
militarily, just as our efforts in the Philippines, Nicaragua, and Co-
lombia began economically in the 1880s and in the following decade or two moved inexorably toward armed conflict. The alien
nature of Arthurian England, its lack of development, and Hank
Morgan's initial success and final failure there recreate allegorically
American expansionist and imperialist efforts in the decades following the Civil War.

   We can now attempt to create an interpretation of *A Connecticut Yankee* based on a full understanding of Hank's heroism and the
role of King Arthur's world. Hank Morgan, a traditional hero making a psychological pilgrimage into the nether world of the self,
comes into conflict with this world and in the end loses to it. Seeing
King Arthur's realm as purely the projection of a Connecticut Yankee's embattled psyche misses the plain political and historical aspects of the novel. Further, to say that a projection of an embattled
psyche defeats the holder of that psyche is meaningless; such a perspective renders the novel sophomoric. In order to understand
what defeats Hank, and in order to appreciate a fuller range of the
novel's concerns, we must come to terms with the world of the novel
as it is painted.

   Further, we can combine the two perspectives I separated earlier in this chapter. The first interprets the world of the novel as
historical allegory. Roger Salomon recognizes the limitations of this
interpretation best in his *Mark Twain and the Image of History*, writing that in *A Connecticut Yankee* "point of view unconsciously wavers
and leads to confusion of meaning because of the fundamental disparity between Twain's predominantly optimistic theory of history
and his personal pessimism" (108). In this abstract construction,
Hank Morgan's attempt to improve Arthur's kingdom according to
the American plan is all good, as it only hurries history's natural
meliorism. Superstition, stupidity, and lack of personal integrity

play evil to this good and become the emblems for Twain's personal pessimism. This interpretation ends by saying that the novel says little because of this "fundamental disparity"; *A Connecticut Yankee* can offer no resolution. But interpreting the world of the novel through allegorical historicity enriches our understanding of this conflict. We can view neither Hank's efforts nor the reigning ideology of King Arthur's world as all good or evil. We can no more endorse Hank's view of the Arthurian citizenry as "human muck" than we can condemn Arthur for his kingliness. Instead, by this interpretation, we see how the good and the bad are not so much in unresolvable conflict with one another as they are the necessarily mixed ingredients of the novel. The confusion Salomon finds we resolve with the understanding that America's massive Gilded-Age industrial and economic development (Hank's grand plan) goes hand in hand with this development's poisonous and doomed mirror-image imperialism (Hank's volcanic eruptions, first of one century onto another, second of fury against the recalcitrant natives).

We can see these divergent interpretive possibilities simultaneously because the novel presents its world allegorically; a realistically rendered world would never be able to put these nearly opposing perspectives together. Recognizing King Arthur's realm as simultaneously representing both a changing America and undeveloped fields for American expansionism encourages two new interpretations of the novel. First, we can begin to understand Hank Morgan, not only as heroic symbol of our own psychological journeys, but simultaneously—turning our attention to hero Hank in his world—as an emblem of that psychological self in history. And second, this reading of Twain's novel offers to the study of history a new interpretation of the era Twain himself named.

Hank Morgan appears to be an individualist: he sends grovelling automata to his man factory where they will learn to think of disloyalty as a higher form of loyalty. He sees his showmanship as a fault, but as his own fault it is worth maintaining. He is so addicted to the cult of himself that when he discovers a man who, like himself, has found his trade and risen to power within it—that is, Dowley—he must try to destroy him. But Hank's individualism, unlike Huck's, grows from egotism and a notion of superiority, the twin psychological fuels of imperialism. An emblem of industrializing America, he has the features of imperializing America. His ideological interest in individualism is undercut by his ego, the same quality which prevents him from fully realizing his heroic potential. Critics have long pointed out the anti-individualism implied by the term 'man factory,' but in fact it is difficult to find any true individualism in Hank Morgan except as it applies to himself. Rather than promote individualism generally or encourage it in others, he turns knights into walking advertisements and views his loyal followers into 52 indistinguishably adorable boys. A handful of characters in the novel retain their individual identity, but only against Hank: Merlin, Hank's nemesis; Morgan Le Fay, his anima; Sandy, who is whatever Hank is not; Clarence, his assistant. Only Arthur, it seems, retains a sufficiently distinguishable self, one not defined in terms of Hank's. And it is Arthur who gives his name to the world which eventually defeats Hank.

But it must also be said that Hank defeats himself. His ideology of individualism has no place in his industrial wonderland. As John Garraty noted above, the new commonwealth is a world of groups, a sharp change from the Jacksonian world that went before. Hank's individualism conflicts with his industrialism. While it seems at first that only one or the other will have to crash, in the end both are destroyed. Hank, his finger forever hovering, as Judith Fetterly notes, above a button or lever, finally pushes one. By this individual action "all our noble civilization-factories went up in the air" (430). On the other hand, the later industrial world destroyed his individuality: "What would I amount to in the twentieth century? I should be foreman of a factory, that is about all; and could drag a seine down street any day and catch a hundred better men than myself" (63). King Arthur's world defeats Hank, but it takes the modern world to destroy him. His individualism fails in an industrialism he can only imagine himself to be a fundamental part of. The machines of the Gilded Age, those he claims at the beginning he can build and design easier than falling off a log, render him no more than a cog, an interchangeable part in a still larger machine. If Hank is divided against himself, it is not because of a fissure between his desires to build and his desires to pull down, between American Industrialism and American Imperialism, but because of the immeasurable distance between the Jacksonian notion of individualism and the Gilded-Age necessity of corporate industrialism. The idea of a powerful individual self must give way to the idea of a group identity in order for industrialism and its partner imperialism to become fact.

This leads us to our second conclusion. Historians have debated the roots of American military imperialism of the 1890s without conclusion. The best arguments as yet mounted I have noted before: that the American Industrial machine produced well beyond domestic capacity to consume and, unable to maintain a favorable trade balance with high-tariff Europe, we expanded our market in the Americas and the Pacific. When European powers threatened these markets we defended them militarily; when local powers resisted our authority we established it with force.

*A Connecticut Yankee in King Arthur's Court* suggests another possibility. Presenting King Arthur's realm as both developing America and as territory for American expansionism encourages us to think about the industrialization of America's Gilded Age as a kind of imperialism against ourselves. The world and ideologies which existed before the Civil War, those shown to be in conflict in *Adventures of Huckleberry Finn*, no longer exist. The war, in part a battle over money, was fought militarily when the increasingly industrialized North decided it had the right to exert its will over the agrarian, slave-holding South. But the war itself promoted the very industrialism which distinguished the North, and the North in the end became as much a victim of economic expansionism as did its enemy. Both were conquered, and what survived from Andrew Jackson's world was a conquered people conquering, turning the tools that defeated them against the next victim. A quick rereading of "The Battle of the Sandbelt," the chapter which understandably causes most critical reluctance to the whole-hearted endorsement of a simpler interpretation of the novel, reveals exactly these ideas. Hank writes of his destruction of all he has built: "We could not afford to let the enemy turn our own weapons against us" (432). If we think of industrialism as an ideological force with the same strength we attribute to colonialism, communism, or capitalism, we can see America of the mid-nineteenth century as a victim of radical ideological change, a change so powerful our own borders could not hold it. Once America had been conquered by this idea, we turned to conquer others with it. Our industrialism therefore becomes our imperialism; the progression from Civil War through industrial development to imperialism occurs naturally. This idea, suggested by this reading of *A Connecticut Yankee in King Arthur's Court*, might offer the outline of an answer to the questions of continuity historians have not resolved in considering the transition between our domestic development in the Gilded Age and our subsequent expansion into the international arena.

This idea remains untried. I am no historian and can do no more than observe that, in my reading of contemporary American historians, I have not found this specific interpretation of the historical movement from American Industrialism to American Imperialism. Whether it withstands the scrutiny of the discipline matters less for the purpose of this work than a secondary discovery. Just as a clear understanding of the history of Jacksonian America allows us to discover a new interpretation of *Adventures of Huckleberry Finn*, so a clear understanding of *A Connecticut Yankee in King Arthur's Court* implies a revised interpretation of a thorny problem in American history. We have, until recently, understood the intertextual structure between literature and history as a matrix which renders novels into uneasy primary documents for the study of history. I believe this demonstrates that the structure of this matrix is much more complex. Throughout his novel Hank Morgan writes of volcanos, of vast changes and boiling tempests below the quiescent surface of a mountain. First it is the nineteenth century itself churning away underground. Later it is his newspaper, his first truly public proclamation of purpose. Perhaps the real volcano in the novel is what Twain later claimed it would take a pen warmed up in hell to write: that just as America had become victim of its own industrial menace, so would it surely menace the rest of the world. That idea itself becomes a volcano ready to explode with a mixed magma of literature and history.

# Part III

Pudd'nhead Wilson

Part III

# 6

✥

# David Wilson's Heroics

*Pudd'nhead Wilson* is a troublesome book. Its ambiguities about race and evil discomfort most readers. Serious critical exploration of the book began in the mid-1950s, and in the decades since readers have found more subjects on which to disagree with one another than they have found in any other work by Mark Twain. After Leslie Fiedler and F. R. Leavis opened the field in their introductions to the novel, critics of lesser rank and more diligence have applied themselves with massively contradictory results. Richard Chase, in his classic *The American Novel and Its Tradition*, seconds Fiedler and Leavis, with qualifications. But after that horn-blowing, critical troops have met in heated battle. Robert A. Wiggins writes in *Mark Twain: Jackleg Novelist* that, if it were not for the claims some critics make for the novel, "one would say little about *Pudd'n-head Wilson* and move on to other matters, content to have assigned the book a place as a minor partial success" (105). Philip Butcher, Michael Orth, Anne Wigger, and others shoot down the novel for selling its noble themes short for the benefit of melodrama. Most other critics content themselves with snaking out a theme or pattern of images in the book. All this work has left only a trail of studies which Barry Wood calls "true, in the sense of demonstrable, without being particularly satisfactory. Each one either omits important events or issues in the book or interprets them as servants to a thesis" (371). A few articles, such as Wood's "Narrative Action and Structural Symmetry in *Pudd'nhead Wilson*," John C. Gerber's "*Pudd'nhead Wilson* as Fabulation," and Clark Griffith's "*Pudd'nhead Wilson* as Dark Comedy," attempt to tackle the book as a whole by taking a structural or generic look at it. It is only since World War II that this novel has found much of a readership. No one has yet come to terms with what makes this book one which modern readers find perhaps the most powerful in Twain's corpus.

No doubt, the book's ticklishness on questions of race and questions of evil accounts for the tale's force. When the marginally-black slave Roxana exchanges her son and her master's in their cradles, we cheer her attack on the system which "daily robbed [her] of an inestimable treasure—[her] liberty" (13), and we expect her child in some way to materialize her revenge. When Tom, this vehicle of hoped-for revenge, grows into a malevolent and selfish prig, all that remains is the dangerous implication that the usurper's breath of black blood causes his baseness. "Thirty-one parts o' you is white, en on'y one part nigger, en dat po' little one part is yo' *soul*. 'Tain't wuth savin'; 'tain't wuth totin' out on a shovel en tho'in' in de gutter" (70), Roxy tells him after one act of craven cowardice. And if we can lay this slave's opinion down to the slave's acculturation Roxy received, we cannot do the same with the comment by the narrator that "'Tom' was a bad baby, from the very begining of his usurpation" (17). Instead we wonder why Twain allowed himself to imply the inferiority of black blood.

Tom's slide from gambling to robbery to murder smells a bit like racism, but Tom does not hold the book's only franchise on evil. The town of Dawson's Landing, while not as dedicatedly evil as Tom, has a share as well. As Mark D. Coburn writes, "The town is the most bigoted of pedagogues, dictating to the citizen what his ambitions and behavior must be. Public opinion is all but omnipotent, and Twain frequently presents 'the town' as if it were a single persona" (210). Following the first idyllic painting of the town, Twain notes, "Dawson's Landing was a slave-holding town, with a rich slave-worked grain and pork country back of it" (4), leaving little doubt as to how we are to view "The scene of this chronicle" (3). This town fawns over the Italian twins, who, as Murial B. Williams shows, might well be con men. It adores its mock nobility and the code duello this nobility prefers to the law. And, in perhaps the surest evidence of its evil, Dawson's Landing undervalues David Wilson, the Eastern-educated outsider and wise man, the man on whom our hopes for the defeat of racism and other evils fall when it becomes clear that neither Tom nor Roxy will deliver the killing blow. But, though Pudd'nhead Wilson lives down his nickname and ignominy, his accomplishments are purely personal. His final act, freeing the Italian twins and revealing Tom's identity as a murderer and a slave, capitulates to the town and restores its fundamental evil undisturbed. These two aspects of the fable disturb all readers; the critical attention shown these points proves this.

We find equally challenging problems closer to the themes I have been detailing in this work thus far. Critics have often asked who is the hero of *Pudd'nhead Wilson*. More than a handful have sided with Roxy, arguing often as not that, if the novel is a tragedy, as Twain observes it is in the comic introduction to "Those Extraordinary Twins" (122) and as many American editions' title pages claim, she is the tragic hero. She rises up against the forces of evil and in the end is defeated by her own, more-evil creation, her son. Critics support their decision to withhold the hero's mantle from David Wilson because of a comment Twain made in a letter to Livy. In response to a noted critic's opinion "that Pudd'nhead was clearly & powerfully drawn & would live & take his place as one of the great creations of American fiction," Twain registers surprise, saying he "never thought of Pudd'nhead as a character, but only as a piece of machinery—a button or a crank or a lever, with a useful function to perform in a machine, but with no dignity above that" (Wecter, *Love Letters*, 291). Other critics disregard this nay-saying of Wilson. They discern the sensibility of the novel in Pudd'nhead's calendar aphorisms and put the tragedy with David Wilson. Though his vindication at the tale's end fits a comic pattern, Wilson's "victory is hollow," as Richard Cracroft writes in "The Ironic Mark Twain: Appearance and Reality in *Pudd'nhead Wilson*," because "Pudd'nhead Wilson has won the applause of fools only by restoring the dubious integrity of racist institutions" (25). Still other critics point out that the title page of the first book publication, in England, read *Pudd'nhead Wilson: A Tale*; the first American publication, in *Century Magazine*, called it simply *Pudd'nhead Wilson*. Critics of this persuasion believe it foolhardy to search for a tragic hero in a novel because it was mislabeled a tragedy. Some of these critics name Pudd'nhead a comic hero and *Pudd'nhead* a comedy. Critics split even this hair. Some side with Leavis in saying the attitude of the book "is remote from cynicism or pessimism" (134) and that Wilson himself is "the poised and preeminently civilized moral center of the drama" (133). But Clark Griffith sees the comedy as Manichean, with darkness victorious at the end. In this case, Wilson becomes "just the addled, amiable dope his nickname makes him out to be" (210). I hope that I can clarify in the coming pages just what sort of a hero we find in *Pudd'nhead Wilson*.

Other critical impediments arise when we try to understand the world of the novel. Readers determined to see Twain as the founder of American Realism find the irreality of Dawson's Landing troublesome. The opening pages of the novel describe the town in plainly allegorical terms: isolated against the river by farmland and hills—like a medieval town, notes David L. Vanderwerken—Dawson's Landing boasts nothing but lovely small houses, fenced and flowered, all perfect, with a cat nearby to "prove title" (3). Twain even withdraws the town from the realm of historical reality by making it, in 1830, an improbable "fifty years old and . . . growing slowly—very slowly, in fact, but still . . . growing" (4). In *Adventures of Huckleberry Finn*, Twain mixed history and realism to represent a living past. In *A Connecticut Yankee in King Arthur's Court* he mixed allegory and history to create a fantastical field for ideas. In *Pudd'nhead Wilson*, he seems to have left out the history altogether. Few critics have been able to establish a cogent argument about the allegorical meaning of Dawson's Landing. George Spangler's "Parable of Property," John Brand's "The Incipient Wilderness," and Michael L. Ross' "Dawson's Landing and the Ladder of Nobility" all present cogent arguments on the nature of this tale's place. But determining the meaning of a fictive place must follow understanding the nature of its fictive reality, and these articles do not truly recognize the irreality of Dawson's Landing. In the next chapter, I will attempt to find a way to blend these critics' insights with an understanding of the book's fictive reality.

My main concerns in this book have been to first understand the sort of heroes Mark Twain has created and then understand the world in which they try to perform their heroic acts. *Adventures of Huckleberry Finn* and *A Connecticut Yankee in King Arthur's Court* present widely varied versions of traditional heroes. Oddly, the heroes of both novels end in similar failure. Huck, a hero of grand proportion, finds himself forced repeatedly into inaction by the great river of history. At the novel's end he simply disappears into the territories and leaves behind only his own mausoleum, in the form of a book. Despite his pugnacious and mechanical leanings, Hank Morgan's heroics show themselves to be psychological. As Morgan has no real personality but only a character type, his journey into the psyche will not aid him personally; it is meant rather as a model for readers. But he finds the combined mass of his ego and Arthurian allegorical historicity overwhelming. He disappears into the twin chasms between who he thinks he is and who he is, and between the present and the past. Both Huck and Hank fail as heroes because something in the way their worlds have been constructed make success within them impossible. In Huck, the traditional hero faces history; of course, history must win. In Hank, the self finds only ego when placed in history; and ego alone will not sustain heroic efforts. *Pudd'nhead Wilson*, presents another sort of hero. Can David Wilson maintain his heroism—that is, to continue to act heroically—in whatever world Mark Twain has constructed to challenge him?

The nature of David Wilson's heroics has attracted significant debate. While no one credits him with the sort of heroism we find in Hank Morgan or Huck Finn, Robert Regan finds him brimming with the sort of traditional heroism which Regan has attached to a stream of Twain figures. For Regan, Tom Sawyer, Hank Morgan, Tom Canty, and David Wilson all follow the model of the Unpromising Hero, the youngest son who, though not as heroic-appearing as the oldest son, wins the prize by cunning, luck, and fortitude. Regan views Wilson as "a man so superior to the citizens of the little Missouri town in which he settles that, incapable of understanding him, they conclude him to be an idiot" (208). Fundamental to this construction of David Wilson's heroism is "The radical, archetypal antagonism" (215) between Tom Driscoll and Wilson, in which Tom becomes the final product of the father-figures' lines. The Unpromising Hero wins his final victory over his evil father or the father's representative. In the trial, Wilson defeats both Tom and the prosecuting Pembroke Howard, the last of the old-line FFV aristocrats. But, Regan has the sense to note, "The Unpromising Hero motif—David Wilson's motif—is not the theme of the novel. The novel's theme is the whole problem of identity—the identity of the slave and the master, of the Negro and the white man, of the guilty and the innocent, of the hunter and hunted, and of the true and false leader" (217). In becoming the elected mayor of Dawson's Landing, Wilson becomes empowered to sort out the issues of identity causing disequilibrium in the town, because in so confused a place only the outsider possesses a reliable identity.

Regan makes many honest and valuable observations about *Pudd'nhead Wilson*, but he bends the novel to conform to his idea. He sees David Wilson's support of the code duello as "one of the most puzzling flaws in the intellectual structure of the novel" (215). Wilson had to support the duel to oppose Tom, Regan argues, even though this support makes him morally culpable; by rendering the duel comic and Wilson passive in it, Regan seems to say, Twain almost makes it appear that Wilson really doesn't support the code. Further, Regan asserts:

> From his first action in the novel (taking the fingerprints of the babies Chambers and Tom) to his last (proving that "Tom" is actually the slave Chambers and a murderer) Pudd'nhead's sole concern, conscious or unconscious, his sole objective, is to reveal the hidden truth of the society in which he lives not as a citizen but as a stranger. (216–17)

This assertion ignores much of the book. Wilson's friendship with the Judge, his interest in palmistry, his acquaintance with the twins, even his participation in the duel, have nothing to do with revealing his society's hidden truth. To make this argument stick, we must agree with Twain that Wilson is nothing but a cog in a machine with a dedicated narrative purpose, and therefore that he has no character outside that purpose. Such a perspective runs counter to readerly experience with the tale, in which David Wilson has more than a mechanical purpose. Remember that when he observes the girl in Tom's room and questions Mrs. Pratt in a way "that would have brought light-throwing answers as to that matter if Mrs. Pratt had any light to throw," he goes "away satisfied that he knew of things that were going on in her house of which she was not aware" (32). This is not the response of either a machine or of a man with only revelation in mind; his personal knowledge matters more to him than the acclaim he might gain by spreading that knowledge. When the vision of the town's hidden truth comes to him—in a dream, of all things; hardly the detective's sharpest tool—Wilson, surprised, "cried out—'It's so! Heavens, what a revelation! And for twenty-three years no man has ever suspected it!'" (104) Finally, Regan's assertion that Pudd'nhead achieves a moderately happy ending runs against the common experience of the novel. We can see this plainly in the very sentence where Regan makes the claim: "Once acquitted, Luigi and his brother Angelo, those still extravagant hold-overs from the original extravaganza, become 'heroes of romance.' But not Pudd'nhead; he is simply 'a made man for good' and the first citizen of Dawson's Landing" (211). The actual passage reads "The Twins were heroes of romance, now, and with rehabilitated reputations. But they were weary of Western adventure, and straightway retired to Europe" (114). Do romantic heroes flee their devotees? Regan ignores the obvious irony behind "heroes of romance" to avoid the same irony in "a made man for good." If Wilson has succeeded, why then do we feel sympathy instead of enthusiasm for him? David Wilson's success has not won him anything worth having.

Let us imagine the slate clean in evaluating David Wilson's heroism. We can agree to a few observations about him. He lacks traditional heroism; his twenty years of patient inactivity in the face of adverse misjudgment demonstrates that. Regan's argument that he conforms to the folk model of Unpromising Hero fails closer examination. Nor can we call him purely mechanical. There is no special reason to trust Twain's judgment on this: a league of others have followed the early critic who saw much more in Wilson's character. Critical failure to name that "something more" does not imply it does not exist. While David Wilson feels pleased with his acceptance in Dawson's Landing when it comes, he cannot be said to strive for it, Eberhard Alsen's article on the subject notwithstanding. While he takes social advantage of situations which come his way, he makes few changes in himself in order to suit his community. Although he gives up the public practice of palmistry, his quarter-century interest in fingerprints remains strong despite its unpopularity; he is not so much a stranger in the town, since everyone seems to know him, as he is an oddball. We have no reason to doubt that he is, as the narrator says, an educated New Yorker seeking his fortune, who has "an intelligent blue eye that had a frankness and a comradeship in it and a covert twinkle of a pleasant sort" (5). While the evidence remains somewhat ambiguous, according to some critics, we must admit the very strong possibility that David Wilson authored the maxims in his calendar. He is the tale's central character: he appears in almost every chapter in the book which, no matter which edition we use for the title, goes by his name. And because of our consensus on all of this, we have a consensus that, though we cannot be sure what kind, David 'Pudd'nhead' Wilson is a hero.

To understand what sort we must also understand what contributes to his heroic position. John C. Gerber describes the type of narrative we are dealing with in his "*Pudd'nhead Wilson* as Fabulation." Though his overall point will have more salience in the next chapter, the notion that the book is a fabulation and not a novel has a tremendous effect on how we view its characters. *Pudd'nhead Wilson* never lets us forget that it is a made-up story. While an unredeemably bad character, such as Tom Driscoll, would strain credulity where realism matters, he belongs in fabulation. In fabulation, too, we expect a hero to counter this villain, and generally we get one who is unerringly good. In this tale, we have David Wilson. Neither the twins, who might be frauds, nor the patricians, who are merely shadows of one another and more of a class than a character, qualify. Roxy crowds for attention, but must be denied from the first, where she exposes her bigotry in her jiving with Jasper (8). Doubters only need consider that her act of rescuing her son also imperils her charge; we know from the outset the impurity of her goodness. While we grow to question the nature of David Wilson's goodness, we do not reject it. Knowing the type of tale we read, we know what sort of hero to expect, and Wilson is our only choice, regardless of the questions he raises.

The fact that we question Wilson's goodness elevates the book above folk-variety fabulation. Clark Griffith observes that

> Wilson *is* different; he is set apart from the rest, I believe, because during fully nine-tenths of the novel which bears his name, he is never once required to do anything. As the pariah-figure, indeed, shunted to the edge of the community from the hour he arrived, he is effectively blocked off from participation in society. This may seem a hardship in his eyes. But where to act at all is, according to the law of life, to act badly, the moral advantages should be apparent to us. In an enforced solitude, puttering among concerns that effect no one else, Wilson remains the rare man whose capacity to be corrupted has not yet been tested. (221)

In this paragraph, Griffith describes Wilson in terms which allow us to see his uniqueness. When we grasp what makes this character unique we can begin where his goodness comes into question. Though we admire uniqueness and the courage it takes an individual to maintain it, uniqueness in a fictional character supposed to be unerringly good raises a moral question: If his behavior is unique, how can we compare it to other acts in order to judge its goodness? If he is simply better than the rest, a shading of character natural to realistic fiction but improper to fabulation, then Wilson's character does not match his form, and Robert Wiggins is right about the quality of the book. But if, instead, David Wilson's character and heroism forces us to reconsider what we understand as goodness, we can agree with Leslie Fiedler in saying that "*Pudd'nhead Wilson* is, after all, a fantastically good book, better than Mark Twain knew or his critics have deserved" (130).

David Wilson's heroism grows in importance through comparison. Only Tom and Roxy are in Wilson's class as characters in the fable; only they can stand beside him for comparison. Many critics have rightly observed the book's deliberate pairing of Tom and Wilson. Barry Wood notes that "Tom represents that disruption of community life that comes with persistent crime and outright lawlessness, exactly balancing the isolated power of law represented by Wilson" (375). Elucidating the theme of property in the book, George Spangler sees a paired opposition on the issue of materialism. "If Tom typifies obsession with property, Wilson is largely dissociated from property, particularly from material success" (31). John Brand, in his article on "The Incipient Wilderness," recognizes how the tale marginalizes both Tom and Wilson on the Western edge of town, with the line between them defining the edge of civilization. And Michael Ross clarifies Tom's biographical likeness to the hero. Tom, "with his ironical and more sophisticated idiom, is sharply distinguished both from his real mother, Roxy, and from his supposed FFV kinsmen. Throughout the novel, he is most closely associated with the other Eastern-educated character, Pudd'nhead Wilson" (251). These likenesses and differences are fundamental to their opposition.

This opposition between Wilson and Tom carries many complications. We cannot assume that because we think we understand the nature of Tom's evil that we understand Wilson's goodness. Alsen's response to Spangler's article points out that David Wilson's vow to Tom—that he would have withheld Tom's case against Luigi and sacrificed his legal launching until Judge Driscoll could have responded more appropriately—is a lie. "If Wilson had really been concerned about the Judge's sense of family honor, he certainly would have kept the case out of court until the Judge returned from his hunting trip later that same day" (39). We cannot know if Wilson's hungering for the spotlight motivates him or not; we can only say that an absolute truthfulness—at least when dealing with a "fickle-tempered, dissipated young goose" (62), as Wilson characterizes Tom just before employing his lie—is not one of David Wilson's virtues. But we knew this from his calendar entry introducing the first chapter: "Tell the truth or trump—but get the trick" (3). Truthfulness is not in and of itself virtuous in this tale; both Tom and Wilson lie.

The true nature of this opposition becomes clearer if we look carefully at the aspects of each character which conflict. Perhaps the firmest opposition comes at each character's first important appearance. Remember that David Wilson tells his joke about the dog "much as one who is thinking aloud" (5), which is to say with the same sort of naturalness we employ in conversations with ourselves. The joke itself displays an "uncanny" misunderstanding of truths the perhaps humorless town knows instinctively; it shows the townfolk that Wilson's brains have been whipped into the creamy oneness of pudding. They are right, in one important sense: Wilson, when he arrives in Dawson's Landing, does not seem able to distinguish between what is said to oneself and what is said to others. Tom begins his life in artifice and has little trouble mastering the differences between the internal and external selves. Though the discovery of his true identity changes him like the "gigantic irruption . . . of Krakatoa" (44), in fact "no familiar of his could have detected anything in him that differentiated him from the weak and careless Tom of other days" (45). Twain explains this simply: "Tom imagined that his character had undergone a pretty radical change. But that was because he did not know himself" (45). Tom's one confusion about socially correct behavior—his foppish Eastern dress—demonstrates only that Tom is capable of making a bad choice in public behavior, not that he in any way confuses the personal and social selves. "The local fashion" suits "the dull country town" (24); these objects virtually stand in for each other as they are presented. When Tom finds he has chosen the wrong field on which to battle his ennui, he accepts conformity in clothing and instead changes location. Tom's point is to battle boredom. Whether he does so with clothes or place seems to matter little to him. Tom dons a plethora of disguises, as though identity, being a matter entirely private, has no value at all.

Contrast Wilson, who "had a rich abundance of idle time, but it never hung heavy on his hands, for he interested himself in every new thing that was born into the universe of ideas" (7). David Wilson is always David Wilson, regardless of the situation or the goal. His participation in the duel, which bothers many critics—who would prefer Wilson impeccable according to some prefashioned moral code perhaps as untenable as the code duello—follows this principle. A friend to both principals in the duel, and having already represented Luigi in court, Wilson fulfills his personal obligation without concern as to the objective morality of the issue. Tom has no secure identity: he knows something is bad and does it anyway. He not only sells his mother down the river to save his own skin, but he also repeats the performance on the request of a stranger (88). He can intend to rob and end up murdering; he can act informed with so little self that even the perspicacious Pudd'nhead cannot imagine him capable of murder. Wilson on the other hand only has identity. Before the end of the tale, his only act is to retain his identity after being cruelly misnamed.

If we compare the explicit thoughts of Tom and Wilson, the point of this opposition comes clear. Even Tom's most honest exposition to himself explodes out of anger at his own birth. "He said to himself that if his father were only alive and in reach of assassination his mother would soon find that he had a very clear notion of the size of his indebtedness to that man" (70). Note that even this absolutely internal expression of Tom's emotional self includes the perception of himself from the outside. He does not think 'I would kill him'; he thinks 'I will show Roxy. . . .' David Wilson, on the other hand, even in his most public scene, does not think of himself in terms of other people's perceptions. He manipulates his performance to suit the crowd, but he does not manipulate his understanding of himself. His one articulated thought in the courtroom scene (109) concerns his own perceptions of Tom's and the audience's responses. To Tom, even the most private thoughts are public performance; to Wilson, even public performance requires the integrity of private thought.

We can grasp the nature of this difference between Tom Driscoll and David Wilson by reading Robert C. Solomon's explanation of Jean-Paul Sartre's notion of authenticity in *From Rational-ism to Existentialism: The Existentialists and Their Nineteenth-Century Backgrounds*:

> It is only looking at ourselves as others see us that we attribute selfhood to ourselves. It is this view of oneself as another which will form one of the foundations of *bad faith*. It is Sartre's explicit task in philosophy (as it was Heidegger's nonexplicit task) to al-low us to break out of this perspective of oneself as another and allow us to see ourselves as ourselves (that is, 'authentically' or 'sincerely'). (274)

We cannot actually blame Tom's specific immorality on his inauth-enticity. But because *Pudd'nhead Wilson* is a fabulation and not a novel, Tom's personal motivations carry less meaning than the sym-bolic associations of his actions, and his evil and inauthenticity fit together as neatly as Wilson's goodness and authenticity. Tom and Wilson are alike in many things, tied structurally, thematically, and narratively in the book, but in the matter of existential authenticity they differ widely. This is the crux of their symbolic opposition.

This interpretation allows us to clear up some of the doubts critics have expressed over David Wilson's heroism, most particu-larly about his acceptance of the dominant morality of Dawson's Landing. We can say that the questions we have about Pudd'nhead's unerring goodness grow out of the difficulty we all have in accept-ing Existentialism's dissociation between conventional morality and the ethics of personal authenticity. David Wilson's capitulation to the foul morality of Dawson's Landing comes to him at no cost psychologically, financially, socially, or ethically; in fact, he gains significantly by it. Only our readerly attachment to an external mo-rality—one we believe better than the town's, to be sure, but still a matter of no importance to "the whole problem of identity"—raises doubts as to David Wilson's heroism. But we must release our at-tachment to preconceived morality if we hope to understand how David Wilson's behavior can represent an existential goodness, as we know his opposition to the evil and inauthentic Tom means he must. We will find the key to that understanding exactly where Wil-son unlocks the mystery of his entire tale: in fingerprints, the oily proof of identity.

Before we can get to Wilson's answer to the problem of identity, we need to explore the second of his oppositions in the book. In the last chapter of the book, Wilson instructs both us and Dawson's Landing in the nature of a certain sort of identity. His instruction destroys Tom—he exists neither literally nor figuratively when the lesson is over—but the instruction only defeats Roxy. "Roxy's heart was broken. . . . Her hurts were too deep for money to heal; the spirit in her eye was quenched, her martial bearing departed with it, and the voice of her laughter ceased in the land" (114). Tom is the tale's perpetrator of evil, but Roxy is his creator. David Wilson's defeat of her must tell us something of his heroism.

Critics love Roxy. Many have pointed out that she is the only complete woman Twain invented. Henry Nash Smith wrote in *Mark Twain: The Development of a Writer* that she is "the only fully developed character, in the novelistic sense, in the book. She has a different order of fictional reality from the figures of fable with which she is surrounded" (179). This seems to mean two things in the book itself: unlike Tom's and Wilson's, her actions are morally mixed; and she has the privilege of acting in ways simultaneously real and grand. She alone seems to perceive the world of Dawson's Landing as we do. As Leavis writes, "Without being in the least sentimentalized, or anything but dramatically right, she plainly bodies forth the qualities that Mark Twain, in his whole being, most values—qualities that, as Roxy bears witness, he profoundly believes in as observable in humanity, having known them in experience" (134). Because of this representation of authorial values, Roxy must act to right the wrongs around her. "Roxy's exchange" of the infants, writes David Vanderwerken, "is an attempt to sabotage the white social feudal structure" (10). We agree with the narrator, who we might argue agrees with Roxy, saying slaves "had an unfair show in the battle of life, and they held it no sin to take military advantage of the enemy—in a small way; in a small way, but not in a large one" (11). So, though Roxy herself may not be fully aware that she is the symbol for our high sentiments, she acts with some consistency as though she is. Roxy's refusal to steal at first, based on a temporary religious rejuvenation, in time subsides enough that she can encourage Tom on his raids. We do not mind this much; Roxy still champions our ethical position by stealing from slave-holders. When Tom's cowardice or perfidy runs counter to the higher moral purpose of disturbing the evil social order, as when he drags Luigi to court or sells Roxy down the river, she lambastes him. Because she more or less consistently holds the higher moral ground, Roxy would be the hero of this fiction, if it were a conventional novel. As further proof, her courage, her intelligence, and her strength get her precisely what similar heroic characteristics have gotten Twain's heroes in *Huckleberry Finn* and *Connecticut Yankee*: failure.

But *Pudd'nhead Wilson* is not a conventional novel, and Roxy's likeness to conventional heroes only reinforces what should by now be obvious: that the real hero of this book is the man who does not fail, though his success might be tragic. Roxy knows this herself. "'Dey ain't but one man dat I's afeard of, en dat's Pudd'nhead Wilson.... He's the smartes' man in dis town ... ; *I* b'lieve he's a witch'" (16). Roxy and Wilson have a sort of equality about them. The acceptance of racism and the code duello readers find so disturbing in the book is in fact the acceptance our two hero-candidates share. Roxy is the only one who can sort out David Wilson's schemes, as with the paired rewards for the twins' lost knife and its thief. They even have scenes which balance one another, as when Wilson, alone in his house, listens in on Roxy's sparring with Jasper (7–9), and when Roxy tells Tom of being a hidden witness to the duel (71–72). Roxy, Michael Ross says, is Twain's leading example of "an aristocracy of nature that is independent of pedigree" (250); we must grant that Wilson, by his very success, is a candidate for the same aristocracy.

In a tale as neatly constructed as *Pudd'nhead Wilson*, individuals who pair also conflict. But where the opposition between Wilson and Tom becomes the moral center of the book's action, the opposition between Roxy and Wilson becomes its spiritual center. In plot, they oppose one another only over Tom. Their other oppositions are the abstract implications of independently derived desires. Wilson seeks two things: "to live down his reputation" (7) and to gain 'revelation' of a 'mystery', words used repeatedly in connection with his work with fingerprints (7, 49, 104). Roxy seeks to avoid the pain of losing her son (Chapter 3) and to obscure the truth of both her son's identity and her own. These practical desires lead Roxy and Wilson to the final courtroom scene, where these desires at last come to battle. Roxy comes out at the short ends of these conflicts over desires. On the material side, and as a result of the same act, Wilson lives down his reputation and Roxy loses her son.

But this settles only one of the two conflicts between Wilson and Roxy. The other concerns their desires to either reveal or obscure identity. While Tom is the practical reward for the victor of the first conflict, he becomes only the symbolic representation of the second. This difference in Tom's position between two possible protagonists emphasizes what we must call the spiritual nature of Wilson's and Roxy's opposition on the issue of identity. Tom symbolizes this opposition—his identity is obscured; he is the visible representation of the conflict imbedded in these opposing abstract desires—but, because he is a symbol and not a reward, he also shows that the book does not truly solve the problem of identity. This abstract opposition outlives the book. Tom's ambiguous identity as the tale closes shows this. Several critics have noted that Tom's final journey down river makes no sense: Chambers was either counted for Tom in Percy Driscoll's estate already, or the Tom-Chambers slave was not part of the estate. In either case, Tom would not be liable for sale. Critics who complain of this as a logical flaw look for realism, but, in this parable of inverted slavery, property stands for identity. The final ambiguity over Tom's position in the ledger books leaves open the question of who won the battle over identity.

David Wilson's defeat of Roxy implies a victor but does not prove one. Whether *Pudd'nhead Wilson* reveals or obscures the nature of identity remains unclear. The division of critical sympathies between Wilson and Roxy for hero shows that readers themselves remain unsure whether they prefer revelation or mystery. This is beyond doubt a spiritual quandary, and the book presents it as such. Critics have explored themes of twinship, medievalism, property, appearance and reality, animals, and Western expansion in *Pudd'nhead Wilson*. No one has yet given a detailed account of religion and spirituality in the book, although Stanley Brodwin's essay on "Blackness and the Adamic Myth" brings out several salient aspects of this theme. Percy Driscoll, he notes (170), behaves like a god in sparing the thieving slaves from a trip down the river, which the narrator tells us "was the equivalent of damning them to hell! No Missouri negro doubted this" (12). Roxy's temporary religious revival saves her from this fate once; she could not be sure it would save her in the future. She switches the children to save her son from a future in hell, using a preacher's parable as her justification, but the act sours. Brodwin sees the fact that "'Tom' was a bad baby, from the very beginning of his usurpation" (17) as a punishment to Roxy for her sin. This is a much more intelligent conclusion than the point of some early critics that this proves that Tom's spot of black blood made him evil; if that were the case his badness would have shown before the usurpation, not as an implied result of it. Brodwin writes, "It is Roxana's fate to be both creator and victim of Tom" (174); "she has played God, and she has been used by men playing God" (176). Brodwin leaps from this to the overarching conclusion that "In the end, there is only the realization that man is tricked by God or Providence and his own sinful nature into thinking that through choice (Roxana) or through the saving grace of ironic humor (Pudd'nhead) he could change destiny and reform the world and himself" (176).

This reaches outside the text. There is, after all, very little reason to believe that Dawson's Landing comes under any Providential eye. Further, Roxy is more powerful than Brodwin gives her credit for, and in the end she is defeated not by God but by Pudd'nhead Wilson. But still, his concern with the book's spiritual material and his observations that "For Roxana, Pudd'nhead is a kind of witch-priest" and "Pudd'nhead, with all his aphorisms about Adam, functions as the servant of God" (171) come with true insight. We must accept that, if there is no actual God in Dawson's Landing, there is at least some force balancing all the pairs of good and evil.

Clark Griffith seems much more on target when he writes "The truth is that, crouched beside the cradles, [Roxy] is less Madonna than Witch, a figure from the outer dark, presiding at an unholy ceremony of changelings. Nothing good can come of her undertaking, for it involves a violation, emphatic and terrible, of the very humanity it was meant to assert" (210). Roxy's darkness, as a thing apart from her blackness, accounts for a host of improbabilities in the book: her decision "to tote along a hoss-shoe to keep off de witch-work" (16) when she visits Wilson; her subsequent lack of fear and occupancy of the haunted house; her ability to convince Tom of the truth of his birth without proof. Her power has aspects of magic to it. It comes not so much from thought and science as from feeling and experience. Her acts do not instruct but protest. As Griffith points out, if

> slavery asserts the supremacy of white to black, it is in actuality
> the very essence of blackness, darkening with corruption every

human heart it touches. . . . It is not simply that what began as
her act of devotion ends up corrupting Roxy, turning her, as she
herself recognizes, into the most miserable of sinners. . . . No,
the full outrage she perpetrated runs deeper still. In defying
blackness, she succeeds only in increasing and intensifying the
black. (219–20)

She uses her spiritual power to obscure identity in the hope that
the confusion will overturn the fundamental blackness of her
world; but the very obscurity of identity between white and black *is*
that fundamental blackness. Neither Roxy nor her magic are evil
in themselves; they promote evil, that is all. David Wilson, in spiritual opposition to Roxy, can only mend the tear she makes, not
eliminate the fabric.

If Roxy wears a black witch's cloak, Wilson wears the habili-
ment of a prophet. His calendar entries indicate this. When the
Judge shows them to the townfolk, "They read those playful trifles
in the solidest earnest, and decided without hesitancy that if there
had been any doubt that David Wilson was a pudd'nhead—which
there hadn't—this revelation removed that doubt for good and all"
(25). But if this revelation removes the town's doubt, it plants our
suspicion that Wilson has extraordinary wisdom. Tom, in trying to
embarrass Wilson in front of the newly-arrived twins, spills more
than he knows: "David's just an all-around genius, a genius of the
first water, gentlemen, a great scientist running to seed here in this
village, a prophet with the kind of honor that prophets generally
get at home" (49). Wilson goes on to prove this japery true by dis-
covering Luigi's murderous past in the Italian's palm. After this,
Wilson behaves in a strikingly irreproachable manner: he is asked
to run for mayor and wins honestly; he keeps Luigi's awful confidence even when the pressure not to mounts; he warns the twins
about the threat behind the Judge's refusal to duel Luigi a second
time. Wilson's prophet-like ability to see the invisible finally comes
clear during the trial. Tom thinks to himself, "The man that can
track a bird through the air in the dark at night and find that bird
is the man to track me out and find the Judge's assassin—no other
need apply. And that is the job that has been laid out for poor
Pudd'nhead Wilson, of all the people in the world!" (102). Wilson
of course does track Tom, through the heavenly revelation of a
dream. In an unpublished paper, Roderick McConnell notes David

Wilson's saintly qualities: his quiet patience, surviving twenty-three "weary long" years before his acceptance; his kindness even to his persecutors; and his dignity, as when he is "deeply gratified" (66) by his nomination for mayor. As the book ends, all this saintly prophet's, this morally refined teacher's "sentences were golden, now, all were marvelous" (114).

This notion of David Wilson as a religious hero should not strike Twain scholars as jarring. By the time *Pudd'nhead Wilson* was published, Twain was already at work on the book he later claimed to have cared the most about, a book he published under a second pseudonym because he feared people would laugh if they thought he had written it. This book is *Personal Recollections of Joan of Arc*. In Joan, Twain found a romantic hero mixed with a religious hero, with both romantic failure and religious vindication documented by history. The Joan he depicts has the gift of prophecy via revelation; she rises to authority by general assent; she has the friendship of the king; she wins her battles as much by wit as by pluck; she is persecuted by a community's willful ignorance; she proves herself at a court trial. We find these same qualities in Pudd'nhead, though, stripped of the authority of history, Twain cannot assert Wilson's sainthood. *Pudd'nhead Wilson* and *Joan of Arc* even share some images and some language. The invisible dragon at the beginning of the later book—about which the narrator, Sieur le Conte, says, "It gives one a horrid idea of how near to us the deadliest danger can be and we not suspect it" (8)—reminds us of Dawson's Landing's invisible dog. Even one of Wilson's aphorisms, about the necessity of ending habits slowly, appears in full in *Joan of Arc*. Religious heroes were on Twain's mind while he wrote *Pudd'nhead*; no doubt its hero picked up some of their characteristics. Clark Griffith acknowledges this. "We are brought to the realization that in a book much about the complexities of twinship, the authentically identical twins are these: . . . demonic Roxy, crouched beside the cradles in 1830, and angelic Wilson, standing erect at the bar of justice in 1853" (221). Between this pair the issue of authentic identity remains in doubt. We have sympathy for the devil who wants to trash the whole stinking system, and we have reverence for the prophet who can teach us the nature of authentic identity.

We can now understand the limits of David Wilson's success, which lie in the dual nature of what we mean by identity. The core issue of *Pudd'nhead Wilson* is not simply identity, but also 'identity,' a term which connotes two contradictory notions. 'Identity' both individualizes and pairs: to say Roxy and Wilson have identity is to say both that they have marks which distinguish them from one another and that, no matter how distinguishable, they are not separable. These two individuals form a single unit. John Brand detects this. He writes in "The Other Half: A Study of *Pudd'nhead Wilson*" that "Dawson's Landing is becoming the seat of a dreadful Nemesis" (14). This nemesis is both separate from and the same as its other. The marginally separated twins represent this relationship emblematically. In one of the vestigia from "Those Extraordinary Twins," Luigi explains saving his brother's life by saying "Suppose I hadn't saved Angelo's life, what would have become of mine? If I had let the man kill him, wouldn't he have killed me, too?" (52)—as though both deaths would result from a single blow. Brand, noting that Tom and Roxy each disguise themselves as the opposite sex, writes, "Both Tom and Roxy are adepts at disguise, both, suggestively, succeeding in flight by pretending to be the other half. In their closeness they are strangers; in their separateness they are akin" (15). This nemesis plagues David Wilson. In the end it disturbs his passivity and forces him to choose to act either for it or against it. In the final trial scene, either he keeps silent about his revelation, risking both his own authenticity and the lives of the twins, or he destroys his own nemesis and thus in an important sense himself.

In *Pudd'nhead Wilson* the two meanings of 'identity' battle. Most all the characters in the book represent in one way or another the notion of likeness. The inseparability of the FFV patriarchs—Robert Regan refers to these men, whose sins inhabit their sons' world, as "the collective father-figure for Pudd'nhead, their odious features covered, but only partially, by an attractive disguise of kindly behavior and gracious living" (214)—demonstrates this essential identity. So too the identity between Thomas à Beckett Driscoll and Valet de Chambre: different only by "a fiction of law and custom," the father of one and by extension the father of both cannot distinguish them. Wilson, the expert in individuation, while giving no evidence that he cannot distinguish the babies, notes their similarity. This fundamental identity or likeness between slave and master is one of the story's few moral compasses: the creation of artificial difference does not change the innate likeness of things. The story of the dog that damns Wilson on his first arrival in Dawson's Landing provides the corollary. Remarking on Wilson's idiocy, one citizen asks, "'What did he reckon would become of the other half if he killed his half? Do you reckon he thought it would live?'" (5) If half the split object is destroyed, the object itself is destroyed.

This notion of the identity of two stretches itself into the far reaches of our imagination. Not only likeness, but also difference become criteria for identity. The tale's insistent twinning of events suggests a moral ecology, where everything is part of one thing. Robert Rowlette's monograph on *Pudd'nhead* documents dozens of these instances (114–17) and notes that the variation on these repetitions often includes reversal: Tom's victory at the first trial and loss at the second, for example. This repetition creates a unity even between events which invert each other and characters who oppose or invert each other. Tom's dressing as a woman and Roxy's dressing as a man, each for the purpose of escape, creates an imaginative bonding of opposites. Tom and Roxy then have an identity. A review of the book makes this obvious; the events in each one's life change the other's fate. The notion of identity which makes a unit of master and slave makes units of other opposites as well. If the FFV patriarchs have identity through their likeness, pairs such as Tom and Wilson or Wilson and Roxy have identity through their opposition. The same rules apply to these units as apply to those which have identity through likeness: the creation of artificial differences does not change their fundamental unity; destroying one destroys both.

But these identities of likeness and opposition describe only one half of what we mean by 'identity.' The other half is individuation. David Wilson champions this idea in the tale, and he does so alone. Roxy's primary act in the novel is to scramble individuals. The Judge, hardly an individual himself, cannot distinguish between angelic children and devilish ones. Explaining the Judge's affection for Tom, Wilson tells the twins, "A devil born to a young couple is measurably recognizable by them as a devil before long, but a devil adopted by an old couple is an angel to them, and remains so, through thick and thin" (93). Tom apparently inherits his father-figures' blindness, repeatedly directing his anger against the wrong people, obvious evidence of an inability to distinguish individuality. When he hears of his mother's mistreatment at the Arkansas plantation, "Tom's heart was fired—with fury against the planter's wife" (86). Tom also misdirects his feelings about the twins: he "hated the one twin for kicking him, and the other one for being the kicker's brother" (74).

On the other hand, from the start, the tale marks Wilson as a man able to distinguish separate identities. He is the only true friend to each of the twins, eerie symbols of identity of likeness and opposition. He never categorizes the people of the town, even though they seek uniformly to give him a new identity. He becomes expert in the only tool available for distinguishing individuality, as his courtroom explanation (108–11) makes clear. And, perhaps most importantly, he never loses track of his own identity. This issue is of central importance in the book. Roxy, "the dupe of her own deceptions" (19), loses perspective on herself as she raises Tom. The Judge knows himself only as a gentleman, not as a human being. Tom has no idea who he is. The twins might well be frauds; we do not know what they believe about themselves and so their possible fraudulence must stand for Angelo's and Luigi's own notions of themselves. Only David Wilson succeeds in holding on to an identity built from within.

In Sartrean terms, the failure to hold on to an internally understood identity is inauthenticity, a result of bad faith. Solomon describes four kinds of bad faith: identifying oneself as a thing; identifying oneself as another person; refusing to recognize the importance of Being-for-others, or in other words being a human among humans; and the denial of one's own freedom (299–301). We can see these forms of bad faith in *Pudd'nhead Wilson*. Roxy, calling herself a slave, becomes an object, an FFV's "chattel, his property, his goods," as Tom puts it, "and he can sell [her], just as he could his dog" (45). The Judge identifies himself as a Driscoll and a gentleman, and this allows him to deny the truth about Tom, as when Pembroke Howard assures him against the rumor of Tom's court case, "You know it's a lie as well as I do, old friend. He is of the best blood of the Old Dominion" (59). Tom has no notion at all of social responsibility, even as enlightened self-interest; the bad faith involved in his selling Roxy down the river needs no discussion. Angelo's recital of the twin's history describes their early life as slavery, and this is in some ways bad faith on the matter of freedom; this issue is extremely complex and I will discuss it in greater detail in the next chapter. Slavery is *Pudd'nhead Wilson's* constant theme.

David Wilson's response to his world differs from the other

characters. Though he acknowledges the condemnation to living as a sort of slavery, Wilson clearly makes a free choice to stay in Dawson's Landing and therefore does not see himself, except in the larger sense of the circumstances of life, as condemned to slavery. He accepts the roles of leader and peacemaker easily. The deepness of his gratification implies that he does not accept power as an aid to determining his identity but as a result of the identity he already has; this is true Being-for-others. I have already pointed out how Wilson's comments to himself about himself demonstrate the clarity with which he sees himself as distinct from the both the people and the objects around him. Though it is extremely difficult to ascribe authenticity to a character in fiction—even more difficult when that character, because of the constraints of fabulation, is meant to represent unerring goodness—we can say at least that David Wilson appears to symbolize authentic individuation, both in his ability to distinguish himself from others and in his ability to distinguish between others.

If we begin to see the tale in terms of conflict between the two sorts of identity, we can understand the nature of David Wilson's heroism. He champions the individual notion of identity. Throughout most of the book he remains inactive, perhaps honoring Sartre's dictum "To be is to do." By his presence alone he threatens Roxy's and Tom's enterprises. His hand is forced in the end by the threat to the twins. Armed with the dreamed revelation of Tom's true identity, he instructs the gathered town in the use of the tools of individuation. Tom makes the actual use of these tools unnecessary—we might say Tom declares his own identity in a final authentic act—by his fainting confession. The narrator refers to Tom in the Conclusion as "Tom," reflecting the nonexistence of his identity or any object to which his name refers. The demon figure Roxy, now defeated, receives appropriate punishment: "In her church and its affairs she found her only solace" (114).

Wilson succeeds only in very limited terms; while he remains authentic and communicates this quality as a new measure of virtue, his material accomplishments come at a high cost. "Wilson's 'success'," Coburn writes, "is only the measure of his limitations: he becomes the chief citizen in a city of the blind" (219). Wilson's Calendar entry before the Conclusion shows he is aware of his own predicament. It reads simply *"October 12, the Discovery. It was wonderful to find America, but it would have been more wonderful to miss it"*

(113). David Wilson makes the necessary sacrifice so that the abstract value of authentic identity will remain intact, but he has destroyed his Nemesis in destroying Tom. As a result, he has destroyed that part of himself we have come to value: his separation from the town. David Wilson has lost his individual identity: he is still Pudd'nhead Wilson, but the town is a town of pudd'nheads. Wilson's attempt to preserve authenticity, both in himself and as an abstract value, does not succeed; the other form of identity, identity as likeness, has won in the end, and Wilson is martyr to the battle. David Wilson's final calendar entry seems to acknowledge that discovery and revelation are two sides of the same coin, but this coin buys nothing but pain.

I have chosen to downplay the twins in this discussion because, without what has preceded, the following makes little sense. Murial Williams points out that, in the absence of the Italians, "We may assume the imposture would have continued undetected. . . . Without the twins, it is logical, assuming the murder, to reconstruct the sequence thus: no suspect, no arrest, no trial, no exposure of Tom" (52). They are the catalyst for events, what Williams calls "an ominous and enigmatic force." We have a typographical clue as to the nature of this force in the capitalization of Twins. In the Norton Critical Edition textual notes we read:

> In a few instances, however, the word 'twins' was written with a lower case *t*, and then—just as clearly—the t was capitalized. Hence, in ambiguous cases, when the word 'twins' is used to refer directly to Luigi and Angelo, it has been capitalized. (180)

These foreigners come from somewhere and disappear again, like the other-worldly visitor Twain later employed as The Mysterious Stranger. They change the world while they are there but offer no judgment on it; they had, after all, seen "some fifteen or sixteen hundred thousand" (31) identical towns. The result of their visit is to destroy Tom, punish Roxy, and 'sivilize' David Wilson, integrating him into the ecology of Dawson's Landing. Clark Griffith sees Angelo and Luigi as representing "the Angelic and the Luciferian"; they are, in any case, twins of light and dark, of conventional good and bad, godly and wild, innocently passive and actively suspect. It is as though they are sent from the world outside of Dawson's Landing to stand for the problem of identity their presence brings to light. Since Dawson's Landing is our world, they are from some other. Perhaps the invisible dog was insufficient provocation to shake the balance of identities; the Twins had to come too. They make it necessary that David Wilson find that invisible dog again, not so that he can rid the community of it, but so that he will kill half of it and then watch while the other half dies. Wilson finds the dog and kills the half that is Tom—a variety of essays on the subject prove that sufficiently—but, as a result, his individuality dies as well. That is what the Twins, the perhaps deific emblem of the ominous and enigmatic, desire. David Wilson saves the Twins, but that saving act only surrenders the very ideal the act is meant to embody. It is an heroic gesture—and an heroic failure.

The hero of this book does much more than act the hero's part. He becomes a prophet of identity. David Wilson lights the way toward a future conception of heroism. He demonstrates an individual—and therefore personally practicable—form of heroism. The fact that our world has trouble recognizing authenticity as heroism in no way diminishes its plain role in *Pudd'nhead Wilson*, or its wider value. This resistance only makes clear exactly what Mark Twain meant when he called his tale a tragedy.

# 7

❧❦❧

# Dawson's Landing

*Pudd'nhead Wilson* begins with an extended description of Dawson's Landing. This captivatingly irreal portrait of the town sets the conditions for everything which follows. Few characters cross the physical boundaries of Dawson's Landing and fewer still its moral restrictions. Just as Twain uses this description to cast his book, so many critics use it to cast their criticism. Leslie Fiedler sees Dawson's Landing as a mythicized Hannibal, somewhat like St. Petersburg, but universalized by being rendered for us from the outside. Louis H. Leiter, in his "Dawson's Landing: Thematic Cityscape in Twain's *Pudd'nhead Wilson*," says the place is presented as though Twain "were trying to make his American town serve as a microcosm for the whole world" (8). Michael Ross points out that we recognize the description of Dawson's Landing "as not a naive, but as a slyly prettified, tableau of Smalltown, USA. It sounds—and is—too good to be true; and before long Twain introduces the fly in the democratic ointment" (245–46)—slavery. David Vanderwerken explains that *Pudd'nhead Wilson*, coming as it does between *A Connecticut Yankee* and *Joan of Arc*, portrays its setting not as a true Missouri antebellum town but as a stylized medieval one. And Mark Coburn writes, "the communal norms of Dawson's Landing, the antebellum Missouri village in which the novel is set, determine every character's thoughts and actions" (210), giving credence to the town's historical veracity but still seeing in it power that a collection of streets, shops, and houses cannot realistically possess. No critic I have read asserts that Dawson's Landing has the sort of realism of *Tom Sawyer*'s St. Petersburg or *Huckleberry Finn*'s Pokeville, Bricksville, or Pikesville. Instead, critics acknowledge that Dawson's Landing is a powerful place, and the purpose of this chapter is to discover the nature and use of its power.

We can say without fear of contradiction that Dawson's Landing is not presented as the setting of realistic fiction, whatever its metaphoric power:

> It was snug little collection of modest one- and two-story frame dwellings whose whitewashed exteriors were almost concealed from sight by climbing tangles of rose vines, honeysuckles and morning-glories. Each of these pretty homes had a garden in front fenced with white palings and opulently stocked with holly-hocks, marigolds, touch-me-nots, prince's feathers and other old-fashioned flowers. (3)

A realistic rendition of setting differentiates house from house, but in Dawson's Landing all the houses look alike: small and white and encased in flowers. Its uniformity tells us immediately of its artificiality; houses do not belong to individuals so much as they belong to members of the town, who for the most part remain as undistinguished from one another as the houses they inhabit. The description reinforces the generality of place with the observation that "a well fed, well petted, and properly revered cat" proves the perfection of the home—any home—in which it is found. We learn that the homes of Dawson's Landing are perfect not because we are told so directly, but because those homes meet the general conditions of perfection, which apply regardless of place. The particularities of the place matter less here than the general conditions it fulfills.

The geographical situation of Dawson's Landing contribute to this image of irreality:

> The hamlet's front was washed by the clear waters of the great river; its body stretched itself rearward up a gentle incline; its most rearward border fringed itself out and scattered its houses about the base line of the hills; the hills rose high, enclosing the town in a half-moon curve, clothed with forests from foot to summit. (3)

The town's uniformity tallies well with its personification: it is a single entity. Dawson's Landing is isolated; nothing at all seems to exist over the hills. Connected by the river to ports of call a thousand miles distant, the town gets regular service only from the little lines; the big ones stop "for hails only" (4). The litany of other rivers and other places more weakens than strengthens the sense

of connection between Dawson's Landing and the other places; after all, nothing particularizes this town, except the fact that we read
about it. The "transient" boats, which stop only for hails, "were
bound every whither and stocked with every imaginable comfort or
necessity which the Mississippi's communities could want" (4). They
have no particular connection with Dawson's Landing; if the town
could supply itself the boats would never stop at all. Because the
place is so isolated it can have its own special reality. We do not
expect the social laws of real towns to apply in Dawson's Landing.
We do not expect law at all and, as John Brand points out in "The
Incipient Wilderness," we get very little of it.

The social structure about which we are told simplifies the
place completely out of reality. The town has a "chief citizen" who
also happens to be "Judge of the county court." The Judge has
three aristocratic equals and this core group determines the social
life and moral customs of Dawson's Landing. Certainly no one
seems to doubt the Judge's right to escort the exotic foreign twins
around town after the reception at Aunt Patsy's. Neither does anyone object to the later duel between the Judge and one of his erstwhile guests, even though duelling had, historically anyway, passed
out of fashion by the 1850s. Most of the remainder of the town's
citizens fill roles as members of the chorus; only Aunt Patsy Cooper
and her daughter Rowena (as hostesses to the twins), the slave
Jasper, and Justice Robinson, politician Buckstone, and constable
Blake (as the nomination committee and functionaries in other
small ways) earn mention by name. Even these characters are simply featured voices from the chorus, pretty much interchangeable
parts of the whole citizenry, which appears to have power only as a
voting mass. But even this power is limited by the Judge's purse
and opinions, as the election results show. The slaves have no
power whatsoever, but they are always around, presumably working the land that provides Dawson's Landing's economic base, but
only presumably since we never see any farming or trade. The rigid
hierarchy comes in for no direct criticism in the book; the tale's
social conscience appears limited to issues of slavery. But what is
meant by 'slavery' in Dawson's Landing remains a question.

It seems unlikely that slavery in Dawson's Landing is identical
to historical slavery in the American South, since the tale creates
doubt as to the very historicity of Dawson's Landing. The series of
errors John O. West and James M. Day note in "Mark Twain's

Comedy of Errors in *Pudd'nhead Wilson*" include a few that bio-graphical critics would argue Twain could not have mistaken and which therefore must be purposeful. Purposeful or not, these errors of geography and history continue the impression of ahistoricity first painted in the opening description. The book implies that the town's founding came in 1780, when St. Louis itself was little more than a French village across the river from a fort. A Mississippi river town growing "very slowly" in 1830 was close to a town dying anywhere else; Western expansion and the development of St. Louis as a center for Western trade led to an explosion of population and land value nearby. The first chapter's comment about the slow growth of Dawson's Landing seems to refer more to the addition of David Wilson, Tom, and Chambers than to the town itself—nothing comes between the comment on growth and the mention of these new people except the roll call of aristocracy. By 1853, when most of the tale occurs, Missouri was hardly a place of peaceful acceptance of slavery. Abolitionism would have made Wilson's restoration of Tom to slavery a political fireball. Except for the presence of slavery and the hovering threat of down-river plantations, there is no evidence of Dawson's Landing's place in time. The town's isolation appears not only physical but historical; time goes by so that people can grow older, not so that systems change, the essence of history according to the Georg Lukacs position I quote in my first chapter. Although Dawson's Landing does change in the course of the book, in ways I will discuss later, all of the town's changes take place between the arrival of the twins and the exposure of Tom's real identity, within the space of a few months in 1853. These changes cannot be constructed as historical any more than Dawson's Landing can be constructed as realistic. Since so little in the tale is historical or realistic, the assumption that the slavery depicted in *Pudd'nhead Wilson* represents the Southern institution implies that, in the book, slavery receives different treatment from any other possibly historical element, that slavery is a significant exception. But from the initial description on, the book presents slavery as a fundamental part of this irreal and ahistorical place.

Instead, these representations of the place and its changes serve purely narrative purposes. John Gerber argues in "*Pudd'n-head Wilson* as Fabulation" that "From the very first we are conscious that it is a imaginative story and that a narrator called Mark Twain is the story teller. The opening sentence of the novel is more formal than 'Once upon a time' but the actual words—'The scene of this chronicle'—have much the same effect" (23). After noting the absurdity and coincidence on which the plot is based, Gerber adds, with ambiguity as to whether reference to the town or the book is intended, "It is a world of make-believe in which excitement, suspense and ingenuity are more important than probability" (27). The picaresque form Twain applied in part to *Adventures of Huckleberry Finn* and *A Connecticut Yankee in King Arthur's Court* allowed his narrators to record more or less real people responding to a more or less real world; satiric commentary on real society traditionally motivates the picaresque. The very movement of the picaresque narrator, normally along a route easily mapped against real places, gives each stop an identity relative to other places. Huck and Hank distinguish place from place on their journeys because particular things happen in each place. But Dawson's Landing, closed to comparison, is never-never land, not a place where a particular thing happens but a place made only to contain this story. Dawson's Landing thus has a universality not because it is like other places, but exactly because it is unlike them. It has no real history, it has almost no real place on a real map, and it has few real people. Because Dawson's Landing lacks particularizing marks, we are free to see it in universal terms. The qualities peculiar to the town only suit it to the tale, not to life; it has no independent existence. Like Twain's later Hadleyburg, it could be any town, so long as the conditions of the place do not preclude the story from happening there.

*Pudd'nhead Wilson's* narratively restricted environment has metonymic representation in slavery. The tale—that is, the entirety of that which is told by this book—defines the town as much as the town defines the story which takes place within its confines. This is why the town of Dawson's Landing itself has qualities we normally associate with character, why we find it easy to accept the language of personification in the description of the town, and why the town acts within the tale as a single persona. Typical novelistic settings offer thematic counterpoint to plot or character—*The Great Gatsby's* ash-heaps, for example, or *Absalom, Absalom!'s* Jefferson—but Dawson's Landing is the *sine qua non* of *Pudd'nhead Wilson*: the plot and characters stand in thematic counterpoint to it.

The restrictive power of Dawson's Landing appears most clearly in the absence of movement of most of the book's characters. David Wilson arrives in this small Missouri town to seek his fortune and immediately runs afoul of the town and so his goals, but still he remains in Dawson's Landing. In fact, he seems never to leave the town for so much as a pleasure trip to St. Louis. The only way out for the aristocracy is death, apparently; Twain excised a section telling of a trip Percy Driscoll took to collect a debt (Rowlette, 87). Even slaves seem unable to go very far, as the early sale of Roxy's fellow slaves locally rather that down the river shows. "I will sell you *here*," Driscoll tells his thieving slaves with natural emphasis, "though you don't deserve it" (12). The twins, at tremendous risk, remain in the town, though they would be far better shed of it. Departure would cost them nothing, staying quite possibly their lives—and still they remain.

This restrictive power fails to restrain two characters, and investigating this failure clarifies for us the nature of this aspect of Dawson's Landing's power. Only Roxy and Tom seem able to leave the town with impunity; the only scenes in the novel which take place outside the confines of Dawson's Landing involve these two. Following the critical habit of thematic interpretation, we could say that, because Roxy and Tom are the products of miscegenation, the town of Dawson's Landing has no power over them. While this is a feature these two characters uniquely share, it is difficult to construct from that an argument about their exceptional freedom. Why would Dawson's Landing control only purebloods? Does whatever ethic the town represents encourage miscegenation or ban its products from town? I cannot conceive of an answer along these lines.

Three other considerations seem more productive to me. The first concerns the relationships between characters discussed in the previous chapter; the second concerns the events which occur outside of Dawson's Landing; and the third concerns the architecture of *Pudd'nhead Wilson*'s world. Tom and Roxy, it has been noted, represent the opposition to David Wilson. Tom, in his irredeemable evil, conflicts with Wilson ethically and narratively. As Tom says to himself:

> All the hard luck comes to me and all the good luck goes to other people—Pudd'nhead Wilson, for instance; even his career has got a sort of little start at last, and what has he done to deserve it, I should like to know? Yes, he has opened his own road, but he isn't content with that, but must block mine. (69)

Tom's freedom of movement can be seen in these symbolic terms: because he has embraced evil and because everything he undertakes comes equipped with its own moral stain, he has no narrative business remaining in Dawson's Landing, which is built to contain a story about the problems of identity. The only conflict he can meaningfully enter into with the town—that of his identity—he shuns. Note that during the only time he questions the nature of his own identity, in his "Why were niggers *and* whites made?" speech (44) and through half of Chapter 10, he is in Dawson's Landing. Once he has quieted his doubt, he runs up to St. Louis again. The town has become the circumstance of a certain sort of dilemma. The dilemma strikes Tom once briefly, and during that time he remains in town. The dilemma is the core of David Wilson's character, so he remains in Dawson's Landing forever.

Roxy opposes Wilson on a symbolic and spiritual level. A part of Roxy's character is her spiritual quest. She refrained from the stealing which resulted in the sale of her fellow slaves because she had got religion at a recent Methodist revival. "She made this sacrifice as a matter of religious etiquette; as a thing necessary just now, but by no means to be wrested into a precedent; no, a week or two would limber up her piety" (11). She is the only character in the book taking a constant recourse into theological matters. Convincing herself of the rightness of switching the babies, she says, "dey ain't nobody kin save his own self—can't do it by faith, can't do it by works, can't do it no way at all. Free grace is de *on'y* way, en dat don't come fum nobody but jis' de Lord" (15). Chastising Tom, she rags him on the poor condition of his soul, the only character in the novel who shows concern with soul, which might be thought of as transcendent identity—a phrase the science-minded and free-thinking David Wilson would likely find oxymoronic. When Roxy asks for mercy at the end, she does not appeal to the court, which has apparently seen nothing illegal in what she has done, but to "de Lord"; we can only conclude she finds herself a "po' misable sinner" (113) in her soul. Roxy's identity transcends the visible world; David Wilson's depends on it. Roxy can leave Dawson's Landing because her identity is a spiritual matter, not a matter of simple creed or fact; Wilson cannot. Like Tom, Roxy engages in few battles which concern the town. The town—not the people who live in Dawson's Landing but the symbolic role Dawson's Landing plays in the story it defines—has restrictive power only over those whose struggles the town recognizes. Pembroke Howard's Presbyterianism comes second to his gentlemen's creed; he stays in Dawson's Landing. Roxy's belief in a diety, a spiritual identity beyond the confines of Dawson's Landing somehow gives her the freedom to leave town. Ending the book in defeat and doubt, she must remain.

But though Roxy and Tom have the freedom to leave Dawson's Landing, both find the world beyond less accommodating to them. Roxy's experiences outside of Dawson's Landing differ from her experiences at home. She leaves the town after Percy Driscoll frees her on his deathbed. "She resolved to go around and say good-bye to her friends and then clear out and see the world—that is to say, she would go chambermaiding on a steamboat, the darling ambition of her race and sex" (22). Roxy realizes her ambition to become a chambermaid and even becomes head chambermaid on the Grand Mogul, but she ends with nothing. Her resolution, to "be independent of the human race thenceforth forevermore if hard work and economy could accomplish it" (33), runs aground when the bank she had entrusted with her savings goes smash. She determines to go home to the helping hand of her old friends. Her return to Dawson's Landing means a reversal of her quest for independence of the human race. We read in detail about one other foray Roxy makes out of town. Agreeing to a year's slavery to save her son's future, Roxy finds that Tom betrays her by selling her down the river. Life on the Arkansas plantation proves as wretched for her as slavery can be. She escapes and arrives disguised at Tom's door. Her son's treachery brings her to the brink of filicide. If Tom had the Judge's courage, he would be as dead. The romantic hero's actions which bring her qualified success in Dawson's Landing bring her failure in the outside world, the sort of heroic failure we saw in Huck and Hank. Her actions are large, her goals just, but the world resists her heroism. In the end, she fails in Dawson's Landing only because David Wilson must succeed; her years of success there must tell us something about the town.

Tom's behavior at home differs from his behavior elsewhere in his consciousness of being watched. In Dawson's Landing, eyes are always on him, but they never see inside him. His black blood worries him for about a week, his one week of self-awareness, but then people see him as he always has been seen, as a mere surface. Roxy "couldn't love him, as yet, because there 'warn't nothing *to* him,' as she expressed it" (46). Just following his worst crime, that against his mother, Tom's reputation at home reaches its apex. "Tom's conduct had been so letter-perfect during two whole months, now, that his uncle not only trusted him with money with which to persuade voters, but trusted him to go and get [it] (*sic*) himself out of the safe in the private sitting-room" (83, error in Norton Critical Edition). Even the normally perspicacious David Wilson cannot see past the surface self of Tom's disguises. "Nothing but a girl would do for me" he tells himself after chance has revealed Tom's true identity "—a man in girl's clothes never occurred to me" (104). In St. Louis, on the other hand, "he found companionship to suit him, and plea-sures to his taste, along with more freedom, in some particulars, than he could have at home" (24). The only companions and plea-sures we know him to have out of town involve gambling; the only freedom he has is from the watching eyes of Dawson's Landing. Out of town, Tom does not disguise himself, he does not steal, he does not murder; at home he does all. The power of Dawson's Landing is not so much to control behavior, as Mark Coburn main-tains, as to offer protective masking. Satirical fiction often shows the falseness of public belief, the hypocrisy between ideas and ac-tions. But Dawson's Landing has no such hypocrisy; except on the issue of identity, there is an exact correspondence between public fiction and public truth. Roxy's grand heroic actions—switching the babies, for example—work there because people in Dawson's Land-ing believe what they see; Tom's disguises succeed for the same reason. These two alone seem to realize the freedom they have be-hind the mask. Their actions out of town bring inescapable re-sults—Roxy's return to slavery, Tom's gambling debts—but the watching eyes of Dawson's Landing see nothing but the surface, believe nothing but fictions.

The very fact that only David Wilson's antagonists have the freedom to leave Dawson's Landing indicates that the world of *Pudd'nhead Wilson* has a symbolic quality. If the entire story took place in the town, we might not easily sense the special conditions which distinguish Dawson's Landing. But, as the tale is constructed, Dawson's Landing's intricate web of public fictions, hierarchy, and morality contrasts with the world outside, which appears to run on the same plan as romantic fiction. While the twins' past lives have the marks of historicity—"when the war broke out my father was on the losing side and had to fly for his life" (27)—Angelo's story does not tally with history any more than the events he tells of tally with reality: paupered and orphaned nobles, who are also vastly educated musical prodigies, are not enslaved for parental debts; but then, identical twins always have the same hair color and complexion. The twins' unhistorical historicity and improbable action form the essence of romantic fiction. We see this also in *Pudd'nhead Wilson's* ties to the romantic theme of the tragic octoroon, which Michael Orth has detailed. "The usual octoroon romance is built around a beautiful girl who is stigmatized in only the faintest degree with Negro blood, but who nevertheless is reduced to slavery and put at the whim of a lecherous master, from whom she is to be rescued by a noble hero" (12). The main story line of *Pudd'nhead Wilson* owes little to this, but Roxy's story, first as a hard-working chambermaid and then as a brutalized slave, fits neatly. These romantic aspects, though, occur outside Dawson's Landing. Inasmuch as romance appears in Dawson's Landing, it comes with Tom's and Roxy's baggage, and the story works in the end to scatter those elements of romance. The world outside of Dawson's Landing runs on rules which do not apply in the town itself.

The emphatic difference between Dawson's Landing and everywhere else —both the natural world we live in and the romantic world we expect from fiction—together with *Pudd'nhead Wilson's* fable-like quality give the town the feel of allegory. But the actual events of the book guide us little when we try to read the town's allegory or understand its lessons. The book's events alone lead us to value social order over individual identity and appearance over reality. With the allegory in view, however, we leave the book with feelings exactly opposite those. What influences us about the town is not so much the events which take place there as the control the town itself exerts over all the people who live there. Though we question the value of the ethics the town promotes, we still recognize that the tale's losers fight against those values, while the winners accept them, no matter how anathematic to their characters. Though Dawson's Landing is presented as a character, it is not presented as an actor: the actions which take place within the town must suit it; that is all. It dictates the circumstance of all action, and this is made noticeable by making it different both from the the world of experience and the world of romantic fiction.

In addition, the presence of "Those Extraordinary Twins" quells the temptation to see Dawson's Landing in comic terms. The vestigia of the farce, its original and contemporary co-publication and the recent textual studies of Herschel Parker and others more than allow a discussion of "Twins" along with *Pudd'nhead Wilson*;

they necessitate it. Leslie Fiedler expressed the belief that, had Twain the courage to publish the integrated manuscript, we would now have "a rollicking atrocious melange of bad taste and half understood intentions and nearly intolerable insights into evil, translated into a nightmare worthy of America" (220). What remains as the afterbirth of *Pudd'nhead Wilson* hardly seems worth saving on its own, a story eight parts nonsense and one part each farce and writerly insight; I have not found it published independently anywhere. But read with *Pudd'nhead Wilson*, it produces a startling effect. *Pudd'nhead Wilson* alone—with its Greek chorus townsfolk, high-relief aristocrats, irredeemable villain, and heroically sympathetic witch—tempts us to laughter. Several critics have read the tale in purely ironic terms because of this. Wilson's calendar entries ought to correct this misperception, but they are so easily read as something apart from the character in the text itself that they do not. Even the passionate ending—one could argue based on the logical flaw of Tom's final sale and the one hundred preceding pages of irony—means to excite laughter instead of sympathy.

But the presence of "Those Extraordinary Twins" discourages this completely. If we compare the two court scenes, we see plainly that the one climaxing the longer tale means itself seriously. We have obvious reason for viewing these scenes together. Not only are all the major players the same, but this is the only scene in "Those Extraordinary Twins" where David Wilson figures prominently. In the farcical trial, Wilson uses sophistry to outwit justice. Against the injudicious Justice Robinson, Wilson subverts normal procedure by demonstrating that, in the absence of firm proof that one or the other of the linked twins administered the kick in question, the jury cannot find either guilty. The outraged Justice responds to the jury:

> You have set adrift, unadmonished, in this community, two men endowed with an awful and mysterious gift, a hidden and grisly power for evil—a power by which each in his turn may commit crime after crime of the most heinous character, and no man be able to tell which is the guilty or which this innocent party in any case of them all. Look to your homes—look to your property—look to your lives—for you have need! (154)

In what way do we find this passage amusing? In what way is it farce? We could say: because the twins are mutants, not really people and so not really subject to law. We could say: because the comically unqualified Justice Robinson has overreacted to what was a perfectly justifiable kick in the pants. We could say: because what happened to the twins is so close to real law, where known criminals walk free due to technicalities. In any case, we accept the humor in this passage which is as much a direct address to both the courtroom and reading audience as is David Wilson's explanation of the nature of fingermarks.

On the other hand, David Wilson wins his trial in *Pudd'nhead Wilson* by the truthful exposure of the identity of the guilty, instead of its willful obfuscation in "Those Extraordinary Twins." The circumstances of the trials themselves differ, of course: one is for a grievous offense, the other for an absurd one; one reads as stagy melodrama, the other as stagy farce; one resolves the conflicts of the plot, the other develops them. But the speeches of David Wilson and Justice Robinson read with striking similarity. But while the question of identity in *Pudd'nhead Wilson* seems of uncertain seriousness, in "Those Extraordinary Twins" it is purely comic. The trial scene there follows Luigi's assertion that he and Angelo are not twins at all and is followed by the absurd duel, "where nobody was in danger or got crippled but the seconds and the outsiders" (159). Its presence makes us absolutely certain about the seriousness of the question of identity in the earlier tale; if one is absurd, the other, so different in so many ways, must not be. In some ways, the twins as Siamese too closely embody the central conflict of *Pudd'nhead Wilson*: Is identity individual or corporate? But if the twins continued as Siamese in the more serious tale, they would by their very oddness become its central feature. Then, the universality of the problem of identity would dissipate in the face of the unique particularity of these mutants. Instead the twins—through the vestigia, the co-publication and the critical awareness—are separated in fact but united in our imagination, just as are Tom and Wilson. The absurd comments Justice Robinson makes about the joined Luigi and Angelo have a special and telling quality when applied to Tom and Wilson. "Those Extraordinary Twins" puts this into focus for us. If Siamese twins have "a hidden and grisly power for evil," so must Tom and Wilson; when we willingly condemn Tom we must also willingly condemn Wilson. This does not prevent our greater sympathy for the one whose ideals more closely match our own, but it does explain in part the inarticulate and unmistakable unease we feel at the conclusion of *Pudd'nhead Wilson*.

The connection between the town and the tale's presentation of slavery now becomes obvious: Dawson's Landing seriously and powerfully determines the actions which take place within it. Freedom, slavery's obverse, thus crowds identity in any full consideration of the novel. I will refer to freedom when discussing the questions provoked by the issue of slavery; the term 'slavery' invites confusion between the particular American institution and the universal problems 'freedom' denotes. Many key elements of plot concern freedom and slavery: the exchange of the babies, Roxy's revelation to Tom, Tom's betrayal of Roxy. This use of freedom in the plot makes it an issue in the book rather than a theme, such as we find in the repeated references to dogs. But freedom is developed thematically as well; even the murder comes to us in its terms: "Without hesitation he drove the knife home—and was free. Some of the notes escape from his left hand and fell in the blood on the floor" (94). Identity is the issue of greater import—in the end it determines who is free and to what degree—but freedom in many ways helps settle the conflict between two forms of identity. If Tom and Wilson have an identity of likeness, what sort of freedom can either be said to have? If individual identity can be reduced to a "mysterious and marvelous natal autograph" (109), what remains to be called freedom? The conclusion tells us that the resolution of identity does two things: it makes Tom a slave, in hell if we are to believe what we are told at the story's beginning; and it grants Chambers whatever measure of freedom exists outside slavery, "a most embarrassing situation" to which Twain refers as "a curious fate" (114). If we knew more about the difference between these two characters' conditions after the tale, we could answer the above questions easily; instead we must struggle a little bit to apprehend them.

Dawson's Landing has a determining and restrictive power which, as emblem of universal slavery, limits and therefore defines this freedom. A number of places in what many call existential fiction function in the same way. The city of Oran, for example, in Albert Camus' *The Plague*, has a similar feel to Dawson's Landing. "Oran is grafted on to a unique landscape, in the center of a bare plateau, ringed with luminous hills and above a perfectly shaped bay. All we may regret is the town's being so disposed that it turns its back on the bay, with the result that it's impossible to see the sea, you always have to go to look for it" (5–6). In Oran, isolation is further enforced by the plague itself, but the result is that Oran takes on an irreal power over the lives of its inhabitants. It ceases to be a place where people live and becomes instead a condition of their lives. For the reader, Oran quickly becomes allegorical: the novel implies that the plague in Oran is life everywhere. For the most part, the sections of the population are monolithic: the people of the town, the authorities, the dead. A few have names, but fewer become characters. In Jean-Paul Sartre's *Nausea*, Roquentin struggles against the sickness brought on by his emerging self-knowledge in the seaside and walled town of Bouville. Although Roquentin does leave Bouville briefly, he and everyone else in the town appear trapped. Even after he has bid all the people he knows in Bouville goodbye, it seems unlikely he will leave. Instead this book ends with an endless repetition of an old jazz song, Roquentin's commitment to write a book, and the information that "tomorrow it will rain in Bouville" (178). Roquentin notes, "I see Bouville. It is a lovely day. I am free: there is absolutely no more reason for living, all the ones I have tried have given way and I can't imagine any more of them. . . . This freedom is rather like death" (156–57). Bouville becomes a tomb for the living. But Bouville is meant to be generalized into a place like life, where freedom seems possible, but where it does not look much different from death. Twain's work offers the same perspective on death and freedom: Pudd'nhead Wilson's quote at the head of Chapter 3, on our debt to Adam for introducing death into the world, only emphasizes the identity between death and freedom implied in the chapter itself.

Robert Solomon explains Sartre's view of situation—a notion which we must translate into setting when contemplating fiction—that

> It is only from the 'correct' *first-person* viewpoint that it becomes evident that we are both free within our situation but yet restricted by it. We are, therefore, both free to choose among alternatives within the situation, but not free to choose the situation itself. Insofar as we are free to choose, Sartre tells us we have *transcendence*; insofar as we are determined by our situation, Sartre tells us we have *facticity*. (274)

In order to understand the relevance of this observation to *Pudd'nhead Wilson* and Dawson's Landing, we must further understand that freedom in this point of view is not the power to act as one wills but the power to confer significance on the situation one is in. Our facticity in a situation does not alter our absolute freedom to assert value where we see it in the situation. Thus Dawson's Landing, Oran, and Bouville determine the lives of the people who live there; those transcendently empowered live freely within that determination.

We have already noted how David Wilson achieves authenticity. We now see that he achieves that *within* Dawson's Landing. Barry Wood notes that with the unmasking of Tom also comes the unmasking of Wilson and of Dawson's Landing. "The new equilibrium which occurs, even though it now included the lawlessness of Tom brought under the control of Wilson's legal intellect, reveals the deeper ironies of a slaveholding situation; for even the most powerful penetration of deception and the unveiling of truth make no lasting mark on this society" (378). We are clearly not discussing an historical society; within a decade of the close of *Pudd'nhead Wilson*, legal slavery ceases. A society this immutable is not a society at all, but rather an allegory for situation. The situation in *Pudd'nhead Wilson* changes—after all, democratic government, with David Wilson elected to head it, has superseded aristocracy in the town—but its determining power does not. Action within such a situation means nothing—"Acts muddy you because they are no more clearly delimited, no more purposeful than the actor" (McMahon, 139)—except as it defines the self within the situation. We can see now that Dawson's Landing becomes the situation within which David Wilson's only and final act leaves him "a made man for good."

Dawson's Landing radically restricts the characters who populate it. "Every character in *Pudd'nhead Wilson*," Mark Coburn writes, "is driven by the need to be accepted by Dawson's Landing and, if possible, to be what the narrator terms a person 'of consequence' in the community" (213–14). Behavior, to be successful, must conform to the town's recognizably peculiar notions of rectitude. Still, we find within the town a widely variable range of unsuccessful behaviors. Characters develop their own patterns of morality within the confines of the town. The FFV aristocrats seem to agree on nothing but the code duello, which means more to them than religion. The townsfolk believe in the literal: Wilson's irony bypasses them, but the Judge's obvious slap at the twins leaves them wondering as to its meaning. Tom's ego creates his morality just as Roxy's passion creates hers. Even the slaves assert their own sort of freedom in taking potshots at the authority over their lives. We can evaluate these various moralities only by noting the degree of success characters have within Dawson's Landing. Roxy's actions, though successful for a time, produce the exact results she sought to avoid. Tom's selfishness leads only to the erasure of self attendant on his role as slave; in the end he is even robbed of his crime, which is laid instead to faulty bookkeeping. The townfolk acknowledge themselves as pudd'nheads, while the aristocrats are variously broken, defeated, and dead, their code now useless. David Wilson's interest in knowledge is an interest in facticity, the inalterable conditions of self *within* which the freedom to determine the significance of that facticity exists. Wilson finds that freedom in authentic identity—and succeeds. Freedom and identity are tied in Dawson's Landing. The only successful freedom there results from an authentic identity.

We can see why the post-war world has found *Pudd'nhead Wilson* a much more attractive book than did preceding generations. We have ourselves begun to see the world in such a way that we can easily interpret Dawson's Landing to represent it. The world of the novel is concentric spheres, with Dawson's Landing at its allegorical center. The next layer is the world of farce, the world of "Those Extraordinary Twins," very much like Dawson's Landing but without its determining power. Beyond that is the world outside of the town, the world of romantic fiction. And beyond that is Mark Twain, presenting us with what Robert Solomon calls "the 'correct' *first-person* viewpoint." Whether or not we share that outer sphere with the tale's narrator depends on how easily we can see the world of Dawson's Landing at the center as an allegorical representation of our own. Richard Lehan writes in *A Dangerous Crossing* that "A literature of the absurd begins by discarding fixed points of reference—God, history, rational philosophy, even the absolute of art—and drives the individual into an unsheltered sense of self" (xiv). Dawson's Landing is a godless, ahistorical, irrational, and artless world; our enthusiasm for David Wilson's heroism must exactly mirror our level of agreement that his world looks, in philosophical outline, like ours. Because, if resolving issues of freedom and identity seems to us the focus of our real lives, then David Wilson's successful solution makes him a true hero. While tradition empowers Huck Finn and Hank Morgan with the appearance of heroism, the actuality of the worlds they occupy defeats them. The power behind their traditional heroism fails when the oral-based world which birthed their types faded under pages of type. Pudd'nhead Wilson, perhaps nothing but a cog in an existential situation, finds that the knowledge of identity brings him an alloyed success far above what his more powerful heroes achieve. In him, we find a hero to believe in.

# Epilogue

I have been at work on this book for more than a year; more than
a decade, counting back to its genesis at Running Press. Working
so hard so many hours tempts me to make some powerful final
statement, but nothing I say now can truly finish what I have done.
A summary is superfluous: an indication of new critical directions
is best left others; and a theoretical treatise a distraction. They
would all serve more to dissipate than conclude this book.

Somehow Mark Twain's endings never let us fully disengage.
Since I have been at work on this book, dozens of people—readers,
not critics—have enthused about Twain's writing to me. Many of
them had read only *Huckleberry Finn* and some short stories; a surprising number had read as much as they could get their hands on.
But invariably the simple mention of Twain brought light to their
eyes. All of them had unanswered questions about the books and
stories. "He's the only writer I reread," a man in his seventies told
me. A middle-aged woman said, "So few books today, or any day I
guess, seem to be about anything except the author's narrow little
world. Mark Twain always seems to write about history, about the
bigger picture." Jonathan Raban notes in *Old Glory*, of his first experience with Huck, "I was living inside the the book" (12); thirty
years later, he floated the length of the Mississippi, still not free of
Twain's novel. It seems you can read to the end of Twain's books,
but you can never finish them.

Perhaps this is why I am so reluctant to write a conclusion. I
do not want to create the impression that I believe my work has
closed a discussion. I said at the beginning that I hoped to open
new pathways to understanding Mark Twain. I do not think those
roads are fully travelled, and I cannot believe that whatever point

they have reached thus far is a destination. Thousands of people have yet to try to close Twain's books; I hope none succeed.

A final question about this project remains for me though. I've divided the book into three parts; what unites them beyond my use of Mark Twain? Several themes come up repeatedly in my work: freedom and slavery, history and historicity, oral traditions and ahistoricity, allegory and realism, symbolism and representation. But something more substantial than themes unites this work. One idea has nagged me throughout; I have allocated it to the epilogue because nothing but speculation lies behind it.

*Adventures of Huckleberry Finn* gathers much of its power from the connection the book has to Jacksonian America. The American dream of independent men and women creating a great nation, not by working together, but by their very independence, comes out of this time. So does our national belief, challenged by Vietnam but now partly recovered, in our natural moral superiority. Huck seems capable of making these dreams reality, and his capitulation to Tom Sawyer's romance, while appropriate to such fantasies, dashes our hopes. Just as the growing furor over slavery spelled the end of Jacksonianism, so historical slavery—in the objectification, torture, and arbitrary manumission of Jim—spells the end of Huck.

*A Connecticut Yankee in King Arthur's Court* brings a dramatic new construction to our understanding of both late nineteenth-century American Industrialism and what Frederic Jameson has called the political unconscious. Blending the comprehension of Hank as psychological voyager with the vision of allegorical Arthurian England as simultaneously 1880s America and the later victims of our expansionism, we see the ease with which we can think of history as a state of mind, a kind of potential narrative, where the events of the past exist independent of the connections we forge between them by the force of imagination. This novel proposes a dream-like past as a stand-in for a nightmare present, and as a result achieves a clearer vision of the time than even modern historians have been able to piece together. But in the end, this imagined past-which-is-the-present overwhelms Hank Morgan's heroic psyche. Hank is defeated by both his ego and his narratized history. But history, simply a society telling itself about itself, is exactly the society's ego. When the actuality of history—the reality of Jacksonian America—defeats its idealized version—the supernaturally empowered shapeshifter Huck—it is not so difficult to understand. Huck is a creature from our prehistory and is himself ahistorical; by writing, Huck puts himself in history's realm and his ahistorical idealism cannot succeed. But *A Connecticut Yankee* shows that it is not only the writing of heroes which necessitates their failure in history, but also the very act of conceiving history which dooms heroic action. Hank's ego defeats him; so does history, the ego of the culture. History, only a representation of the past and not the past itself, still must be conceived before the heroic act of attempting to change history may begin. Heroes and history are both imaginary conceptions, but history necessarily pre-exists the hero we make to change it; it thus determines the hero and cannot in fact be changed by him.

Imagine now where this leaves Mark Twain. His years of effort on *Huckleberry Finn* produced in 1884 a novel showing the limits of heroic action in the realistic field of history. He wrote of the land of his youth, recapturing a time when magic seemed possible, and discovered just how impossible it really was. So he turned his attention for the next several years to the heroics of adulthood and his adult world. This more sedentary, psychological heroism proved even less effective against history; the very act of conceiving history defeats from the start the heroism meant to change it. Twain's own purchase into the wild world of Gilded Age mechanization and speculation only confirmed this. He forever bragged of his latest financial coup, but in fact his financial games lost him most of the money he made by his writing, his speaking, and his marriage. Twain looked to the past through the eyes of Huck Finn and saw the hopelessness of idealism. He looked at his own world through the eyes of Hank Morgan and saw the egotism and vanity behind industrial superiority. Personal and financial reversals forced his retreat to Europe to contemplate—what? He had looked for heroes in his past and came up empty. The search for present-day heroes proved even more discouraging. What could he contemplate next, heroes in the future?

Mapping out his later writing, we find that is truly what Twain did contemplate. He returned to his hapless Captain Stormfield riding rockets to the wrong heaven. He explored the terrors of an amateur scientist drying out under the microscope of "The Great Dark." He dedicated years to his work on Joan of Arc, Christian Science, Adam, and Satan, never giving in to religion himself, but questing after an understanding of the role faith must play in futuristic heroism. And, whether by luck or wisdom, he discovered the hero of the future not exclusively in religion or exclusively in science but in mixing the two up in his Mississippi Valley boyhood home.

*Pudd'nhead Wilson*, published in 1894, recreates the time shift of *A Connecticut Yankee* by turning the historical reality of *Huckleberry Finn* into an allegorical representation of the future. In this future world, history—now de-narratized into the more general term 'situation'—retains its power over individual lives, but David Wilson—by his scientific knowledge of that situation and by his continued authenticity in the tempting face of bad faith—demonstrates what sort of heroism remains to us. If actual history cannot be turned back, and if the very act of conceiving history defeats the ability to conceive anything which can defeat it—if, in short, situation determines all possible thought and action—heroism must mean a full and moral control of the possibilities situation leaves us. Twain represented this in the fable form he prefered in his later years; Heidegger and Sartre articulated the same positions philosophically in the decade following Twain's death.

I cannot prove Twain intended any of this, though I suspect that, if we could question him on it now, he would wink, smile . . . and claim absolutely his ability not only to reconceive a national past but also to foreshadow an intellectual future. I can only note that Mark Twain's books remain in our reading repertoire for two important reasons. First, because they force us to confront the limited possibilities for personal heroism. If Huck Finn, able to die and be reborn, able to adopt new identities at will, able to turn his back on 'sivilizing' society without fear, if Huck cannot even free from slavery a single strong, intelligent, capable man, how can we hope to perform acts even smaller? And if Hank Morgan, a giant among pygmies, a frighteningly competent technician, cannot keep himself from amorality and egotism when granted the small power of entering directly into his own psyche, how can we expect ourselves to combat the personal demons within us, armed with only childhood and dreams of adulthood? David Wilson succeeds not by supernatural power or psychological rectitude, but by simple knowledge and simpler faith. Through science he learns his situation. By acting only through his true self he retains his authenticity. That he does not revolutionize the immoral situation under which he lives matters little; it can only be minimally revised anyway, and not so much by individual action as by a confluence of actions. At least he ends the tale in significantly better shape than he begins it. In fiction, as anywhere, that is success. Because we can learn this from Mark Twain, we keep reading him.

Second, Twain's fiction allows us to understand not only our own history but also history itself in a new way. In *Adventures of Huckleberry Finn*, history carries Huck like the Mississippi, determining what he can and cannot achieve. The reality of Jacksonian America can withstand any amount of idealism, however charmingly represented. History, the novel shows, is an inescapable force. Twain, writing in the 1880s of a time half a century past, saw the power of history overwhelming his present as easily it overwhelmed Huck's. We, reading of a time a century and a half past, feel the same force. In *A Connecticut Yankee in King Arthur's Court*, history becomes a product of the mind, a place we create to subsequently determine our own limits. Writing of his own time under the allegorical guise of sixth-century England, Twain diagrams the connection between American Industrialism and American Imperialism in a painfully poignant way: he demonstrates that we are the victims of our own industrialization, not simply its beneficiaries, and that Industrialism is an historical force which first defeated us and then strained our borders to try its power elsewhere. Remarkably, Twain's disillusionment with heroes led him to map out in *Pudd'nhead Wilson* a conception of the world which would succeed the one he did not survive. Not only do Mark Twain's books transform our understanding of our history, but they also reconstruct history themselves through the conflict between heroes and their worlds: Jacksonian America through the 1884 *Huckleberry Finn*, the Gilded Age through the 1889 *Connecticut Yankee*, his unseen future, our existential present, in the 1894 *Pudd'nhead Wilson*.

I have written an epilogue in spite of myself, and I find I like it. Perhaps I was not so ambivalent about a conclusion as I imagined, or perhaps I have only achieved the appearance of a conclusion by forcing the otherwise diligent research and thought the body of this book represents into the dizzy world of speculation. I am drawn to speculation, I realize, because I have not yet gotten to the bottom of Mark Twain's writing. I have not discussed the beauty of his prose, or the power of his imagery, or the magic in his stories. But there is plenty of time ahead—for me and for others—to keep reading Twain and telling others what we see there, in the hope that they will see it too. And perhaps then, they will themselves have a new vision of this marvelous fiction.

# Bibliography

Allen, Gerald. "Mark Twain's Yankee." *New England Quarterly* 39, 1966 (Dec) 435–46.

Allen, Jerry. *The Adventures of Mark Twain.* Boston: Little, Brown, 1954.

Alsen, Eberhard. "Pudd'nhead Wilson's Fight for Popularity and Power." *Western American Literature* 7, 1972 (2) 135–43.

Anderson, Frederick, ed. Introduction to *Pudd'nhead Wilson and Those Extraordinary Twins.* San Francisco: Chandler, 1968. (Facsimile of First Edition.) In The Norton Critical Edition, Sidney E. Berger, ed. New York: W.W. Norton, 1980.

———, ed. *Mark Twain: The Critical Heritage.* The Criticial Heritage Series, B. C. Southam, ed. New York: Barnes and Noble, 1971.

Anderson, Kenneth. "The Ending of Mark Twain's *A Connecticut Yankee in King Arthur's Court.*" *Mark Twain Journal* 16, 1969 (4) 21.

Aspiz, Harold. "Lecky's Influence on Mark Twain." *Science and Society* 26, 1962 (Winter) 15–25.

Asselineau, Roger. *The Literary Reputation of Mark Twain from 1910 to 1950: A Critical Essay and a Bibliography.* Paris: M. Didier, 1954.

Baetzhold, Howard G. *Mark Twain and John Bull: The British Connection.* Bloomington: Indiana University Press, 1970.

Baldanza, Frank. *Mark Twain: An Introduction and Interpetation.* New York: Barnes and Noble, 1961.

Banta, Martha. "Escape and Entry in *Huckleberry Finn.*" Modern Fiction Studies 14, 1968 (Spring) 79–91.

Bassett, John Earl. *"Huckleberry Finn*: The End Lies at the Beginning." *American Literary Realism* 1, 1967 (1) 89–98.

Beaver, Harold. *Huckleberry Finn.* Boston: Allen & Unwin, 1987.

———. "Run, Nigger, Run: *Adventures of Huckleberry Finn* as a Fugitive Slave Narrative." *Journal of American Studies* 8, 1974 (Dec) 339–61.

Beck, Warren. "Huck Finn at Phelps Farm." *Archives des lettres modernes* 13, 1958 (Juin-Sept) 1–31.

Bell, Bernard. "Twain's 'Nigger' Jim: The Tragic Face Behind the Minstrel Mask." *Mark Twain Journal* 23, 1985 (1) 10–17.

Bell, Michael Davitt. "Mark Twain, 'Realism', and *Huckleberry Finn*." In Louis J. Budd, ed. *New Essays on "Adventures of Huckleberry Finn."* New York: Cambridge University Press, 1985.

Bellamy, Gladys Carmen. *Mark Twain as Literary Artist*. Norman: University of Oklahoma Press, 1950.

Belson, Joel Jay. "The Nature and Consequences of the Loneliness of Huckleberry Finn." *Arizona Quarterly* 26, 1970 (Fall) 243–48.

Benardete, Jane Johnson. "*Huckleberry Finn* and the Nature of Fiction." Massachusetts Review 9, 1968 (Spring) 209–26.

Berger, Arthur Asa. "Huck Finn as an Existential Hero." *Mark Twain Journal* 18, 1976 (2) 12–17.

Berkove, Lawrence I. "The Reality of the Dream: Structural and Thematic Unity in *A Connecticut Yankee*." *Mark Twain Journal* 22, 1984 (1) 8–14.

Bier, Jesse. *The Rise and Fall of American Humor*. New York: Holt, Rinehart, 1968.

Billon, Frederic L. *Annals of St. Louis in Its Early Days Under the French and Spanish Dominations 1764–1804*. New York: Arno Press, 1971.

Blair, Walter. *America's Humor*. New York: Oxford University Press, 1978.

———. *Horse Sense in American Humor*. Chicago: University of Chicago Press, 1942.

———. *Mark Twain & Huck Finn*. Berkeley: University of California Press, 1960.

———. "Was *Huckleberry Finn* Written?" *Mark Twain Journal* 19, 1979 (4) 1–3.

Blues, Thomas. *Mark Twain and the Community*. Lexington: University of Kentucky Press, 1970.

Bode, Carl, ed. *American Life in the 1840s*. Garden City, New York: Anchor, 1967.

Branch, Watson. "Hard-Hearted Huck: 'No Time to be Sentimentering.'" *Studies in American Fiction* 6, 1978 (Fall) 212–18.

Brand, John M. "The Incipient Wilderness: A Study of *Pudd'nhead Wilson*." Western American Literature, 7, 1972 (2) 125–34.

———. "The Other Half: A Study of *Pudd'nhead Wilson*." *Mark Twain Journal* 21, 1982 (2) 14–16.

Breashear, Minnie M. and Robert M. Rodney, eds. *The Art, Humor and Humanity of Mark Twain*. Introduction by Edward Wagenknecht. Norman: University of Oklahoma Press, 1960.

Briden, Earl F. "Huck's Great Escape: Magic and Ritual." *Mark Twain Journal* 21, 1982 (2) 17–18.

———. "*Pudd'nhead Wilson* and the Bandit's Tale in *Gil Blas*." *Mark Twain Journal* 19, 1978 (1) 16–18.

Bridgman, Richard. "Mark Twain and Dan Beard's Clarence: An Anatomy." *Centennial Review* 31, 1987 (Spring) 212–27.

Brodwin, Stanley. "Blackness and the Adamic Myth in Mark Twain's *Pudd'nhead Wilson*." *Texas Studies in Literature and Language* 15, 1973, 167–76.

Brooks, Van Wyck. *The Ordeal of Mark Twain*. New York: Dutton, 1920.

Brown, Clarence A. "*Huckleberry Finn*: A Study in Structure and Point of View." *Mark Twain Journal* 12, 1964 (4) 10–15.

Brown, Spencer. "*Huckleberry Finn* for Our Time: A Re-reading of the Concluding Chapters." *Michigan Quarterly Review* 6, 1967 (Winter) 41–46.

Browne, Ray B. *Heroes of Popular Culture*. Bowling Green, OH: Bowling Green University Press, 1972.

Bryce, James. *The American Commonwealth*. Louis M. Hacker, ed. New York: G. P. Putnam's Sons, 1959.

Budd, Louis J. *Critical Essays on Mark Twain, 1867–1910*. Boston: G. K. Hall, 1982.

———. *Critical Essays on Mark Twain, 1910–1980*. Boston: G. K. Hall, 1983.

———. *Mark Twain: Social Philosopher*. Bloomington: Indiana University Press, 1962.

———. *Our Mark Twain: The Making of His Public Personality*. Philadelphia: University of Pennsylvania Press, 1983.

———. "Southward Currents under Huck Finn's Raft." *Mississippi Valley Historical Review* 46, 1959: 222–37.

———, ed. *New Essays on "Adventures of Huckleberry Finn."* New York: Cambridge University Press, 1985.

Burg, David F. "Another View of *Huckleberry Finn*." Nineteenth-Century Fiction 29 (Dec) 299–319.

Butcher, Philip. "'The God-fathership' of *A Connecticut Yankee*." CLA Journal 12, 1969 (March) 189–98.

———. "Mark Twain Sells Roxy Down the River." *CLA Journal* 8, 1965 (June) 225–33.

Byers, John R., Jr. "The Pokeville Preacher's Invitation in *Huckleberry Finn*." *Mark Twain Journal* 18, 1977 (4) 15–16.

Cady, Edwin. *The Light of Common Day: Realism in American Fiction*. Bloomington: Indiana University Press, 1971.

Campbell, Joseph. *The Hero with a Thousand Faces*. New York: Pantheon, 1949.

Camus, Albert. *The Plague*. New York: The Modern Library, 1948.

Canby, Henry Seidel. *Turn West, Turn East: Mark Twain and Henry James*. Boston: Houghton Mifflin, 1951.

Caron, James E. "Pudd'nhead Wilson's Calendar: Tall Tales and a Tragic

Figure." *Nineteenth Century Fiction* 36, 1982 (March) 452–70.

Carrington, George. *The Dramatic Unity of "Huckleberry Finn."* Columbus: Ohio State University Press, 1976.

Carter, Everett. "The Meaning of *A Connecticut Yankee.*" American Literature 50, 1978: 418–40.

Carton, Evan. *"Pudd'nhead Wilson* and the Fiction of Law and Custom." In Eric J. Sundquist, ed. *American Realism: New Essays.* Baltimore: Johns Hopkins University Press, 1982.

Cecil, L. Moffitt. "The Historical Ending of *Huckleberry Finn*: How Nigger Jim Was Set Free." *American Literary Realism* 13, 1980, 280–83.

Champagny, Robert. *Humanism and Human Racism: A Critical Study of Essays by Sartre and Camus.* The Hague: Mouton, 1972.

Chase, Richard. *The American Novel and Its Tradition.* New York: Doubleday, 1957.

Christopher, J. R. "On the *Adventures of Huckleberry Finn* As a Comic Myth." Cimmaron 18, 1972 (Jan) 18–27.

Coburn, Mark D. "'Training is Everything': Communal Opinion and the Individual in *Pudd'nhead Wilson.*" Modern Language Quarterly 31, 1970 (1) 209–19.

Collins, William J. "Hank Morgan in the Garden of Forking Paths: *A Connecticut Yankee in King Arthur's Court* as Alternative History." *Modern Fiction Studies* 32, 1986 (Spring) 109–14.

Covici, Pascal Jr. *Mark Twain's Humor: The Image of a World.* Dallas, TX: Southern Methodist University Press, 1962.

Cox, James M. *Mark Twain: The Fate of Humor.* Princeton, NJ: Princeton University Press, 1966.

———. *"Pudd'nhead Wilson*: The End of Mark Twain's American Dream." *South Atlantic Quarterly* 58, 1959: 351–63.

Cracroft, Richard H. "The Ironic Mark Twain: Appearance and Reality in *Pudd'nhead Wilson.*" Mark Twain Journal 21, 1983 (3) 24–26.

Cronin, Frank C. "The Ultimate Perspective in *Pudd'nhead Wilson.*" Mark Twain Journal 16, 1971 (1) 14–16.

Cross, Randy K. *"Huckleberry Finn*: The Sacred and the Profane." Mark Twain Journal 21, 1982 (2) 27–28.

Cummings, Sherwood. "Mark Twain's Acceptance of Science." *Centennial Review* 6, 1962 (Spring) 245–61.

David, Beverly R. "Mark Twain and the Legends for *Huckleberry Finn.*" American Literary Realism 15, 1982 (Fall) 155–65.

Davis, Thadious M, ed. *Black Writers on "Adventures of Huckleberry Finn:" A Hundred Years Later.* Mark Twain Journal 22, 1984 (2).

Denton, L.W. "Mark Twain on Patriotism, Treason, and War." *Mark Twain Journal* 17, 1974 (2) 4–7.

Desmond, John F. *"Huckleberry Finn* and the Failure of Anamneusis." *Mark Twain Journal* 21, 1983 (4) 8–10.

# Bibliography

DeVoto, Bernard. *Mark Twain's America*. Boston: Little, Brown, 1932.

———. *Mark Twain at Work*. Cambridge: Harvard University Press, 1942.

Diamond, Sigmund, ed. *A Nation Transformed*. New York: Braziller, 1963.

Dinan, John S. "Hank Morgan: Artist Run Amuck." *Massachusetts Studies in English* 3, 1972 (Spring) 72–77.

Dobson, John M. *Politics in the Gilded Age*. New York: Praeger Publishers, 1972.

Donaldson, Scott. "Pap Finn's Boy." *South Atlantic Bulletin* 36, 1971 (May) 32–37.

Doyno, Victor A. "Over Twain's Shoulder: The Composition and Structure of *Huckleberry Finn*." Modern Fiction Studies 14, 1968 (Spring) 3–9.

Duram, James C. *Mark Twain and the Middle Ages*. Wichita, KS: Wichita State University Press, 1971.

Dyson, A. E. "Huckleberry Finn and the Whole Truth." *Critical Quarterly* 3, 1961 (Spring) 29–40.

Eastman, Max. "Mark Twain and Socialism." *National Review* 10, 1961 (March 11) 154–55.

Eliot, T. S. Introduction to *The Adventures of Huckleberry Finn*. New York: Chanticleer Press, 1950.

Emerson, Everett H. *The Authentic Mark Twain: A Literary Biography of Samuel Clemens*. Philadelphia: University of Pennsylvania Press, 1984.

Ensor, Allison. "The 'Opposition Line' to the King and the Duke in *Huckleberry Finn*." *Mark Twain Journal* 14, 1968 (3) 6–7.

Faulkner, Harold U. *Politics, Reform and Expansion*. New York: Harper and Row, 1959.

Feinstein, George. "Vestigia in *Pudd'nhead Wilson*." Twainian 1942 (May) 1–3.

Ferguson, Delancey. *Mark Twain, Man and Legend*. New York: Russell and Russell, 1965.

Fetterly, Judith. "Disenchantment: Tom Sawyer in *Huckleberry Finn*." *PMLA* 87, 1972 (Jan) 69–74.

———. "Yankee Showman and Reformer: The Character of Mark Twain's Hank Morgan." *Texas Studies in Literature and Language* 14, 1973 (Winter) 667–79.

Fiedler, Leslie. "'As Free as Any Cretur . . .'" *The New Republic* 133, 1955 (Aug 15) 17–18, (Aug 22) 16–18.

Fienberg, Lorne. "Twain's Connecticut Yankee: The Entrepreneur as Daimonic Hero." *Modern Fiction Studies* 28, 1982 (Summer) 155–67.

Finkelstein, Sidney. *Existentialism and Alienation in American Literature*. New York: International Publishers, 1965.

Fisher, Marvin and Michael Elliott. "*Pudd'nhead Wilson*: Half a Dog Is Worse Than None." *Southern Review* 8, 1972 (3) 533–47.

Foner, Philip S. *Mark Twain: Social Critic*. New York: International Publishers, 1958.

Ford, Thomas W. "The Miscegenation Theme in *Pudd'nhead Wilson*." Mark Twain Quarterly 10, 1955: 13–14.

———. "Pudd'nhead Wilson's Calendar." *Mark Twain Journal* 19, 1978 (2) 15–19.

Foucault, Michel. *The Archaeology of Knowledge*. New York: Pantheon, 1972.

———. *Power/Knowledge*. New York: Pantheon, 1980.

von Frank, Albert J. "Huck Finn and the Flight from Maturity." *Studies in American Fiction* 7, 1979 (Spring) 1–15.

Fraser, John. "In Defence of Culture: *Huckleberry Finn*." Oxford Review 6, 1967 (Michaelmas) 5–22.

Gardner, Lloyd C., ed. *A Different Frontier: Selected Readings in the Foundations of American Economic Expansion*. Chicago: Quadrangle Books, 1966.

Gargano, James W. "*Pudd'nhead Wilson*: Mark Twain as Genial Satan." *South Atlantic Quarterly* 74, 1975 (Summer) 365–75.

Garraty, John. *The New Commonwealth*. New York: Harper, 1968.

Gaston, Georg Meri-Akri. "The Function of Tom Sawyer in *The Adventures of Huckleberry Finn*." *Mississippi Quarterly* 27, 1974 (Winter) 33–39.

Gattell, Frank Otto and McFaul, John M., eds. *Jacksonian America, 1815–1840*. Englewood Cliffs, NJ: Prentice-Hall, 1970.

Geertz, Clifford. *The Interpretation of Cultures*. New York: Basic Books, 1973.

———. *Local Knowledge*. New York: Basic Books, 1983.

Geismar, Maxwell. *Mark Twain: An American Prophet*. Boston: Houghton Mifflin, 1970.

———. *Mark Twain and the Three R's: Race, Religion, Revolution—and Related Matters*. Indianapolis: Bobbs-Merrill, 1973.

Gerber, John C. "*Pudd'nhead Wilson* as Fabulation." *Studies in American Humor* 2, 1975 (Spring) 21–31.

———, ed. *American Humor*. Scottsdale, AZ: Arete Publications, 1977.

Gibson, William M. *The Art of Mark Twain*. New York: Oxford University Press, 1976.

Girgus, Sam B. "Conscience in Connecticut: *Civilization and Its Discontents* in Twain's Camelot." *New England Quarterly* 51, 1978 (Dec) 547–60.

Gollin, Richard, and Rita Gollin. *Huckleberry Finn* and the Time of the Evasion." Modern Language Studies 9, 1979 (Spring) 5–15.

Grant, Douglas. *Twain*. Edinburgh: Oliver and Boyd, 1962.

Gribben, Alan. "Removing Mark Twain's Mask: A Decade of Criticism and Scholarship." *ESQ* 26, 1980: 100–108, 149–71.

Griffith, Clark. "*Pudd'nhead Wilson* as Dark Comedy." *ELH* 43, 1976 (2) 209–26.

Gross, Theodore L. *The Heroic Ideal in American Literature*. New York: The Free Press, 1971.

# Bibliography

Haines, James B. "Of Dogs and Men: A Symbolic Variation on the Twin Motif in *Pudd'nhead Wilson*." *Mark Twain Journal* 18, 1977 (3) 14–17.

Hansen, Chadwick. "The Character of Jim and the Ending of *Huckleberry Finn*." Massachusetts Review 5, 1963 (Fall) 45–66.

———. "The Once and Future Boss: Mark Twain's Yankee." *Nineteenth-Century Fiction* 28, 1973 (June) 62–73.

Harris, Neil, ed. *Land of Contrasts: 1880–1901*. New York: Braziller, 1970.

Harris, Susan K. *Mark Twain's Escape From Time: A Study of Patterns and Images*. Columbia: University of Missouri Press, 1982.

Harrison, Stanley R. "Mark Twain's Requiem for the Past." *Mark Twain Journal* 16, 1972 (3) 3–10.

Hart, John E. "Heroes and Houses: The Progress of Huck Finn." *Modern Fiction Studies* 14, 1968 (Spring) 39–46.

Haslam, Gerald W. "*Huckleberry Finn*: Why Read the Phelps Farm Episode?" *Research Studies* 35, 1967 (Sept) 189–97.

Hauck, Richard Boyd. *A Cheerful Nihilism*. Bloomington: Indiana University Press, 1971.

Havard, William C. "Mark Twain and the Political Ambivalence of Southwestern Humor." *Mississippi Quarterly* 17, 1964 (Spring) 95–106.

Henderson, Harry B. III. *Versions of the Past: The Historical Imagination in American Fiction*. New York: Oxford, 1974.

Hill, Hamlin. *Mark Twain: God's Fool*. New York: Harper, 1973.

Hoffman, Daniel. *Form and Fable in American Fiction*. New York: Oxford University Press, 1961.

Hoffmann, Michael J. "Huck's Ironic Circle." *Georgia Review* 23, 1969 (Fall) 307–22.

Hogan, Jerry B. "*Pudd'nhead Wilson*: Whose Tragedy Is It?" *Mark Twain Journal* 20, 1980 (2) 9–12.

Holland, Laurence B. "A 'Raft of Trouble': Word and Deed in *Huckleberry Finn*." *Glyph* 5, 1979: 69–87.

Holmes, Charles S. "*A Connecticut Yankee in King Arthur's Court*: Mark Twain's Fable of Uncertainty." *South Atlantic Quarterly* 61, 1962 (Fall) 462–72.

Hoogenboom, Ari, and Olive Hoogenboom, eds. *The Gilded Age*. Englewood Cliffs, NJ: Prentice-Hall, 1967.

Hopkins, Crale De Vaul. "Patterns of Modernist Thought in Mark Twain's Late Writings." Dissertation, Duke University, 1975.

Howell, Elmo. "Uncle Silas Phelps: A Note on Mark Twain's Characterization." *Mark Twain Journal* 14, 1968 (3) 8–12.

Howells, William Dean. *My Mark Twain, Reminiscences and Critcisms*. New York and London: Harper, 1910.

Hoy, James F. "The Grangerson-Shepherdson Feud in *Huckleberry Finn*." *Mark Twain Journal* 18, 1976 (1) 19–20.

Hughes, Langston. Introduction to *Pudd'nhead Wilson*. New York: Bantam, 1959.

Inge, M. Thomas, ed. *The Frontier Humorists: Critical Views*. Hamden, CT: Archon, 1975.

———, ed. *Huck Finn Among the Critics: A Centennial Selection*. Frederick, MD: University Publications of America, 1985.

James, Stuart B. "The Politics of Personal Salvation: The American Literary Record." *Denver Quarterly* 4, 1969 (Fall) 19–45.

Jameson, Fredric. *The Political Unconscious*. Ithaca, NY: Cornell University Press, 1981.

Johnson, Ellwood. "Mark Twain's Dream Self in the Nightmare of History." *Mark Twain Journal* 15, 1970 (1) 6–12.

Johnson, James L. *Mark Twain and the Limits of Power: Emerson's God in Ruins*. Knoxville: University of Tennessee Press, 1982.

Kaplan, Harold. *Democratic Humanism and American Literature*. Chicago: University of Chicago Press, 1972.

Kaplan, Justin. *Mr. Clemens and Mark Twain, a Biography*. New York: Simon and Shuster, 1966.

Kazin, Alfred. "Almost Perfect." *Library Journal* 87, 1962 (Nov 15) 4243–45.

Keetch, Brent. "Mark Twain's Literary Sport." *Mark Twain Journal* 18, 1976 (2) 7–10.

Kesterson, David B. ed. *Critics on Mark Twain*. Coral Gables, FL: University of Miami Press, 1973.

Ketterer, David. "Epoch-Eclipse and Apocalypse: Special 'Effects' in *A Connecticut Yankee*." *PMLA* 88, 1973 (Oct) 1104–14.

Khouri, Nadia. "From Eden to the Dark Ages: Images of History in the Work of Mark Twain." *Canadian Review of American Studies* 11, 1980, 151–74.

King, Bruce. *"Huckleberry Finn." Ariel* 2, 1971 (Oct) 69–77.

Kolb, Harold H., Jr. "Mark Twain, Huck Finn, and Jacob Blivens: Gilt-Edged, Tree-Calf Morality in *Adventures of Huckleberry Finn*." *Virginia Quarterly* 55, 1979, 653–69.

Kolin, Philip C. "Mark Twain, Aristotle, and *Pudd'nhead Wilson*." *Mark Twain Journal* 15, 1970 (3) 1–4.

Krause, Sydney J. "Huck's First Moral Crisis." *Mississippi Quarterly* 18, 1965 (Spring) 69–73.

———. *Mark Twain as Critic*. Baltimore: Johns Hopkins University Press, 1967.

Krauss, Jennifer. "Playing Double in *Adventures of Huckleberry Finn*." *Mark Twain Journal* 21, 1983 (4) 22–23.

Kravec, Maureen T. "Huckleberry Finn's Aristocratic Ancestry" *Mark Twain Journal* 18, 1976 (2) 19–20.

Kreuter, Kent Kirby. *The Literary Response to Science, Technology and Indus-*

*trialism: Studies in the Thought of Hawthorne, Melville, Whitman, and Twain.* Ann Arbor, MI: University Microforms, 1964.

Lahood, Marvin I. "Huck Finn's Search for Identity." *Mark Twain Journal* 13, 1966 (3) 11–14.

Leacock, Stephen Butler. *Mark Twain.* New York: Haskell House, 1974.

Leary, Lewis. *A Casebook on Mark Twain's Wound.* New York: Crowell, 1962.

———. *Mark Twain.* Minneapolis: University of Minnesota Press, 1960.

Leaver, Florence B. "Mark Twain's *Pudd'nhead Wilson.*" *Mark Twain Journal* 10, 1956 (2) 14–20.

Leavis, F. R. "Mark Twain's Neglected Classic: The Moral Astringency of Pudd'nhead Wilson." *Commentary* 21, 1956 (Feb) 128–36.

Lehan, Ricard. *A Dangerous Crossing.* Carbondale: Southern Illinois University Press, 1973.

Leiter, Louis H. "Dawson's Landing: Thematic Cityscape in Twain's *Pudd'nhead Wilson.*" *Mark Twain Journal* 13, 1965 (1) 8–11.

Levy, Alfred J. "The Dramatic Integrity of Huck Finn." *Ball State University Forum* 20, 1979 (Spring) 28–37.

Levy, Leo B. "Society and Conscience in *Huckleberry Finn.*" *Nineteenth Century Fiction* 18, 1964 (March) 383–91.

Light, James F. "Paradox, Form, and Despair in *Huckleberry Finn.*" *Mark Twain Journal* 21, 1983 (4) 24–25.

Light, Martin. "Sweeping Out Chivalric Silliness: The Example of *Huck Finn* and *The Sun Also Rises.*" *Mark Twain Journal* 17, 1974 (3) 18–21.

Liljegren, Sten Bodvar. *The Revolt Against Romanticism in American Literature as Evidenced in the Works of S. L. Clemens.* New York: Haskell House, 1964.

Long, E. Hudson. *Mark Twain Handbook.* New York: Hendricks House, 1957.

Lukacs, Georg. *History and Class Consciousness.* Cambridge, MA: MIT Press, 1971.

Lynn, Kenneth S. *Mark Twain and Southwestern Humor.* Westport, CT: Greenwood Press, 1972.

———. "Welcome Back From the Raft, Huck Honey!" *American Scholar* 46, 1977 (Summer) 338–47.

Macnaughton, William R. *Mark Twain's Last Years as a Writer.* Columbia: University of Missouri Press, 1979.

Mailloux, Steven. "Reading *Huckleberry Finn*: The Rhetoric of Performed Ideology." In Louis J. Budd, ed. New Essays on "Adventures of Huckleberry Finn." New York: Cambridge University Press, 1985.

Manieere, William R. "Huck Finn, Empiricist Member of Society." *Modern Fiction Studies* 14, 1968 (Spring) 57–66.

———. "'No Money for to Buy the Outfit': *Huckleberry Finn* Again." *Modern Fiction Studies* 10, 1964 (Winter) 341–48.

———. "On Keeping the Raftsmen's Passage in *Huckleberry Finn*." *English Language Notes* 6, 1968 (Dec) 118–22.

Mann, Carolyn. "Innocence in *Pudd'nhead Wilson*." *Mark Twain Journal* 14, 1968 (3) 18–21.

Marks, Barry A. "The Huck Finn Swindle." *Western American Literature* 14, 1979 (Summer) 115–32.

Marshall, Gregory. "Blood Ties as Structural Motif in *Huckleberry Finn*." *Mark Twain Journal* 21, 1982 (2) 44–46.

Marx, Leo. *The Machine in the Garden: Technology and the Pastoral Ideal in America*. New York: Oxford University Press, 1964.

———. "Mr. Eliot, Mr. Trilling, and *Huckleberry Finn*." *American Scholar* 22, 1953 (Fall) 423–40.

May, Ernest R. *Imperial Democracy: The Emergence of America as a Great Power*. New York: Harcourt, Brace, 1961.

Maynard, Reid. "Mark Twain's Ambivalent Yankee." *Mark Twain Journal* 16, 1968 (3) 1–4.

McCollough, Joseph B. *"Pudd'nhead Wilson*: A Search for Identity." *Mark Twain Journal* 18, 1978 (4) 1–5.

———. "Uses of the Bible in *Huckleberry Finn*." *Mark Twain Journal* 19, 1978 (3) 4–5.

McIntyre, James P. "Three Practical Jokes: A Key to Huck's Changing Attitude Toward Jim." *Modern Fiction Studies* 14, 1968 (Spring) 33–37.

McKay, Janet Holmgren. "'An Art So High': Style in *Adventures of Huckleberry Finn*." In Louis J. Budd, ed. *New Essays on "Adventures of Huckleberry Finn*." New York: Cambridge University Press, 1985.

———. *Narration and Discourse in American Realistic Fiction*. Philadelphia: University of Pennsylvania Press, 1982.

McKee, John DeWitt. "Three Uses of the Arming Scene." *Mark Twain Journal* 12, 1965 (3) 18–21.

McMahan, Elizabeth E. "The Money Motif: Economic Implications in *Huckleberry Finn*." *Mark Twain Journal* 15, 1971 (4) 10–15.

McMahon, Joseph H. *Humans Being: The World of Jean-Paul Sartre*. Chicago: University of Chicago Press, 1971.

McNamara, Eugene. *"Adventures of Huckleberry Finn*: Chapter One as Microcosm." *Mark Twain Journal 18, 1977 (4) 17–18*.

Metzger, Charles R. "*Adventures of Huckleberry Finn* as Picaresque." *Midwest Quarterly* 5, 1964 (April) 249–56.

Meyers, Marvin. *The Jacksonian Persuasion*. Palo Alto, CA: Stanford University Press, 1960.

Michelson, Bruce. "Huck and the Games of the World." *American Literary Realism* 13, 1980, 108–21.

Miller, Bruce E. *"Huckleberry Finn*: the Kirkegaardian Dimension." *Illinois Quarterly* 34, 1971 (Sept) 55–64.

Miller, Douglas T. *The Nature of Jacksonian America*. New York: Wiley, 1972.

# Bibliography

Miller, Jim Wayne. "Pudd'nhead Wilson's Calendar." *Mark Twain Journal* 13, 1966 (3) 8–10.

Miller, Robert Keith. *Mark Twain*. New York: Ungar, 1983.

Millichap, Joseph R. "Calvinistic Attitudes and Pauline Imagery in *The Adventures of Huckleberry Finn*." *Mark Twain Journal* 16, 1971 (1) 8–10.

Mills, Nicolaus C. "Social and Moral Vision in *Great Expectations* and *Huckleberry Finn*." *Journal of American Studies* 4, 1970 (July) 61–72.

Mitchell, Lee Clark. "'Nobody But our Gang Warn't Around': The Authority of Language in *Huckleberry Finn*. In Louis J. Budd, ed. *New Essays on "Adventures of Huckleberry Finn."* New York: Cambridge University Press, 1985.

Morgan, Howard W. *Unity and Culture in the United States, 1877–1900*. London: Penguin, 1971.

Morsberger, Robert E. "*Pudd'nhead Wilson* and the Iron Mask." *Markham Review* 7, 1978 (Winter) 25–27.

Nieder, Charles. *Mark Twain*. New York: Horizon, 1967.

Norman, Dorothy. *The Hero: Myth, Image, Symbol*. New York: World, 1969.

Oehlschlaeger, Fritz H. "*Huck Finn* and the Meaning of Shame." *Mark Twain Journal* 20, 1981 (4) 13–14.

Oliver, Nancy. "New Manifest Destiny in *A Connecticut Yankee in King Arthur's Court*." Mark Twain Journal 21, 1983 (4) 28–32.

Opdahl, Keith M. "'You'll Be Sorry When I'm Dead': Child-Adult Relations in *Huck Finn*." *Modern Fiction Studies* 25, 1980: 613–24.

Orth, Michael. "*Pudd'nhead Wilson* Reconsidered or The Octoroon in the Villa Viviana." *Mark Twain Journal* 14, 1969 (4) 11–15.

Ostrom, Alan. "Huck Finn and the Modern Ethos." *Centennial Review* 16, 1972 (Spring) 162–79.

Paine, Albert Bigelow. *Mark Twain, a Biography*. New York: Harper, 1912.

Parker, Herschel. *Flawed Texts and Verbal Icons*. Evanston, IL: Northwestern University Press, 1984.

Pearce, Roy Harvey. "Huck Finn in his History." *Etudes Anglaises* 14, 1971 (Summer) 283–91.

Percy, Walker. *Lost in the Cosmos*. New York: Farrar, Straus and Giroux, 1983.

Pessen, Edward. *Jacksonian America*. Homewood, Illinois: Dorsey Press, 1969.

Pettit, Arthur G. *Mark Twain and the South*. Lexington: University of Kentucky Press, 1974.

Piacentino, Edward J. "The Significance of Pap's Drunken Diatribe Against the Government in *Huckleberry Finn*." *Mark Twain Journal* 19, 1979 (4) 19–21.

Pribek, Thomas. "Huck Finn: His Masquerade and his Lessons for Lying." *American Literary Realism* 19, 1987 (Spring) 68–79.

Quirk, Tom. "'Learning a Nigger to Argue': Quitting *Huckleberry Finn*." *American Literary Realism* 20, 1987 (Fall) 18–33.

———. "The Legend of Noah and the Voyage of Huck Finn." *Mark Twain Journal* 21, 1983 (3) 21–23.

Raban, Jonathan. *Old Glory: An American Voyage*. New York: Simon and Shuster, 1981.

Raglan, Lord FitzRoy Richard Somerset. *The Hero*. London: Methuen, 1936.

Ramsey, Robert Lee. *A Mark Twain Lexicon*. Columbia: University of Missouri Press, 1938.

Rank, Otto. *The Myth of the Birth of the Hero*. New York: Vintage, 1964.

Regan, Robert. *Unpromising Heroes: Mark Twain and His Characters*. Berkeley: University of California Press, 1966.

Robinson, Forrest G. *In Bad Faith*. Cambridge, MA: Harvard University Press, 1987.

———. "The Silences in *Huckleberry Finn*." Nineteenth Century Fiction 37, 1982 (June) 50–74.

Rodney, Robert M. *Mark Twain International*. Westport, CT: Greenwood Press, 1982.

Rogers, Franklin R. *Mark Twain's Burlesque Patterns*. Dallas, TX: Southern Methodist University Press, 1960.

Rogers, Rodney O. "Twain, Taine and Lecky: The Genesis of a Passage in *A Connecticut Yankee*." *Modern Language Quarterly* 34, 1973 (Dec) 436–47.

Rose, Marilyn Gaddis. "*Pudd'nhead Wilson*: A Contempoarary Parable." *Mark Twain Journal* 13, 1966 (2) 5–7.

Ross, Michael L. "*Pudd'nhead Wilson*: Dawson's Landing and the Ladder of Nobility." *Novel* 6, 1973: 244–56.

Rourke, Constance. *American Humor*. New York: Harcourt Brace, 1931.

Rowlette, Robert. *Twain's* Pudd'nhead Wilson: *The Development and Design*. Bowling Green, OH: Bowling Green University Popular Press, 1971.

Rubenstein, Gilbert M. "The Moral Structure of *Huckleberry Finn*." *College English* 18, 1956 (Nov) 72–76.

Rubin, Louis D. Jr. "Mark Twain and The Language of Experience." *Sewanee Review* 71, 1963 (Fall) 664–73.

Rust, Richard Dillworth. "Americanisms in *A Connecticut Yankee*." *South Atlantic Bulletin* 33, 1968 (May) 11–13.

Salomon, Roger Blaine. *Mark Twain and the Image of History*. New Haven: Yale University Press, 1961.

Sapper, Neil G. "'I Been There Before': Huck Finn as Toquevillian Individual." *Mississippi Quarterly* 24, 1970 (Winter) 35–45.

Sartre, Jean-Paul. *Nausea*. New York: New Directions, 1964.

———. *Troubled Sleep*. New York: Knopf, 1950.

Sattelmeyer, Robert and Crowley, J. Donald, eds. *One Hundred Years of*

*"Huckleberry Finn": The Boy, His Book, and American Culture.* Columbia: University of Missouri Press, 1985.

Scanlon, Lawrence E. "'They're After Us' Again." *Mark Twain Journal* 13, 1966 (1) 20–21.

———. "Unheroic Huck." *East-West Review* 2, 1969 (Winter) 99–114.

Schell, Edgar T. "'Pears' and 'Is' in *Pudd'nhead Wilson.*" *Mark Twain Journal* 12, 1963 (2) 12–15.

Schlesinger, Arthur M. Jr. *The Age of Jackson.* Boston: Little, Brown, 1953.

Schmitz, Neil. *Of Huck and Alice.* Minneapolis: University of Minnesota Press, 1983.

———. "The Paradox of Liberation in *Huckleberry Finn.*" *Texas Studies in Literature and Language* 13, 1971 (Spring) 125–36.

———. "Twain, *Huckleberry Finn*, and the Reconstruction." *American Studies* 12, 1971 (Spring) 59–67.

Schonhorn, Manuel. "Mark Twain's Jim: Solomon on the Mississippi." *Mark Twain Journal* 16, 1968 (3) 9–11.

Schroth, Evelyn. "Mark Twain's Literary Dialect in *A Connecticut Yankee.*" *Mark Twain Journal* 19, 1978 (2) 26–28.

Seelye, John. *The True Adventures of Huckleberry Finn.* Evanston, IL: Northwestern University Press, 1970.

Seib, Kenneth. "Moses and the Bullrushes: A Note on *Huckleberry Finn.*" *Mark Twain Journal* 18, 1977 (4) 13–14.

Sewell, David R. *Mark Twain's Languages: Discourse, Dialogue, and Linguistic Variety.* Berkeley: University of California Press, 1987.

Sidnell, M.J. "Huck Finn and Jim: Their Abortive Freedom Ride." *Cambridge Quarterly* 2 (Summer) 203–11.

Simonson, Harold. *The Closed Frontier: Studies in American Literary Tragedy.* New York: Holt, Rinehart and Winston, 1970.

Simpson, Claude M., ed. *Twentieth Century Interpretations of* Adventures of Huckleberry Finn: *A Collection of Critical Essays.* Englewood Cliffs, NJ: Prentice-Hall, 1968.

Sloane, David E. E. *Mark Twain as Literary Comedian.* Baton Rouge: Louisiana State University Press, 1979.

Smith, Henry Nash. *Democracy and the Novel: Popular Resistance to Classic American Writers.* London: Oxford University Press, 1978.

———. *Mark Twain's Fable of Progress: Political and Economic Ideas in "A Connecticut Yankee."* New Brunswick, NJ: Rutgers University Press, 1964.

———. *Mark Twain: The Development of a Writer.* Cambridge, MA: Harvard University Press, 1962.

———, ed. *Mark Twain: A Collection of Critical Essays.* Englewood Cliffs, NJ: Prentice-Hall, 1963.

Smith, Page. *The Nation Comes of Age.* New York: McGraw Hill, 1981.

———. *The Rise of Industrial America.* New York: McGraw Hill, 1984.

Solomon, Andrew. "Jim and Huck: Magnificent Misfits." *Mark Twain Journal* 16, 1972 (3) 17–24.

Solomon, Jack. "Huckleberry Finn and the Tradition of the *Odyssey*." *South Atlantic Bulletin* 33, 1966 (March) 11–13.

Solomon, Robert C. *From Rationalism to Existentialism.* NP: Humanities Press, 1972.

Sommers, Jeffrey. "'I Never Knowed How Clothes Could Change A Body Before': The Dual Function of Clothing in *Huckleberry Finn*." *Mark Twain Journal* 20, 1981 (4) 19–21.

Spangemann, William. *Mark Twain and the Backwoods Angel.* Kent, OH: Kent State University Press, 1966.

Spangler, George M. *"Pudd'nhead Wilson*: A Parable of Property." *American Literature* 42, 1970 (1) 28–37.

Spofford, William K. "Mark Twain's Connecticut Yankee: An Ignoramus Nevertheless." *Mark Twain Journal* 15, 1970 (2) 15–18.

Stein, Allen F. "Return to Phelps Farm: *Huckleberry Finn* and the Old Southwestern Framing Device." *Mississippi Quarterly* 24, 1971 (Spring) 111–16.

Stone, Albert. *The Innocent Eye: Childhood in Mark Twain's Imagination.* New Haven, CT: Yale University Press, 1961.

Strickland, Carol Colclough. "Of Love and Loneliness, Society and Self in *Huckleberry Finn*." *Mark Twain Journal* 21, 1983 (4) 50–51.

Tatham, Campbell. "'Dismal and Lonesome': A New Look at *Huckleberry Finn*." *Modern Fiction Studies* 14, 1968 (Spring) 47–55.

Tenney, Thomas Asa. *Mark Twain: A Reference Guide.* Boston: G. K. Hall, 1977. (Annual updates in *American Literary Realism*.)

Thomas, Brook. "Language and Identity in *Adventures of Huckleberry Finn*." *Mark Twain Journal* 20, 1981 (3) 17–21.

Thorpe, Willard. *American Humorists.* Minneapolis: University of Minnesota Press, 1964.

de Tocqueville, Alexis. *Democracy in America.* Ed. by J.P. Mayer, trans. by George Lawrence. Garden City, NY: Doubleday and Company, 1969.

Toles, George E. "Mark Twain and *Pudd'nhead Wilson*: A House Divided." *Novel* 16, 1982 (Fall) 55–75.

Towers, Tom H. "Love and Power in *Huckleberry Finn*." *Tulane Studies in English* 23, 1978, 17–37.

———. "Mark Twain's *Connecticut Yankee*: The Trouble in Camelot." In Ray B. Browne, ed. *Challenges in American Culture.* Bowling Green, OH: Bowling Green University Press, 1970.

Trachtenberg, Alan. "The Form of Freedom in *Adventures of Huckleberry Finn*." *Southern Review* 6, 1970 (Oct) 954–71.

Trilling, Lionel. *The Liberal Imagination.* New York: Viking, 1950.

Tucker, John Sutton, ed. *Mark Twain's "The Mysterious Stranger" and the Critics.* Belmont, CA: Wadsworth Publishing, 1968.

Turnbull, Deborah Berger. "Hank Morgan as American Individualist." *Mark Twain Journal* 20, 1980 (2) 19–21.

Twain, Mark. *Adventures of Huckleberry Finn*. Berkeley: The Mark Twain Library, University of California Press, 1986.

———. *The Complete Short Stories of Mark Twain*. Ed. by Charles Neider. Garden City, NY: Doubleday, 1957.

———. *A Connecticut Yankee in King Arthur's Court*. Berkeley: The Mark Twain Library, University of California Press, 1984.

———. *Personal Recollections of Joan of Arc*. New York: Harper and Brothers, 1899.

———. *Pudd'nhead Wilson and Those Extraordinary Twins*. The Norton Critical Edition, Sidney E. Berger, ed. New York: W. W. Norton, 1980.

———. *The Unabridged Mark Twain*. Philadelphia: Running Press, 1976.

Vales, Robert T. "Thief and Theft in *Huckleberry Finn*." *American Literature* 37, 1966 (Jan) 420–29.

Vanderwerken, David L. "The Triumph of Medievalism in *Pudd'nhead Wilson*." *Mark Twain Journal* 18, 1977 (4) 7–10.

Van Deusen, Glyndon G. *The Jacksonian Era, 1828–1848*. New York: Harper, 1959.

Vogelback, Arthur Lawrence. *The Publication and Reception of "Huckleberry Finn" in America*. Durham, NC: Duke University Press, 1939.

de Vries, Jan. *Heroic Song and Heroic Legend*. New York: Oxford University Press, 1963.

Wagenknecht, Edward. "Huckleberry Finn as the Devil's Disciple." *Boston University Studies in Fiction* 18, 1970 (Spring) 20–4.

———. *Mark Twain: The Man and His Work*. Norman: University of Oklahoma Press, 1967.

Wagner, Jeanie M. *"Huckleberry Finn and the History Game." Mark Twain Journal* 20, 1980 (1) 5–9.

Ward, John William. *Andrew Jackson—Symbol for an Age*. New York: Oxford University Press, 1953.

Warren, Robert Penn, "Bearer of Bad Tidings: Writers and the American Dream." *New York Review of Books*, March 20, 1975, 12–19.

Weaver, Thomas, and Merline A. Williams. "Mark Twain's Jim: Identity as an Index to Cultural Attitudes." *American Literary Realism* 13, 1980 (Spring) 19–30.

Wecter, Dixon. *The Hero in America*. New York: Scribners, 1941.

———. *Sam Clemens of Hannibal*. Boston: Houghton Mifflin, 1952.

———, ed. *The Love Letters of Mark Twain*. New York: Harper, 1949.

Wells, Anna Mary. "Huck Finn, Tom Sawyer and Samuel Clemens." *PMLA* 87, 1972 (Oct) 1130–31.

Werge, Thomas. "Huck, Jim and Forty Dollars." *Mark Twain Journal* 13, 1965 (1) 15–16.

West, John O. and James M. Day. "Mark Twain's Comedy of Errors in *Pudd'nhead Wilson*." *Mark Twain Journal* 22, 1984 (1) 43–44.

Wigger, Anne P. "The Composition of Mark Twain's *Pudd'nhead Wilson* and 'Those Extraordinary Twins': Chronology and Development." *Modern Philology* 55, 1957 (Nov) 93–102.

Wiggins, Robert. *"Pudd'nhead Wilson*: A Literary Caesarean Operation." *College English* 25, 1963 (Dec) 182–86.

Williams, James D. "Revision and Intention in Mark Twain's *A Connecticut Yankee*." *American Literature* 36, 1964 (Nov) 288–97.

———. "The Use of History in Mark Twain's *A Connecticut Yankee*." *PMLA* 80, 1965 (March) 102–10.

Williams, Murial B. "The Unmasking of Meaning: A Study of the Twins in Pudd'nhead Wilson." *Mississippi Quarterly* 33, 1980 (1) 39–53.

Williams, Philip. "Huckleberry Finn and the Dialectic of History." *Essays and Studies in English Literature and Language* 51–2, 59–98.

Williams, William Applegate. *The Roots of the Modern American Empire*. New York: Random House, 1969.

Wilson, James D. *"Adventures of Huckleberry Finn*: From Abstraction to Reality." *Southern Review* 10, 1974 (1) 80–94.

———. "Hank Morgan, Philip Traum and Milton's Satan." *Mark Twain Journal* 16, 1973 (4) 20–21.

Winters, Donald E. "The Utopianism of Survival: Bellamy's *Looking Backward* and Twain's A Connecticut Yankee." *American Studies* 21, 1980 (Spring) 23–38.

Wood, Barry. "Narrative Action and Structural Symmetry in *Pudd'nhead Wilson*." In *Pudd'nhead Wilson and Those Extraordinary Twins*. The Norton Critical Edition, Sidney E. Berger, ed. New York: W. W. Norton, 1980.

Woodard, Fredrick and MacCann, Donnarae. *"Huckleberry Finn* and the Traditions of Blackface Minstrelsy." *Interracial Books for Children Bulletin*, 15, 1984 (1 and 2) 4–13.

Young, Philip. *Three Bags Full: Essays in American Fiction*. New York: Harcourt, Brace, Jovanovich, 1972.

# Index

# Index